IT'S **BIGGER** THAN HIP HOP

M.K. Asante, Jr.

IT'S BIGGER THAN HIP HOP

The Rise

of the

Post—Hip—Hop

Generation

ST. MARTIN'S PRESS NEW YORK

www.stmartins.com

Library of Congress Cataloging-in-Publication Data

Asante, Molefi K., 1981–
    It's bigger than hip hop : the rise of the post-hip-hop generation /
M. K. Asante, Jr.—1st ed.
        p. cm.
    Includes bibliographical references and index.
    ISBN-13: 978-0-312-37326-9
    ISBN-10: 0-312-37326-0
    1. African Americans—Social conditions. 2. African Americans—Intellectual
life. 3. African Americans in popular culture. 4. African Americans—Race
identity. 5. Popular culture—United States. 6. Hip hop—United States.
7. Rap (Music)—History and criticism. 8. Music—Social aspects—United
States. 9. African American youth—Attitudes. I. Title.
E185.61.A725 2008
305.235089'96073—dc22

                                                                    2008019523

First Edition: September 2008

10 9 8 7 6 5 4 3 2 1

For My People

CONTENTS

acknowledgments

MUCH LOVE

To the most high and the ancestors.

To my mother and father for their unshakable love.

To Maya, queen, for her anchored illumination.

To my family all around the world for their support.

To Lawrence Ross, Manie Baron, and Monique Patterson for making this book a reality.

To my teachers and mentors for their wisdom: Maya Angelou, Amiri Baraka, Charles Fuller, Kenny Gamble, Walter Lomax, Mumia Abu-Jamal, Kofi Opoku, Maulana Karenga, Monifa Love Asante, Dolan Hubbard, bell hooks, Haki Madhubuti, Jim Brown, Assata Shakur, Michael Eric Dyson, George Carlin, Haile Gerima, Keith Mehlinger, Cornel West, Lennox Dingle, and Kevin Howie.

To my comrades for their light: Dead Prez, Daahoud Asante, Sunni Patterson, Mos Def, Struggle, Chuck D, Owen 'Alik Shahadah, Eka Asante, Immortal Technique, Head-Roc, Eshon Burgundy, Black Ice, Greg Corbin, Jared Ball, Jeff Chang, Saul Williams, Davey D, Jon

Sistrunk, Jeremy Glick, Joan Morgan, Jamilah Abu-bakare, William Jelani Cobb, Shalana Austin, Dustin Felder, Ben Haaz, Pierce Freelon, Reiland Rabaka, Deen Freelon, Ursula Rucker, Mark Anthony Neal, Kameelah Rasheed, Lauryn Hill, Amy Goodman, Imani Perry, Ahmed Artis, Allissa Hosten, Louba Durand, Kiri Davis, Abraham Osuna, Christina Garces, Zamani-Ra, and Nasir Allen Asante.

To the photographers and visual artists whose work appears in this book: Ellis Marsalis, LaToya Ruby Frazier, Jamal Thorne, Hank Willis Thomas, Theodore A. Harris, Jason Woods, Maya Freelon Asante, Paul D'Amato, Don Ryan, Nathaniel Donnett, Chris Metzger, and Jose Alamillo.

To my students at Morgan State University for teaching me. To researchers Ryan Bowens and Marquita Brown for their assistance.

To the everyday people who inspire me daily.

To the revolutionaries, activists, and organizers who refuse to accept the status quo.

To my brothers and sisters locked down (they can't imprison your soul!).

To hip-hop.

To you.

AWAKENING

When you make an observation, you have an obligation. This is the piece of poetry that I try to live by. It's what prompted these pages and, last November, motored me through the nothingness of rural Pennsylvania to conduct a writing workshop in prison—the pen.

As I pulled up to the facility—a colorless lump of concrete strangled with jagged concertina wire—rain fell, flickering like old film. Inside, I huddled with a dynamic group of inmates, all young, all black, and all bent on not being broken. After the workshop, I was taken to visit the cell block where they spent the bulk of their days and nights. On my way out, I noticed that Jordan King, a participant in the workshop, was the only one on the block whose bed did not have a mattress.

"No mattress?" I asked, puzzled.

"I have one, but I don't sleep on it," he told me.

"What do you sleep on?" I pried.

"The hard floor, the steel frame, anywhere but on this," he asserted as he hunched beneath the bunk and flashed a flimsy mattress. "See," he stated, as he reburied the cot, "I can't sleep on that. It's too comfortable and I don't trust comfort in a place like this because it numbs you to the reality of where you really are and why."

Just as the frigid floor and steel frame told Jordan, in that raspy voice of reality, where he was, this book—by snatching the mattresses from beneath our slumbering selves—is about where we are today and where we want to be tomorrow.

Each generation must out of relative obscurity
discover its mission,
fulfill it, or betray it.
—FRANZ FANON

IT'S **BIGGER** THAN HIP HOP

chapter 1.
THE POST-HIP-HOP GENERATION

Now, as then, we find ourselves bound, first without,
then within, by the nature of our categorizations.
— JAMES BALDWIN

All the fresh styles always start off
as a good lil' hood thang;
look at blues, rock, jazz, rap . . .
By the time it reach Hollywood it's over,
but it's cool, we just keep it goin' make new shit.
— ANDRÉ 3000

"The hip-hop generation," a tag typically rocked by Blacks and browns born after the Civil Rights and Black Power movements, certainly captured the essence of the rebellious, courageous, creative, politically discontent teens and twenty-somethings of the 80s and 90s. But "nah, not today," says Alton Smith, a nineteen-year-old poet from North Philly who counts himself among a new generation of world-changers that believe—he tells me as our Black bodies climb into the night—"It's bigger than hip hop."

With its sands scattered to the winds of the world, hip hop joins

1

scores of other vibrations that are born in the Black community, but that live, thrive, and reproduce all over the world. More than just an integral part of pop culture, hip hop has shaped the perceptions of people, especially young ones, wherever they are. Take, for instance, Planète Rap, a hip-hop clothing store whose front window is tatted with images of a heat-holdin' 50 Cent, located on the posh Grande Boulevard in Paris. Or the Ghanaian teenager who, as I hoofed through his neighborhood in Accra, greeted me with "What's good, my nigga?" Although these examples straddle some stereotypes, there are many others—like the marriages between hip-hop groups and grassroots organizations in São Paulo, Brazil, the emergence of revolutionary Palestinian female emcee Sabreena Da Witch, or the East African hip-hop groups Kalamashaka and Kwanza Unit whose raw rhymes routinely expose government corruption in the region—that

3-piece suit: $250

new socks: $2

9mm Pistol: $79

gold chain: $400

Bullet: ¢60

Picking the perfect casket for your son:

priceless.

Photo: Hank Willis Thomas

demonstrate how the adoption of hip hop outside of the U.S. has been collectively constructed.

In its homeland, "hip hop," says Alton, "empowered my dad's generation to be better, to stand up, to stop the violence." He flashes a yellowed Polaroid of his father who, in 1980, eight years before Alton was born, founded a rap group. "But it just don't do that now." Alton's disappointment is amplified by an urban crisis that has recently stolen the life of his seventeen-year-old cousin.

"I stay at a funeral," he sighs, then roll-calls a few names of the young Black men, boys even, who are among the over four hundred murder victims in Philadelphia in 2007. "But turn on the radio and what do you hear? You hear, 'I'll kill you nigga, I'll kill you nigga,'" he says, trying to shrug off the senselessness. When the murder rate is higher for Blacks in Philadelphia—the city of brotherly love—than it is for U.S. troops in Iraq and Afghanistan, young men like Alton search for ways to interrupt this wretched cycle of death and despair.

Although Alton sees the hip hop of his father's generation as empowering, he acknowledges that the economic dominance of all things hip hop during his own time has brought many voices into the mainstream that, prior, were barely heard and never listened to in that space.

"Yeah, but at what price?" quizzes Tiffany Coles, a twenty-one-year-old "Seventh Wardian" from New Orleans who, as we motor through the ruins of her desolate city, says that hip hop's mainstream success reminds her of Rosie Perez's monologue in *White Men Can't Jump*. "Sometimes when you win, you really lose, and sometimes when you lose, you really win, and sometimes when you win or lose, you actually tie, and sometimes when you tie, you actually win or lose." For Tiffany, hip hop's dive into the mainstream was a win for the handful of corporations and artists who grew rich, but a significant loss for those who it is supposed to represent.

"I want to be a part of the generation that's going to rebuild this city and fight against the officials in this city who are trying to keep us out. I love hip hop, but if the hip-hop generation ain't about doing this kind of work"—she points to a battered home with the word HELP scrawled into the boards that block the windows and doors—"then we need something else."

Hip hop, like the Black musical oxygen that preceded it—blues, gospel, jazz, soul—cannot be looked at in a vacuum because the artists owe their lives to the context of their births. A discussion of the blues, then, without a discussion of slavery and Black southern life would not just be incomplete, but lame, too. A discussion on hip hop, in the same way, must include what Dr. Jared Ball, hip-hop professor and 2008 Green Party presidential candidate, calls "its proper context of political struggle and repression." Without this context, we are left, as Fred Hampton trumpeted one balmy Chicago afternoon, with "answers that don't answer, explanations that don't explain and conclusions that don't conclude."

Putting hip hop in its proper context means understanding the inextricable link between Black music and the politics of Black life. Dr. Martin Luther King, Jr., reflecting in his autobiography on the role of Black music during the Civil Rights Movement, called the freedom songs the "soul of the movement" and even stressed the overriding importance of the lyrics, the message:

> They are more than just incantations of clever phrases designed to invigorate a campaign; they are as old as the history of the Negro in America. They are adaptations of songs the slaves sang—the sorrow songs, the shouts for joy, the battle hymns, and the anthems of our movement. I have heard people talk of their beat and rhythm, but we in the movement are as inspired by their words. "Woke Up This Morning with My Mind Stayed on Freedom" is a sentence that needs

no music to make its point. We sing the freedom songs for the same reason the slaves sang them, because we too are in bondage and the songs add hope to our determination that "We shall overcome, Black and white together, We shall overcome someday." These songs bound us together, gave us courage together, helped us march together.

Going beyond the naïve idea that Black music is simply entertainment helps us to better understand the current crisis. "It seems to me that if the Negro represents, or is symbolic of, something in and about the nature of American culture, this certainly should be revealed by his characteristic music," is how poet Amiri Baraka (then LeRoi Jones) puts it in *Blues People.* So, in that way, to observe contemporary hip hop is to observe ourselves; an observation that, for Alton, Tiffany, and others, not only blares problems loud enough to drown out seductive samples or head nod–inspiring bass lines, but turns them toward redefinition.

The current crisis isn't just that rap music, hip hop's voice box of values and ideas, has drifted into the shallowest pool of poetic possibilities, or even that most of today's hip hop betrays the attitudes and ideals that framed it in the same way that, say, the U.S. Patriot Act neglects the principles—*at least in theory*—espoused by the framers of the constitution. Many young people—myself, age twenty-five, included—who were born into the hip-hop generation feel misrepresented by it and have begun to see the dangers and limitations of being collectively identified by a genre of music that we don't even own. And it is our lack of ownership that has allowed corporate forces to overrun hip hop with a level of misogyny and Black-on-Black violence that spurs some young folks to disown the label "hip-hop generation."

The balance, here, as Tiffany measures, is remembering "that the stuff on BET and on the radio, which is mainly negative, is not all of hip hop." So while Tiffany is skeptical of the label "hip-hop generation," she embraces the contributions of emcees who, in the triumphant tradition of Black arts, have employed the medium as a means to elevate, uplift, and inspire collective change. At the same time, she realizes that "most people 'round here won't listen to it if it's not on the radio."

Part of the crisis is centered around the distribution mechanisms for hip hop. Although hip hop is the cultural expression of young Black America, we do not control how the cultural expression is disseminated. Instead, multinational corporations like Viacom, Clear Channel, and Vivendi, through their radio and television outlets, control how most people hear and see hip hop. When I ask my students at Morgan State—an urban, predominantly Black university—about emcees like Immortal Technique, Talib Kweli, and Dead Prez, an overwhelming majority of them reveal that they've never even heard of them. This is tragic because the aforesaid emcees are among a select few that address the social and political issues that affect them most. This is partly due to the unfortunate reality that rappers whose lyrics fall into the abyss of negativity are not usually demarcated as "negative" or "ignorant"; however, emcees who rhyme against self-destruction are always marginalized as "conscious," "alternative," or "political" rappers, tags that sling them into categorical ghettos and thus help to place them outside the earshot of the masses.

While it is important to acknowledge that mainstream rap is not all of rap, it's also important to acknowledge the effect that the mainstream has on aspiring emcees. When Alton, for instance, says that the rappers from his neighborhood are rapping about killin' niggas, they are imitating the models of success that they see on TV and hear on the radio. In that way, the mainstream has a dominating effect and is able to dictate the direction of the culture and art.

All of this is against the ambivalent backdrop of globalization, the fog of an unjust war, the impending consequences of the corporate desecration of mother nature, and the apex of an unprecedented urban crisis. These are problems that hip hop, as art, culture, and community, has failed to respond to, and we are now at a generational tipping point, the moment when a dramatic shift is more than a possibility; it's a certainty. And while a dramatic shift is certain (and can be felt already), the outcome is not. History teaches us that both action and inaction lead us to dramatic shifts. If the post-hip-hop generation chooses to act, what values, whose ideas, will inform that action? If they choose not to act, not to "wake up," as it were, whose values and ideas will be imposed upon them?

The term "post-hip-hop" describes a period of time—*right now*—of great transition for a new generation in search of a deeper, more encompassing understanding of themselves in a context outside of the corporate hip-hop monopoly. While hip hop may be a part of this new understanding, it will neither dominate nor dictate it, just as one can observe the civil rights generation's ethos within the hip-hop generation, yet the two remain autonomously connected.

Post-hip-hop is an assertion of agency that encapsulates this generation's broad range of abilities, ideals, and ideas, as well as incorporates recent social advances and movements (i.e., the women's movement, the antiwar movement, gay rights, antiglobalization) that hip hop has either failed or refused to prioritize. How can one, for instance, dialogue progressively about gender issues within a space dominated by sexism and phallocentrism? Or take seriously notions of cooperative or participatory economics within a space that espouses guerilla capitalism? Or talk seriously about the end of war—over *there* and right *here!*—within a space that promotes violence? Of course these elements are not exclusive to the hip-hop generation and are mere reflections of American culture on the whole. Saul Williams, in an open

letter to Oprah Winfrey, points out that the ideologies that govern
hip hop also govern America:

> *50 Cent and George Bush have the same birthday (July 6th). For a*
> *Hip Hop artist to say "I do what I wanna do/Don't care if I get*
> *caught/The DA could play this mothafukin tape in court/I'll kill you/*
> *I ain't playin'" epitomizes the confidence and braggadocio we expect*
> *and admire from a rapper who claims to represent the lowest denomi-*
> *nator. When a world leader [George Bush] with the spirit of a cowboy*
> *(the true original gangster of the West: raping, stealing land, and pil-*
> *laging, as we clapped and cheered) takes the position of doing what he*
> *wants to do, regardless of whether the UN or American public would*
> *take him to court, then we have witnessed true gangsterism and*
> *violent negligence.*

When we consider hip hop's origins and purpose, we understand it is a
revolutionary cultural force that was intended to challenge the status
quo and the greater American culture. So, its relegation to reflecting
American culture becomes extremely problematic if one considers the
radical tradition of African-American social movements—which have
never been about mirroring dominant American culture.

Post-hip-hop is not about the death of rap, but rather the birth of
a new movement propelled by a paradigm shift that can be felt in the
crowded spoken-word joints in North Philadelphia where poet Gregory "Just Greg" Corbin tells a crowded audience, "So these cats will
rhyme about Rick Ross before they talk about African holocaust /
rhyme about Pablo Escobar before they talk about how many bodies
was lost." A shift that can be felt at the krump-dance dance-offs in
Los Angeles where young pioneer Tight Eyez proclaims, "We're not
gonna be clones of the commercial hip-hop world because that's been
seen for so many years. Somebody's waitin' on something different,

another generation of kids with morals and values that they won't need what's being commercialized or tailor-made for them; custom-made, because I feel that we're custom-made. And we're of more value than any piece of jewelry . . . or any car or any big house that anybody could buy." And a shift that can be seen on a tattered stoop on the corner of Flatbush Avenue in Brooklyn where Rashard Lloyd, a high school senior and budding community activist, grumbles when I ask him, "What does hip hop mean to you?" After a moment of contemplation, he makes clear, "Hip hop don't speak *to* or *for* me."

While Rashard's attitude may surprise those who mistake the ring tones, reality shows, and glossy advertising campaigns as indicators of hip hop's dominance, it shouldn't. Trailblazers of every generation have always sought radical alternatives to what corporate America deems cool. According to "The U.S. Urban Youth Market: Targeting the Trendsetters," a study conducted by research and analysis firm Packaged Facts, Black youths like Rashard "possess an overriding desire to remain outside of the mainstream." Claire Madden, vice president of marketing for Market Research, the parent company of Packaged Facts, says that once "there is a perception from urban youth that these manufacturers [companies and artists] are ignoring their origins, they are named sell-outs and it is only a matter of time before they fall."

In order to understand the rise of the post-hip-hop generation, it's imperative to understand the foundations of hip hop. Although West African in its derivation, hip hop emerged in the Bronx in the mid-seventies as a form of aesthetic and sociopolitical rebellion against the flames of systemic oppression. This rebellion, on one hand, was musical because rap music was a radical alternative to disco, which excluded many Blacks and Latinos in the inner cities. As Kurtis Blow, one of hip hop's first commercially successful rappers, told me as we drove through the South Bronx on a hip-hop tour bus packed with European tourists,

"At that point, everybody everywhere was completely disco crazy. Hip hop was a rebellious mutation of disco that stemmed from the cats in the South Bronx and Harlem who couldn't afford the bourgeois Midtown discos. Instead, hip hop took to the streets, the parks, the community centers, block parties. Hip hop represented the same freshness of view that drew me to Malcolm X." It's critical that Blow links hip hop to Malcolm because it is this connection that represents hip hop's most potent and dominant sense of rebellion. Put another way, the force that created Malcolm was the same force that created hip hop—a visceral energy aimed at transforming (or at least voicing) the conditions of oppressed people. This was not simply hip hop's promise, but its reality.

Its quintessence was epitomized in the late 1980s during hip hop's Stop the Violence Movement with the anthem "Self Destruction," a collaborative effort by the era's most well-known rappers, including KRS-One, who proclaimed: "To crush the stereotype here's what we did / We got ourselves together / So that you could unite and fight for what's right."

Although hip hop was founded on the principles of rebellion, over the past decade it has been lulled into being a conservative instrument, promoting nothing new or remotely challenging to mainstream cultural ideology. Even in the midst of an illegitimate war in Iraq, rap music remains a stationary vehicle blaring redundant, glossy messages of violence without consequence, misogyny, and conspicuous consumption. As a result, it has betrayed the very people it is supposed to represent; it has betrayed itself.

Saul Williams, a poet whose musical combination of hip hop, rock, techno, and a cappella Black oration might be called post-hiphop, asks us, "So what is hip hop? Well, with Public Enemy and KRS-One, hip hop became the language of youth rebellion. But now, commercial hip hop is not youth rebellion, not when the heroes of hip hop like Puffy are taking pictures with Donald Trump and the heroes of capitalism—you know that's not rebellion. That's not 'the street'—that's Wall Street." And it is this reality that prompts Chuck D—an emcee that represented the Black youth rebellion in the eighties and nineties—to ask the question today: *How You Sell Soul to a Soulless People Who Sold Their Soul?*

The popular commercialism of hip hop, which has resulted in a split from those it's supposed to represent, is not new. In fact, it goes in part by the same name: hip. Just as the hip-hop generation was charged by rap, the hip era of the fifties and sixties was fueled by jazz. In *The Conquest of Cool,* an exploration of the bond between advertising and counterculture, Thomas Frank describes the co-opting of hip through "hip consumerism" as "a cultural perpetual motion machine in which disgust with the falseness, shoddiness, and everyday oppressions of consumer society could be enlisted to drive the ever-accelerating wheels of consumption."

In hip's case, and the same is true for hip hop, Scott Saul, professor of English at Berkeley, points out that "it [hip] moved from a form of African-American and bohemian dissent to become the very language of the advertising world, which took hip's promise of authenticity, liberation, and rebellion and attached it to the act of enjoying whatever was on sale at the moment." Today, young people have been tricked into seeing their acts of consumerism as acts of rebellion.

No one knows what will be next, or if their generation will sell it. However, the post-hip-hop ethos allows the necessary space for new ideas and expressions to be born free from the minstrel toxins that have polluted modern hip hop.

Although post-hip-hop is not about music, per se, the music that is and will be created is critical as it is the soul of a new movement, functioning as a soundtrack to a fresh set of attitudes, ideas, and perspectives. All forms of art are fundamental to the post-hip-hop generation, as art possesses the remarkable ability to change not only what we see, but how we see.

The late Martinican writer Frantz Fanon once said, "Each generation, out of relative obscurity, must discover their destiny and either fulfill or betray it." The post-hip-hop generation must be brave enough to fully engage in exploration, challenge, and discovery, acts that will ultimately result in a revelation of contemporary truths that will help define us, and, in turn, the world.

KEEPIN' IT REAL vs. REEL

His shadow, so to speak,
has been more real to him than his personality.
—ALAIN LOCKE

The authentic fake.
—UMBERTO ECO

It's a paradox we call reality
So keeping it real will make you a casualty
of abnormal normality.
—TALIB KWELI

I greet you at the beginning of what I hope is the last round of a great battle; an intense struggle that has raged across the treacherous battlefields of media, with blood spilling into our national imaginations, for centuries. A conflict in which victory is a prerequisite to our collective freedom, but that, unfortunately, we've been losing.

RING ANNOUNCER: In this corner, wearing sheen Black skin crafted by the Most High and manufactured from struggle, standing tall with the weight of her/his people upon her/his broad shoulders, with the ability to solve problems and do the right thing—The Real Black.

[Crowd boos]

RING ANNOUNCER: And, in this corner, wearing blackface crafted in the most high–rise board rooms by gray suits at white corporations, standing down and being a weight on her/his people, with the ability to kill niggas for fun, pimp a bitch, shuck, jive, and make lies the truth—The Reel Black.

[Crowd erupts in cheers]

I wish, of course, that the above was an effort in fiction, but unfortunately, these images—skillfully spidering into our world and forcing themselves into our lives, our ways of thinking, of seeing—are as real as we believe them to be. "The first step," a young man from Chicago's South Side tells me as we build our collective future, "is thinking outside the box, but then that's hard because the box [TV, mass media] tells us what to think." Any twenty-first-century discussion of our world, across race, gender, and class lines, must acknowledge and take seriously the notion, the reality, that young people of today derive the bulk of their ideas not from traditional institutions, but from the growing number and more intrusive forms of mass media.

"He was a nice middle class nigga / but no one knew the evil he'd do when he got a little bigger," Tupac rhymed in "Shorty Want to Be a Thug" through my sputtering speakers as I drove down a desolate, police tape–furled North Philly neighborhood in search of a tall, chestnut-colored man with thin hair and long facial features.

I found *him*.

"Peace," I lobbed as I climbed out of my car.

" 'Sup, Malo," he greeted me as I walked into the part-liquor, part-bodega, part-Chinese food spot where we agreed to meet. Hearing that name—"Malo"—took me back. Malo, the last part of my middle name Khumalo, was what I preferred to be called in my early teenage years. When people would ask what my name meant, I would ignore the Swahili definition of Khumalo, which means "prince," and instead offer the Spanish definition of *"malo,"* which simply means "bad." I'm reminded of my adolescent confusion every time I snatch a glimpse of my brown bicep where, at fourteen years old, I engraved "MALO" in Old English typeface into my young skin on the day that I was both arrested and expelled from school.

Our warm embrace was interrupted by the screeching of bicycle wheels.

"Yo, what's the deal?" hurled a grown man, his face engulfed in a serrated beard, as he zoomed in on a bright-pink kids' Huffy.

" 'Sup, nigga," he threw back as the rider pulled up.

After a three-way dap was exchanged, I watched the two as they told lies to each other; lies about "bitches" that they "fucked" and "bitch-ass niggas" who they "fucked up." After each lie, they'd laugh and dap again. It was pure performance. But neither of them would ever acknowledge themselves as actors, instead it ended with:

"Uzi, you's a real-ass nigga, man. I'm out," the bearded man said as he peddled off, disappearing around the corner.

"Uzi?" I turned to him and asked, thinking about the dysfunctional family of submachine assault guns.

"Yeah—yo, that's what niggas call me 'round here," he briefed me.

Uzi? I'm not callin' him that, I thought to myself. *His mama ain't name him Uzi.*

In fact, not only did his mama not name him Uzi, but she would adamantly disapprove of the name. I knew this, of course, because she's my mother, too. Our mother—the soft-spoken Queen from Brooklyn—who asks me, every time my big brother is arrested, every time the police trample her door down in search of her firstborn son, or every time the word "nigga" flies from his blunt-burnt lips, "Where does he get it from?"

"I don't know, Mom—not from you, though," I usually say in assurance, trying to prevent my mother from blaming herself. It's not her fault, it's no *one's*.

My brother, whom I hadn't seen or spoken to in a year because I was away in school and he didn't have a phone, was my childhood and adolescent hero—a "true thug." I used to boast about him to my awestruck middle-school crew. That was ten years ago. On this day, our reunion, he was homeless, jobless, and on the run from the police.

"Let's go for a ride," I suggested. I wanted to talk about his performance; to dig deeper into what I remember "Malo" going through as a teenager and what I suspected my brother was still going through. I figured the car ride would be my opportunity.

"Yeah, c'mon," I said, as we pulled off.

Just ask him. Just ask him why he's frontin', I urged myself.

"So, what's the deal, man?" I asked him.

"What you mean?"

"From my heart, don't take this the wrong way. But sometimes I feel like you're frontin'. Puttin' on an act. You know I know the *real* you," I explained, putting it all out there.

After a round of awkward silence: "I'm stuck, man. Trapped. Like this is who I've gotta be," he tells me.

Interestingly, my brother's feeling of entrapment (and he's not alone) supports an idea that writer Alice Walker dubs "prison of image," whereby society's stereotypes function not as errors, but rather forms of social control. In my brother's case, this prison of image led him to multiple stints in prison proper.

When Black men and women find themselves trapped inside the hellholes of the prison industrial complex, we usually point to poverty, inadequate schools, and/or broken households—all symptoms of institutional racism—as primary antagonists. In my brother's case (and he's not alone), his symptoms were different—since he was raised in a middle-class, two-parent household. However, the cancer of racism was the same. This does not mean escaping personal responsibility; however, many in the post-hip-hop generation have recognized that perhaps the most pervasive form of racism, one that is seldom tagged as such but cuts across geographic, gender, age, and class lines, is representation vis-à-vis mass media. Even in the face of relative progress made in electoral politics and education, African-Americans have made hardly any progress on the critical front of representation in mass media. Of course most Black men and women are in the prison system as a result of poverty rather than pop culture; however, the bombardment of negative stereotypes exacerbates an already dire crisis even further and in some cases, like my brother's, creates crises out of relative stability.

If one simply (and unfortunately) turns on the TV or radio, images of people of African descent remain virtually unchanged from the racist stereotypes promoted before and during slavery. Although there have been minor updates to the Black shadow cast on screen, the formula has remained fixed. Fixed, for the Black woman, has been Jezebel, the lewd mulatto; Sapphire, the evil, sex-crazed manipulative bitch; and Mammy, the Aunt Jemima nurturer whose sexuality has been so removed that she is best portrayed by Martin Lawrence (*Big Momma's House*), Tyler Perry (*Diary of a Mad Black Woman*), or Eddie Murphy (*Norbit*). For the Black man, fixed has been Bigger Thomas, the white-woman-crazed brute; Jack Johnson, the hypersexed, hyper-athletic super thug; and Uncle Tom, the asexual sidekick.

Realizing the damage these images had upon the psyches of both

Blacks and whites, Frederick Douglass, in 1848, denounced minstrel shows as "the filthy scum of white society, who have stolen from us a complexion denied to them by nature, in which to make money, and pander to the corrupt taste of their white fellow citizens." Despite this, however, these stereotypes were highly profitable both economically and politically and continued to invade every form of media available. An early instruction manual for would-be cartoonists advised students:

The colored people are good subjects for action pictures: they are natural born humorists and will often assume ridiculous attributes or say side-splitting things with no apparent intentions of being funny. . . . The cartoonist usually plays on the colored man's love of loud clothes, watermelon, crap shooting, fear of ghosts, etc.

These same characters and stereotypes, introduced at the dawn of cinema when D. W. Griffith's *The Birth of a Nation,* a film that depicts the KKK as national heroes, became the first Hollywood blockbuster, are still alive and well today. Moreover, because of advances in technology and distribution, they have become even more pervasive and widespread and thus more damaging.

The hip-hop and post-hip-hop generations, the first groups to grow up in legally desegregated America, possess a worldview that has not been shaped by the sociopolitical institutions that our parents and grandparents were a part of, many of which, because of desegregation, have since withered away. Where the Black church, community centers, and family were once the primary transmitters of values and culture, today it's a potent mass media concoction of pop music, film, television, and digital content—all of which are produced and disseminated through a small handful of multinational corporations.

Evidence of this intensified mass media onslaught can be seen, for instance, in the astronomical increase in advertising. Corporations, aware that "pop music, film and fashion are among the major forces transmitting culture to this generation," as noted in Bakari Kitwana's *The Hip-Hop Generation,* have intensified their efforts to reach us. Consider that in 1988, corporations spent $100 million on advertising targeted at children. By 1998, that number ballooned to $2 billion, and today that number exceeds more than $6 billion. In addition, the nature of these ads has morphed from straightforward product promotion to manipulative, sly programming interwoven into shows dubbed "reality" that are anything but. The reality is that while corporate America has realized the vast influence mass media has on youth, national leadership has been lethargic in addressing the ramifications of this reality. This is an area where the post-hip-hop generation, born amid a digital information age and having learned from the mistakes of both the hip-hop and the civil rights generations, must take the lead. Examples of the post-hip-hop generation taking initiative on this can be seen in the proliferation of organizations and individuals dedicated to media education, awareness, and literacy. Individuals like Kiri Davis, a young filmmaker who, at sixteen, directed *A Girl Like Me,* an award-winning short documentary, illustrate the damage of stereotypes on young African-Americans. In the film, Kiri places a black doll and a white doll in front of the children and asks them to choose the doll that is the nicest, the most beautiful, and the doll that they'd prefer to play with. Fifteen out of the twenty-one children preferred the white doll. When asked why he chose the white doll as "the nice doll," one child responded "because he's white." Kiri tells me that although she was saddened by the children's responses, "it's up to us to change that, to create new images and celebrate ourselves."

James Baldwin once said that in order to understand "what it means to be a Negro in America," we must engage in "an examination of the myths we perpetuate about him." These myths, then and now, are perpetuated primarily by white institutions looking to both meet their bottom line and, by creating and reinforcing "myths" of Black inferiority, justify racist state oppression in the minds of the rulers and the ruled.

Before, during, and after slavery, the white corporate and political structure recognized that control over the Black image is not simply important to enslaving and oppressing Blacks, but absolutely central. Central to both the masses of whites who needed to believe, as "Christians," that Blacks were not human beings in order to oppress them, or at least not oppose their oppression. And central for Blacks, on the other hand, because these images not only imposed an inferiority complex but also validated their oppression. After all, "It must be remembered that the oppressed and the oppressor are bound together within the same society; they accept the same criteria, they share the same beliefs, they both alike depend on the same reality," Baldwin added. It should be noted that even before European enslavers hit the West African shores of Elmina or Gorée Island, they'd produced and disseminated images of Blackness that supported the notion of white supremacy and justified the institution of slavery. Those that profited from slavery realized early on that their domination was contingent upon their control over how Blackness was portrayed. This notion of image control has been an important one for America not just in its subjugation of Africans, but in various other ideological conflicts. Italians, for instance, have long acknowledged that during World War II, the real victory for America came not from landing in Anzio or Salerno, but rather from Hollywood films that sold Italians on the idea of an American consumer society. The physical battle, in that regard, was a mere technicality.

In her essay "Black Feminism: The Politics of Articulation," filmmaker Pratibha Parmar writes that "Images play a crucial role in

defining and controlling the political and social power to which both
individuals and marginalized groups have access." She concludes by
reminding us that "the nature of imagery determines not only how
other people think about us but how we think about ourselves."
Without media education and literacy, "we just slot in, we buy into it
and accept their depiction of us," a young woman explains at a media
awareness conference in Newark.

Dominant images teach us, as a young girl once confided in me,
"to hate myself. My hair. My skin. The way I talk. Everything."
They tell Black women that their natural state is not beautiful; that
they are mere sex objects and "nappy-headed hoes" and push Black
men "toward a fantasy of Black hypermasculinity" where "Blackness
means a primal connection to sex and violence, a big penis and relief
from the onus of upward mobility," as John Leland puts it in *Hip:
The History.*

This means that the images produced by and for whites to justify
Blacks' oppression, images of savages, of laziness, of pimpism and
gangsterism, have been embraced by Blacks. It means that the images
that taught white people to hate Blacks, to oppress them, have ultimately resulted in *Blacks* hating *Blacks.* And it is this reality that is
most tragic. Tragic, not simply because these images are produced,
but because they have been accepted and internalized and even repro-
duced. Baldwin writes in "My Dungeon Shook" that his grandfather
"was defeated long before he died because, at the bottom of his heart,
he really believed what white people said about him." I knew, as I
looked at my brother, that he, we, made the same mistake.

"His shadow, so to speak, has been more real to him than his personality," is the way Harlem Renaissance scholar Alain Locke, discussing the challenges of the New Negro, put it in his 1925 article
"Enter the New Negro." Locke was attempting, by collecting and

publishing the writings of Blacks during his time, to redefine
Blackness in the popular imagination. He recognized that the New
Negro had to defy the dominant stereotypes not just in art, but in
everyday life. He writes:

> Could such a metamorphosis have taken place as suddenly as it has
> appeared to? The answer is no; not because the New Negro is not here,
> but because the Old Negro had long become more of a myth than a
> man. The Old Negro, we must remember, was a creature of moral de-
> bate and historical controversy. His has been a stock figure perpetuated
> as an historical fiction partly in innocent sentimentalism, partly in
> deliberate reactionism. The Negro himself has contributed his share to
> this through a sort of protective social mimicry forced upon him by
> the adverse circumstances of dependence. So for generations in the
> mind of America, the Negro has been more of a formula than a
> human being—a something to be argued about, condemned or de-
> fended, to be "kept down," or "in his place," or "helped up," to be wor-
> ried with or worried over, harassed or patronized, a social bogey or a
> social burden.

It's startling that today, more than eighty-five years later, we are dealing with the same shadow, a shadow not even cast by our own Black
bodies. A shadow that, as Locke writes, is "fiction," but is paraded as
real. And this is *reel* Blackness.

With rap videos, movies, music, news, advertisements, our minds
have been shaped by one-dimensional, stereotypical, racist, and, most
of all, limiting images of what Blacks can be. Because of the post-hip-
hop generation's overexposure to media-recepting technologies, these
images—a multiplex of comfortable violence, sexism, machismo, and
conspicuous consumption—bombard us 24-7. Although they may not

reflect our reality, their sustained and continuous presence can determine it—determine the real.

The reel becomes the real.

In 1994, at twelve years old, I stayed in the house for nearly a year. When I did go outside, I didn't wander beyond the ring of our home phone.

Why?

Because I couldn't miss the call from my brother.

Brrrinnnnggg. Brrrinnnnggg.

I was the first to pick it up.

"'Ello," I would say in a budding, out-of-breath voice.

"You have a collect call from the state correctional facility," the operator would say in monospeak. A smile would split across my face as I pressed 1 and accepted the call.

"What's up, lil' brother?" My big brother would ask sincerely. A few minutes into our conversation, he'd say the magic words: "Play somethin' for me," and he called the other inmates to the phone so they could huddle up and listen to my selections. I remember putting the phone to the speaker on my boom box and bumpin' "Life's a Bitch" off of Nas's *Illmatic*:

> *Keepin' it real, packin' steel, gettin' high*
> *'Cause life's a bitch and then you die.*

As a preteen, I became a remote prison DJ and as I rocked the crowd of inmates, I began to see just how powerful hip hop was as my brother and the other inmates erupted in awe, repeating, like scripture, the lines: "Keepin' it real, packin' steel, gettin' high / 'Cause life's a bitch and then you die." It was clear then, as it is now, that the hip-hop generation was using rap music, almost exclusively, to shape, develop, and define both public personas and personal identities.

Although for the hip-hop generation, "keeping it real" became the ultimate barometer of one's character, the post-hip-hop generation realizes that because we do not control how "real" is constructed, defined, and disseminated, this image is not real at all. Rap may serve as the most visceral example of the performance of reel. As writer William Jelani Cobb, in *To the Break of Dawn,* writes, " 'Real' is to the rap industry as 'All-Natural' is to the fast food supplier, as 'New and Improved' is to the ad agency. As 'I Solemnly Swear' is to the politician." Hip-hop culture, and in particular rap music, is particularly unique in this because "The blues artist may sing about evil, but is not required to be it or live it. The rapper is judged by a different set of credentials—the ability to live up to his own verbal badness. To get down to the denominator, hip hop has come to understand itself in the most literal of terms," concludes Cobb.

"I'm trapped between me as a person and me as J.O. the rapper," Baltimore emcee John Jones, who has just come home from serving jail time, tells me. "When I was inside [prison], I was rappin' a lot more positive. But now that I'm out, my rhymes is more on some negative stuff because that's what people want to hear. It's a different kind of prison," he explains. This prison is erected by the need to respond to stereotypical and racist portrayals of Blackness and maintained by our cultural obsession with the "real" and inability to see through the traps. This crowds and distorts not only the aesthetic space that Black artists create in, but also the average Black woman or man, like J.O. or my brother for example. Under the banner of "keeping it real," the hip-hop generation has been conditioned to act out a way of life that is not real at all. The hip-hop *industry* (as opposed to the hip-hop *community*) has been successful in framing an authentic Black identity that is not intellectual, complex, creative, educated, or diverse, but a monolith of violence (only against other Blacks!) and sexism. These images are not just harmful domestically, but are beamed around the world as a statement about universal Blackness. As a student in London I experienced, firsthand, the effects of this global distortion when my Nepalese roommate, once he discovered we'd be living together, asked to be transferred because he "feared for his life." After a discussion, he confessed that his irrational fears were not the result of ever being around Black folks (he hadn't), but consuming, in Nepal, the negative images about African-Americans. "I thought you'd shoot me," he confessed to me later.

This ethos translates to hip-hop films, as well. Hood films, unlike, say, Italian mafia flicks, are supposed to capture and define what it means to be Black. Take, for example, the fictional film *Menace II Society* whose official tagline was "This is the truth. This is what's real." Filmmaker Byron Hurt, whose documentary *Hip-Hop: Beyond Beats & Rhymes* premiered at the Sundance Film Festival in 2006, introduces the film with this observation:

> *We're like in this box. In order to be in that box—you have to be strong, you have to be tough, you have to have a lot of girls, you have to have money, you got to be a playa or a pimp, you have to be in control, you have to dominate other men, other people. If you're not any of those things, people call you soft or weak or a pussy or a chump or a faggot, and nobody wants to be any of those things so everybody stays inside the box.*

So why do we continue to stay in these boxes? Perhaps it's because of the American golden rule: those with the gold make the rules. So, essentially, white teenage boys, the primary consumers of rap music, spend billions of dollars on images and music produced by white corporations that reinforce these stereotypes. Fixed on meeting bottom lines, corporations in turn leverage their excessive amount of capital and power to produce, perpetuate, promote whatever's on sale—thus employing a disproportionate influence on our minds.

This process of white consumerism, which is age-old, has taught Blacks that there are hefty profits to be made by living *down* to white expectations. Many of today's artists feel as prominent Harlem Renaissance novelist Jessie Fauset did when her first novel, *There Is Confusion,* was rejected because, as one editor put it, "white readers don't expect Negroes to be like this."

"Yo, I'll kill you nigga . . . I'm moving kilos of coke . . . I'm strapped with AKs, semis, Glocks, shit from Russia . . . yaddy, yaddy, yah," J. O. tells me about the topics young Black rappers feel they have to discuss. "That's the shit that most niggas is on. Why? Even though it ain't true, 'cause if it was you'd be under the jail, they know, just like I know, that that's the shit that sells. Negativity. Drugs. Guns. Bitches. There really is not an alternative. You either rap like that or you don't sell. That's where you gotta come from if you wanna make it."

"Even if that's not really you?" I ask.

"Yup," he confirms.

My brother felt the same way.

In the hip-hop world, keeping it real has become the measuring stick for one's connection to the ghetto. The ghetto has become the repository of all that is real, and everything else is not. The problem with this is that the ghetto in mass media is not the real ghetto.

The ghetto doesn't exist and the Gulf War never happened. French theorist Jean Baudrillard shocked people when he published the book *The Gulf War Did Not Take Place.* Baudrillard argued that the war was largely a TV event, experienced by the masses more like a video game than an actual situation of war. Baudrillard explained this theory as hyperreality and asserted that we can no longer distinguish between imitation and reality—and that we often prefer the imitations because they have been gutted of any societal consequences.

The ghetto then, as most experience it through mass media, doesn't exist either. It, too, is reel. Wrenched out of its sociopolitical and racial injustice context, it is transformed into an urban playground. It allows people to listen to "ghetto music," without examining the issues that allow such a place to exist.

"What makes it so difficult is to know that we need to be doing other things. . . . They want [Black artists] to shuck and jive, but they don't want us to tell the real story because they're connected to it," says rapper David Banner, who is a graduate of Southern University in Baton Rouge, where he also served as president of the student government. Banner is right on; whites and even upwardly mobile Blacks who consume reel "ghetto" music have made a fetish out of Black disenfranchisement. And because the music is *lite,* they are not forced to deal with the reality that it is racist policies—exclusionary zoning laws, real estate industry discrimination, redlining, parasitic corporate development, and the Department of Transportation's highway projects that tear apart viable Black communities—that create the ghetto in the first place.

On the Black-hand side, Blacks in the ghetto see a highly stylized, depoliticized version of their environment, and on the other, Blacks outside of the ghetto are told their experience is inauthentic. In this market-driven environment, truly important ideas about love, caring, and service are disregarded as incidental or lost completely. For those of us who are already battling issues of inadequate education or poverty, warding off these harmful ideological ideas is even more challenging.

This might help explain a recent article in the *San Francisco Chronicle* entitled "Suicide Rate Climbing for Black Teens: Move to Middle Class May Cause Identity Crisis," which details a federal study that shows the suicide rate for Black teens has been rising dramatically. Unlike white and Latino teens, the Black teens who commit suicide tend to come from higher socioeconomic backgrounds than the general African-American population. Many social psychologists speculate that this increase is due to identity crises perpetuated by the mass media.

In bell hooks's provocative analysis on Black masculinity, *We Real Cool: Black Men and Masculinity,* she furthers the discussion, stating:

> *While we often hear about privileged black men assuming a ghetto gangsta-boy style, we rarely hear about the pressure they get from white people to prove they are "really black." . . . This pressure is part of the psychological racial arsenal for it constantly lets educated black people, especially black males, know that no amount of education will allow them to escape the imposition of racist stereotypes. Often in predominantly white educational settings, black males put on their ghetto minstrel show as a way of protecting themselves from a white racialized rage. They want to appear harmless, not a threat, and to do so they have to entertain unenlightened folks by letting them know "I don't think I'm equal to you. I know my place. Even though I am educated I know you think I am still an animal at heart."*

Writer Kheven Lee LaGrone believes that middle-class "Black teens are stuck between the plantation and the ghetto." In the article "The 90s Minstrels," he asks,

> *Do they feel they are treated like minstrels, the black American "other," or as a "nigger/nigga" defined by white suburbia? This is important, since for many black suburban youth, gangsta rap may represent their only connection to the inner city and to what they consider "true" blackness.*

The real Blackness hooks and LaGrone write about, and that my brother spent his life chasing, isn't real at all. It's reel: from the ignorant, womanizing, hypermasculine thug to the oversexed, loud, quick-to-get-an-attitude-over-nothing bitch. It's all reel.

In the case of my brother, who is a few years north of thirty, I hold on to grains of hope that someday he might turn things around, redefine himself and climb out of the prefabricated box he's in. For some though, it's too late.

The late Russell Tyrone Jones—also known as Joe Bananas, Dirt McGirt, Dirt Dog, Ason Unique, Big Baby Jesus, Osirus, and most commonly Ol' Dirty Bastard—died frontin'. Much like my brother, ODB spent his adult life dancing between jail, welfare, and stints with rap success. And also like my brother, ODB vehemently denied his middle-class upbringing, and instead promoted a poverty-stricken, dangerous one (as if being Black wasn't enough). In "Caught Up," he raps:

> *I'm a ghetto nigga dog so I get it how I live*
> *Got money, lock 'em off, fuckers still I got drama*
> *Got two strike dog and five baby mamas.*

"I was furious," said William Jones, ODB's father. "You know, that story about him being raised in the Fort Greene [Brooklyn] projects on welfare until he was a child of thirteen was a total lie," he added. When Jones talked to his wife about their son's bogus claims of ghettoship, her response was simple: "He did it for publicity." Of course he did. ODB understood that boasting racist and classist stereotypes about Blacks would reaffirm them in the minds of a largely white consumer market. This would explain the correlation between ODB's run-ins with the law and simultaneous spikes in record sales.

ODB's story reminds us that most artists feel that in order to "make it," they need to portray a stereotypical image that is marketable to white America. As a result, artists like ODB downplay their middle-class origins and artists who are from the ghetto avoid portraying and calling out the savage injustices that created their condition. When *Time* magazine covered gangsta rapper Ice-T's upbringing, they noted that "Although he lived in Windsor Hill, a middle-class section of L.A., he claims he began hanging with a rough crowd. He plays up these tough-guy roots to legitimize his hard raps."

It is this type of rhetoric and these decisions by culture makers that has caused "Black" to become synonymous with the "reel ghetto." It is like a person who is seeking to become something that he is not because he is so worried that he will not be accepted by the masses as real. But real is as real believes and lives. You can find it anywhere. Julie Dash, the filmmaker responsible for such works as *Daughters of the Dust* and *The Rosa Parks Story*, reminds me that, "Our lives, our history, our present reality is no more limited to 'ghetto' stories than Italian Americans are to the Mafia, or Jewish Americans are to the Holocaust."

In an article by social commentator Harold Clemens entitled " 'Ghetto'—The New N-Word," he describes this usurpation of the Black experience. He writes that the word " 'ghetto,' when used colloquially as an adjective, is the most racist, derogatory word in the common lexicon, given its so subtle insinuations and layers. Employed to mean 'uncouth,' 'unruly,' or 'parvenu,' 'ghetto' is the most popular new code word to stigmatize blacks." He goes on:

> *Evidence of this relationship is the commonality of statements like, "You can be black and not be ghetto," which sounds a hell of a lot like the formerly popular, "You can be black and not be a nigger." People even make comments like "ghetto-ass, white boy." The first remark*

obviously insinuates black people are usually "ghetto," or at least that people that are "ghetto" are usually black. The latter obviously insinuates that white boys, and white people in general, usually aren't "ghetto," since the identification, "white boy," is necessary to complete the description.

The ghetto experience in our history in America is an important one, mainly because it represents our historic and contemporary socioeconomic struggles for liberation. Because the reel ghetto experience has been highly profitable, it has left all Blacks—in the ghetto or outside of it—feeling inauthentic. The reality is that young, nonviolent Black men are born into a world that has already pegged them as violent criminals. Further, they treat and mistreat them based on this falsehood. It's no surprise then that many youths explained their decision to act out as a giving-in of sorts to a reality that is fixed. The mentality becomes, "If you're going to treat me like a criminal, I may as well get what I can get," because ultimately both fates are the same. My brother and ODB became what society viewed them as, which is always unfortunate.

When I see young people like Alyce Bush, the founder of Roots to Freedom, a grassroots nonprofit organization dedicated to providing an alternative to the negative images that sabotage our reality, I'm hopeful that we will find a rhythm that helps those of us who have sought authenticity through combing through the most inauthentic places.

In Richard Wright's *Black Boy,* Bigger Thomas remarks, "Having been thrust out of the world because of my race, I had accepted my destiny by not being curious about what shaped it." My brother, ODB, and countless others felt that they could not challenge the perceptions. One does not have to go along with any image imposed upon them by the outside. We are not simply to be acted upon; in some real senses we are actors ourselves, making the world go 'round, and choosing to be what we choose to be. Poet Saul Williams reminds us that "Right now, we are unable to imagine world peace. Why? Because our imaginations have been stolen from us. We can imagine World War III because we've seen it in every movie, every TV show, etc. We cannot imagine world peace because we've never seen it before." If it's not up to the post-hip-hop generation to create alternatives that will reveal their infinite possibilities, then who will produce these images?

Tupac once told us, "Stop being cowards and let's have a revolution, but we don't wanna do that. Dudes just wanna live a caricature, they wanna be cartoons, but if they really wanted to do something, if they was that tough, all right, let's start a revolution." That revolution may not be televised, but with the advent of digital and Web technology, the post-hip-hop generation is utilizing forms of new media to challenge, discover, and influence how we think about our world.

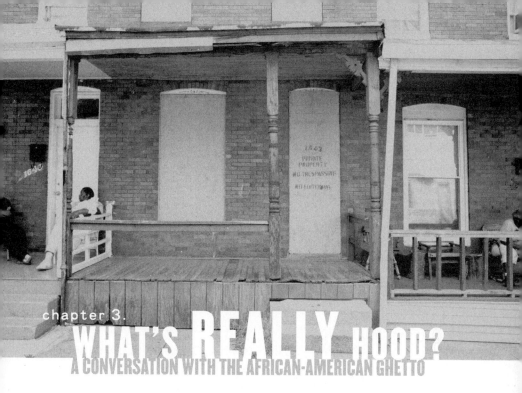

chapter 3.
WHAT'S REALLY HOOD?
A CONVERSATION WITH THE AFRICAN-AMERICAN GHETTO

> A ghetto can be improved in only one way:
> out of existence.
> —JAMES BALDWIN

First off, thanks for granting me this interview.

No problem. It's time for me to set the record straight.

About . . . ?

About me. Who I am. And actually, more importantly, why I am who I am.

See, people who live in me know me on an intimate and visceral level, while people who live elsewhere probably know what I look like. However, most of these folks, residents and nonresidents alike, don't understand who I really am.

Is it important that they know who you really are?

Is it important? It's essential. Imperative. Especially for the post-hip-hop generation. They are going to be the ones whose decisions will

affect me the most. They've been fed a hyperrealistic, inadequate por-
trait of who I am and if not dealt with it will cause confusion and
vital opportunities will be lost. Basically, they need to understand me
in order to fully understand themselves.

All right then, so, who are you? Who is the African—American ghetto?

I'm a place where people are and have historically been forced to live.

Which people?

All types of people: brilliant, courageous, beautiful, crazy, funny, tal-
ented, strong, injured, soulful. All types. Geeks. Shoemakers. Scholars. Comedians. Athletes. Scientists. Lovers. The whole spectrum.

The common denominator is that they're economically poor and
African-American.

I'm curious about your name, "Ghetto." What does it mean? Where does it
come from?

Linguists trace it back to the Italian words *"getto"* (to cast off) and
"borghetto" (small neighborhood), the Venetian slang "gheto," the
Griko *"ghetonia"* (neighborhood), and the Hebrew word *"get"* (bill of
divorce).

The first time my name was written was when English traveler and
writer Thomas Coryat, on a foot journey through Europe, described
"the place where the whole fraternity of the Jews dwelleth together,
which is called the Ghetto."

And what year was that?

1611.

Early in its usage it meant a walled-off and gated section in cities
where Jews were confined. The word was mostly used in Italy, near
port cities like Venice where a lot of Jews lived and worked. Jews were

placed under strict regulations, forced to live together, and put on curfews that prevented them from being out at certain times. As if that wasn't enough, sumptuary laws forced Jews to wear special star-shaped yellow badges and yellow berets, identifying themselves as Jews and opening themselves up to taunts and attacks by Christians who were the majority.

Damn. Did other writers back in the day write about your name?

Yeah, lots. In 1879, British writer Dean Farrar writes about the ghetto in *Life of St. Paul.* Edward Dowden, a nineteenth-century literary critic, makes many references to ghettos in his analysis of Percy Bysshe Shelley. British author Israel Zangwill wrote the books *Children of the Ghetto* and *Dreamers of the Ghetto,* both biographical studies. In 1908, Jack London in *Martin Eden* explains that his characters "plunged off right into the heart of the working-class ghetto." Despite its usage by these writers, it wasn't widely discussed or popular.

When did it become widely known?

The word blew up in the mid-1930s when the Nazis took power and set up ghettos that, just like in previous times, confined Jews into cramped, tightly packed areas of the inner cities of Eastern Europe. However, unlike previous ghettos in Europe, these ghettos were im-poverished, overcrowded, and disease-plagued areas enclosed by stone or brick walls, wooden fences, and barbed wire. And, if Jews tried to leave, the penalty was death.

So it was death either way?

Adolf Eichmann, a top Nazi official, came up with what he called the "Final Solution to the Jewish Question," a program of system-atic genocide that attempted to eradicate the entire Jewish popula-tion in Europe. In preparation, Eichmann began to move all Jews into ghettos. The Nazis, between 1939 and 1945, set up more than three hundred Jewish ghettos in the Soviet Union, the Baltic states, Romania, Czechoslovakia, Poland, and Hungary. During the Holocaust, nearly all the Jews in the ghettos were killed—so yes, death either way.

Do you see yourself as being related to those Jewish ghettos of Europe?
Of course. Take the Warsaw ghetto, as an example of institutional overcrowding, where Jews, who were 30 percent of the population, were forced to live in 2.4 percent of the city's area—about ten people per room. Most apartments had no sanitation, piped water, or sewers. Starvation was rife.

So, similarly, during my birth in America, Urban Renewal (which, behind closed doors, was called "nigger removal") was all about systematically uprooting Blacks from sections of the city deemed "valuable," then forcing them into projects. For every ten homes that they destroyed, they only built one new unit in the projects—institutional overcrowding.

Many things are the same: the social isolation; the normalized terror by authorities; and state-sponsored racism, to name a few.

And what about other ghettos around the world—do you see yourself as related to them?
Of course. Every ghetto—from Soweto to L'île-Saint-Denis, from Brixton to Chiapas, from favelas to shantytowns—I am one with.

Why?
'Cause oppression is oppression is oppression, man.

Some people say that you're a "state of mind"?
Which people?

Um—

I say survival is a state of mind. That's where soul comes from.

And what's soul?

Soul is graceful survival against impossible circumstances.

That's heavy. All right now, can you talk about your roots as the Black
American ghetto?

Definitely.

All right, so, 40 Acres & A Mule is not just the name of Spike Lee's
film company, it's also the colloquial term for the reparations that
were supposed to be issued to enslaved Africans after the Civil War—
forty acres of farmland and a mule to cultivate that land. The official
name was Special Field Orders, No. 15, and it was issued on January
16, 1865, by Maj. Gen. William Sherman.

So what happened?

Well, when President Abraham Lincoln was killed, Andrew Johnson,
his replacement, revoked Sherman's orders. The very few Blacks who
had already received land had it quickly taken away.

Abolishing slavery with no restitution is like opening the door to a
prison cell, while leaving all other exits bolted, chained, and locked,
and telling an inmate that "they are free." The cell door, although
perhaps the most confining, is but a multitude of forces that keeps
the prisoner imprisoned.

Anyway, without any restitution, Blacks were forced into a vicious
cycle of sharecropping, also known as Slavery II, where they paid rent
to white landowners from their yearly yield. This form of neoslavery
also occurred later in South Africa and Zimbabwe where it was illegal
for Blacks to own their own land. Sharecropping is a vicious cycle because, by the end of the year without fail, the sharecropper is always

in debt, meaning he can never free himself from the land. This, coupled with de-citizenizing Jim Crow laws, made it impossible for Blacks to own land in the South, binding them—through the law—in the shallow pits of poverty.

That was in the South. What about in the North?

Around the times I just mentioned, 1865–1876, Blacks comprised less than 5 percent of industrial northern cities like Detroit, Chicago, Philadelphia, et cetera. Blacks in the North, because of racism and discrimination, weren't allowed to work in factories or join unions, which reduced them to the lowest, dirtiest, grimiest, nastiest jobs— jobs no one else would do.

Beginning around 1914, though, large numbers of Blacks started moving to industrial hubs like New York City, Philadelphia, Baltimore, Maryland, Detroit, Chicago, et cetera.

Because things were so bad in the South?

It was "*so* bad" everywhere. But mainly because World War I, which began in 1914, called for a lot of unskilled factory workers. And you know when America needs weapons, they don't care who makes 'em.

Blacks kept coming North, looking for work, even after the war was over. During the twenties alone, over two million Blacks came North in hopes of a better life. You had a lot of Blacks looking for work in an already impossible job market, then the Depression hits.

But that affected pretty much everybody, right?

Yeah, everybody was affected. But while everybody was affected, you must remember: Blacks were the first to get fired when things got bad and the last ones to get hired once things finally picked up. But that wasn't the worst of it by any stretch of the imagination. What happened next was unconscionable:

President Franklin D. Roosevelt cut Black people out of his plan to alleviate the poverty of the national Depression.

How?

It was clear that Social Security—which provided benefits to retirees and the unemployed, and a lump-sum benefit at death—and Mandatory Minimum Insurance were proven methods of reducing and alleviating poverty.

Roosevelt drafted these programs under his Committee on Economic Security, and they were passed by Congress under his New Deal. One of the major problems was that both of these acts excluded domestics and agricultural workers, who made up more than two-thirds of the Black workforce. Then with all of—

Can you—

Can you let me finish?

My bad.

I haven't even got to the worst part yet.

All right, please continue.

Where was I?

FDR was cutting Black people out of all his programs.

Right, right. The Federal Housing Administration was also developed under FDR. This organization guaranteed mortgages for up to 90 percent of the purchase price, which meant that people who wanted to buy a home only had to cough up 10 percent rather than the 25 percent to 30 percent required before the FHA. The FHA made home ownership possible again—which was an important part of recovering from the Depression. In the thirty-five years after its creation, home ownership skyrocketed.

What was the catch?

The catch was that the FHA refused to guarantee mortgages in Black communities due to a process called redlining. In most of these places, Blacks couldn't receive loans at all. Once the FHA refused to give loans to Blacks, private lenders replicated the government's policy and position, which, really, was about denying Black humanity.

Can you talk about what redlining is and how it affected you?

The term "redlining" was coined in the 1960s by activists in Chicago. It refers to a process where affluent or white neighborhoods were outlined in blue and considered type "A"; working class neighborhoods were outlined in yellow and considered type "B"; and of course, Black neighborhoods were outlined in bloodred ink and considered type "D." These maps were created for FHA manuals as well as private lenders. The FHA advised banks to stay away from areas with "inharmonious racial groups" and recommended that municipalities enact racially restrictive zoning ordinances and prevent Black home ownership.

During the second great migration (1940–1970), when 4.5 million Blacks came North, industrial cities decided to segregate the industrial from the residential areas. Remember, during this time, Blacks had absolutely no political power and overt racism was at an all-time high. Therefore many Black areas were tagged as industrial neighborhoods.

And what did that industrial tag mean?

The industrial tag prevented these neighborhoods from undergoing any new construction and even limited the improvements that could be made.

So, why didn't Blacks just leave these redlined areas?

Those redlined areas were me. I told you earlier that I'm a place where people are forced to live, because of discrimination via racism in the real estate market and segregation. Blacks could not, I repeat *could not*, live where they pleased, even if they had the money, and because of those things I just mentioned, they probably didn't.

So you've been around for a long time?

Well yes, but I didn't always look like I do now.

See, during the sixties and before, Blacks, although segregated and isolated, lived in me very viably. I was anchored by Black-owned businesses and Black-run institutions. Believe it or not, "crime" during this period was not a problem in me. But then . . .

Crack?

Whoa—not yet, slow down. That's later.

Way before crack, there was "nigger removal," as it was sometimes called by government officials.

Okay, yeah, you mentioned that earlier.

Right. Officially dubbed Urban Renewal, this program was designed to transform poor neighborhoods into new, architecturally attractive structures that would attract tourists and increase business. The Urban Renewal program had its shaky origins in the Housing Act of 1949, but it did not get under way in a serious fashion until 1954, when the Eisenhower administration made several changes in the law.

Of course I was chosen for Urban Renewal because the people who lived there didn't have any political power. Whites during this time made all the decisions for Blacks with no input or say from Blacks.

Under Urban Renewal, I was razed and rebuilt and the Blacks who lived in me were forced out.

When you say "forced out," what do you mean?
I mean forced out. Eminent domain, the process whereby the state seizes private property for government or private use, gives the government the authority to *jack* residents.

Where did the displaced Blacks go?
Uncle Sam decided that they needed to construct new areas for these displaced Blacks to live. So they built shabby, health-hazardous, cheap housing in me called housing projects.

For every ten homes they destroyed, they built one unit in the projects.

So is this why you are the way you are today?
Not quite—there are a few more things that happened to me that I feel contributed significantly to who I am today.

On top of "nigger removal," the federal interstate system had a devastating effect on me physically and psychologically. When I wasn't razed for Urban Renewal, they would build highways that went right through me and separated my people from others. This created further isolation for Blacks and it simultaneously created insulation for whites as they fled to the suburbs.

Thanks to these new highways, though, whites could get into the city when they needed to. Between 1950 and 1970, 70 million whites fled the city and moved to the suburbs. The reason this white flight was so devastating is that whites took jobs with them when they left and eventually moved businesses out of me and into the suburbs.

Soon after, the factories left, too. See, post–World War II the factories had been one of the primary ways for Blacks to climb out of the quicksand of poverty. However, those jobs fled with the whites.

To the suburbs?

No, overseas. Multinational corporations got out of me and headed for places like India, Indonesia, and other impoverished nations of the world. Places where the wages are dramatically less, unions are illegal, there are no environmental or labor laws. So, they've got twelve-year-olds working sixteen hours, making pennies per day. When companies don't go overseas, they use prison labor instead of creating real jobs, which is, in essence, slave labor. I mean, the rates they pay prisoners rivals what they might pay a child in an impoverished country.

Major corporations do this?

American Airlines, Boeing, Compaq, Dell, Eddie Bauer, Chevron, Hewlett-Packard, Honeywell, IBM, JCPenney, TWA, McDonald's, Microsoft, Motorola, Nordstrom, Pierre Cardin, Revlon, Sony, Texas Instruments, Victoria's Secret, and Toys "R" Us, to name a few.

In addition, the mechanization of many low-skilled jobs left a lot of people well below the poverty line. So jobs in the domestic and service sectors are all that's left for low-skilled workers. Since 1975, however, these jobs have been declining in real dollars and in relation to other sectors.

What about Black professionals?

Integration was another fierce blow to me.

After the end of legal segregation, the Black middle class—who had traditionally been instrumental in creating, maintaining, and patronizing businesses in me—bounced. They, too, fled for the burbs, leaving the poorest of the poor behind.

Finally, Blacks left me in a mad exodus along with the whites at the end of legal segregation.

That reminds me of a Malcolm X speech.
Which one?

It's called "Message to the Grassroots." He says,

> *This modern house Negro loves his master. He wants to live near him. He'll pay three times as much as the house is worth just to live near his master, and then brag about "I'm the only Negro out here." "I'm the only one on my job." "I'm the only one in this school." You're nothing but a house Negro. And if someone comes to you right now and says, "Let's separate," you say the same thing that the house Negro said on the plantation. "What you mean, separate? From America? This good white man? Where you going to get a better job than you get here?" I mean, this is what you say. "I ain't left nothing in Africa," that's what you say. You left your mind in Africa.*

[A chuckle is shared]

I know this is kind of off topic, but I gotta ask: Why are there so many damn check-cashing places, liquor stores, and take-out Chinese restaurants in you?
Actually, not off topic at all. I just told you that the Black middle class fled. Well, when affluent Blacks left me and bounced to the suburbs, the businesses, following the money, left, too. To give you a popular example, there were, during segregation, more than three

hundred Black movie houses around the country. You're a filmmaker, right? Tell me how many are there now.

Okay, let's see, um—

Exactly.

So with the flight or destruction of viable Black businesses, that left only the businesses you mentioned—the businesses whose primary goal is to capitalize on Black poverty. Check-cashing spots capitalize and exploit low-wage earners unable to afford a bank account and who need quick money; pawnshops capitalize on poor folks who need to liquidate personal valuables in order to make rent. Fast-food Chinese restaurants, through the thick bulletproof glass, capitalize on the Black poor by offering food—very unhealthy food that the owners admittedly don't eat—to Blacks at a low monetary cost but with high health costs. And liquor stores, which can be found on nearly every corner, capitalize on the depression and despair that come with being poor and living in me.

Rick James once commented: "One thing 'bout the ghetto, you don't have to worry, it'll be there tomorrow." That said, where do you see yourself in ten years?

It all depends.

On . . . ?

What it has always depended upon: the people.

What are some of the things you'd like to see the post—hip—hop generation do? Things they could do that would improve you and the lives of the people who live in you?

How much time you got? [Laughter]

Tell me what time it is.

All right, first, the post-hip-hop generation should understand the relationship between poverty and health. That's something that we haven't talked about yet and it's absolutely essential.

Lack of income, clean water, food, and access to medical services and education are all related to poverty and health—and all of this is intensified in me. Because of urban diets and environments, people in me have extremely high rates of diabetes, hypertension, heart disease, and asthma. Not only are my residents more likely to have illnesses, but because they are poor, they are more likely to be limited by these conditions. Health issues prevent many from working or, at the least, limit their productivity—ultimately lowering income.

Asthma, lead poisoning, malnutrition, anemia, ear infections—all of these are not only costly to treat or even diagnose, but all lead to permanent impairments. So, for example, children who live in me are twice as likely to suffer from lead poisoning, which many, many studies have shown has serious effects on the brain causing learning problems, hyperactivity, coordination issues, aggression, erratic behavior, and brain damage. There is a lot of lead in much of the housing in me, especially in the projects, so children are exposed to lead.

See, health is connected to everything. Both lead poisoning and asthma are severe problems on their own; however, they mushroom because they greatly diminish a child's school performance and are the leading causes of absenteeism. Not to mention many children are malnourished, which leads to headaches, lack of concentration, frequent colds, and fatigue. You would think that schools in me would be more equipped to deal with these kind of issues, but they are actually given less funds. It's a systematic holocaust.

Every illness, especially untreated, makes it more difficult to deal with an already extremely difficult environment. People who live in mc are more likely to work and live in conditions that are detrimental to their health.

What do you—

Oh, not to mention that just being poor—period—and the stress from poverty is a huge detriment to one's health.

Dr. King, in a book called *Where Do We Go From Here: Chaos or Community?* said—

Are you paraphrasing?

No, I memorized it. It's that good. He said,

> *The children's clothes are too skimpy to protect them from the Chicago wind, and a closer look reveals the mucus in the corners of their bright eyes, and you are reminded that vitamin pills and flu shots are luxuries which they can ill afford. The "runny noses" of ghetto children become a graphic symbol of medical neglect in a society which has mastered most of the diseases from which they will too soon die. There is something wrong in a society which allows this to happen.*

What do you think can be done about this?

People need universal health care, for starters, to begin to climb out of the desolate pits of poverty. Right now, nearly all of my citizens, and more than 43 million Americans in total, are uninsured and it doesn't have to be like this. Congressman Jim McDermott (D-WA), for example, proposes a single payer plan that would provide coverage for all Americans without increasing total costs, every year; however, it's never been approved. Moreover, this is what the people want—not just my people, but most Americans. A USA/Harris poll recently conducted showed that 77 percent of the general public believes the government should provide universal health care.

The other important thing is unemployment insurance. Unemployment insurance keeps people who have been laid off above the poverty level; however, the way it's structured now, 60 percent of people who are laid off don't receive any temporary monies. We must do this. It would mean no person willing and ready to work should be living in poverty.

Another thing is expanding Supplemental Security Income, a program that provides benefits to those permanently disabled, and workers' compensation, a program that provides benefits to workers who have been injured on the job. Everyone who cannot work should receive benefits. Right now, people who have been temporarily disabled from injuries caused off the job cannot receive benefits from either program. What's worse is that even those who are permanently disabled—by mental illness, disability due to addiction, and hard-to-prove conditions like back pain—are not eligible to receive any benefits.

How much would all this cost?

That can't be determined for sure, but consider this: in 1999, the "poverty gap," which is the amount of money needed to raise all the incomes to at least the poverty line, was $65 billion. Yearly Social Security income is $500 billion. And the tax cut we got in 2001 was $1.3 trillion. America has the loot.

Why are your schools, some of which I attended, failing?

Because poor African-Americans are forced into me, my schools are almost completely segregated. Secondary and elementary schools are funded mainly through local taxes, so my schools have much fewer resources per child and significantly less money to fund education.

My students are bringing noneducational issues like hunger, domestic violence, homelessness, abuse, and many other personal problems that demand greater resources. However, despite this, my schools are getting far less money than, say, suburban schools, which don't have to deal with these issues.

Can I read you a passage? I came across it recently and it echoes this point.

Sure, go ahead.

This is from *Savage Inequalities: Children in America's Schools* by Jonathan Kozol:

> "Don't tell students in this school about 'the dream.' Go and look into a toilet here if you would like to know what life is like for students in this city."
>
> Before I leave, I do as Christopher asked and enter a boys' bathroom. Four of the six toilets do not work. The toilet stalls, which are eaten away by red and brown corrosion, have no doors. The toilets have no seats. One has a rotted wooden stump. There are no paper towels and no soap. Near the door there is a loop of wire with an empty toilet-paper roll.
>
> "This," says Sister Julia, "is the best school that we have in East St. Louis."
>
> Almost anyone who visits in the schools of East St. Louis, even for a short time, comes away profoundly shaken. These are innocent children, after all. They have done nothing wrong. They have committed no crime. They are too young to have offended us in any way at all. One searches for some way to understand why a society as rich and, frequently, as generous as ours would leave these children in their penury and squalor for so long—and with so little public indignation. Is this just a strange mistake of history?

That's the sad reality.

Along the same lines, the late, great artivist Ossie Davis once said, "I believe the ending of poverty is the cultural assignment of our time." Do you agree?

Yes, and racism in this country is intertwined with poverty—so yes, poverty and racism. I mean, in America, the richest nation in the world, on any given night, 562,000 American children go to bed hungry.

Do you think the U.S. government cares?

Follow the money, the budget, and you'll see what the government cares about. The U.S. budget represents not only political and economic interests, but moral ones as well. Don't believe what politicians tell you their priorities are, look at the budget and decide for yourself.

A child is born into poverty every forty-three seconds, and without health insurance every minute in America. This is public information.

One of the most common misconceptions is that the government can't solve the poverty problem and that everything that could possibly be done has been tried. The government can in fact solve the problem and it's not that expensive. The reality is they haven't been willing to consider eradicating poverty in this country.

So what do we do?

Didn't Frederick Douglass say that "Power concedes nothing without a demand. It never did and it never will."

Yeah, he did.

Well, there you go.

It's up to the people, in me and outside of me, to make this a priority. Demand justice and true equality.

But they don't understand because of misrepresentation. That's why I agreed to this interview.

KRS—One once said, "It's not a novelty, you can love your neighborhood
without loving poverty." Do you agree with that?

Most definitely. Poverty is nothing to love. My image has been dis-
torted and misrepresented, though, so you have a white media that
both glorifies and demonizes me at the same time, while never really
addressing who I am.

So I take it you feel misrepresented?

Of course. There is me, as I am, with all of the institutional, political,
economic, and structural racist policies, and then there is my image
that fails to address any of this in a real way.

The misrepresentation leads to a public consensus about my residents. They believe, both those who reside elsewhere and, sadly, those
who reside in me, that their poverty is their fault. That they are lazy,
addicted, sexually promiscuous, and so on and so forth, and that this
is the reason for the poverty, when the reality, as I've touched upon, is
completely different. To give you a quick example, most people who
live in me are not addicted to drugs or alcohol, don't engage in criminal activity, and are not on welfare. This would come as a shock to
those who absorb the images on TV and in movies and the rhymes of
mainstream rappers.

America is a very individualistic society. So, as a result, poor people
are blamed for their poverty and the rich are credited with their
wealth, disregarding inheritance, class privilege, resources, et cetera. I
mean, Bush is as responsible for his wealth as most of my residents
are for their poverty.

Yeah. So do you think this has political ramifications?

Definitely. If the majority of Americans think that the poor are poor
because of their own faults, then they'll also believe that the poor
should get out of it on their own. They believe the poor are undeserving.

All of this is reinforced by popular culture, which literally makes fun of poor people. Their lack of education is laughed at, their squalor glorified, their struggle criminalized. People certainly don't want to change the policies.

There's this big thing about "pulling yourself up by the bootstraps."
You can't pull yourself up by the bootstraps if you don't have any damn shoes!

What about the violence in you?
Violence? [shrugs]

Well?
Was Nat Turner violent?

Uh, I'm not—
Reminds me of Nat Turner, because he was not violent, he was responding to slavery, which was violent. The conditions in which my residents live are violent. There's always been this attempt to demonize my residents. They call survival after a hurricane "looting." They call protests against a system that keeps them poor "riots."

Look, man, as long as I'm around, there will be desperation. What do you expect if you put the poorest folks together in one area, take away jobs, destroy social networks, police the hell out of them, harass them—I mean, seriously, what do you expect?

Is there anything else that you'd like to tell the post—hip—hop generation?
Organize, organize, organize. The time is now.

Thanks for your time.
Peace.

chapter 4.

IT'S BIGGER THAN HIP HOP

We were born into an unjust system;
we are not prepared to grow old in it.
—BERNADETTE DEVLIN

"And finally, how does it feel to be just twenty-three years old—and a *professor?*" asked the energetic host of the Pacifica radio program on which I was being phone interviewed.

"I haven't started yet, however, the thing—"

"I'm sorry, brother Asante, I'm afraid that's our time," she informed me.

"Oh," I grunted, feeling cheated.

"It was nice talking to you. Good luck to you this semester at Morgan State University."

"A'ight, thanks, peace," I said as I disappointedly hung up the phone.

I wanted to answer the question. I wanted to say that I truly was excited about the position; however, just as our interview was prematurely amputated, I was convinced that my professorship would be, too.

A few years before I was hired, artivist Amiri Baraka was offered the position of poet laureate of New Jersey by then-governor Jim Mc-Greevey. Baraka—perplexed that he, given his highly publicized radical politics—would be offered a state gig, warned McGreevey, "You're gonna get in trouble," as he accepted the job. Sure enough, within a few months, after Baraka wrote and recited his book-length post-9/11 poem, "Somebody Blew Up America," there was trouble. The poem asks: "Who have the colonies / Who stole the most land / Who rule the world / Who say they good but only do evil / Who the biggest executioner / Who made Bush president? / Who believe the confederate flag need to be flying? / Who talk about democracy and be lying?" When Baraka refused to resign at the governor's request, McGreevey, lacking the power to fire Baraka, opted to abolish the position altogether, thus giving Baraka the distinct moniker as the first and last poet laureate of New Jersey. On a similar note, I felt I was destined to become the first and last twenty-three-year-old professor ever appointed.

Why?

Because most colleges and universities, especially historically Black schools, are conservative institutions. I have the audacity to believe that poverty can and must be eradicated; that health care can and must be made free; that prisons should be converted into schools and rehabilitation centers; and that war is not the answer—thus making me, in the eyes of those that seek to conserve the unjust world as it is, a "radical." Additionally, I understand that the exercise of education is never neutral. Education, in this turbulent time, is either engaged in integrating and conforming young minds to accept and maintain the world they've inherited or it is an exercise in liberation by which young women and men create, imagine, and participate in the transformation of their world. Because I coveted the latter—*the transformation of the world*—I knew that my job was not secure. For, in order to transform the world, one must challenge and confront the institutions that train and graduate custodians of the status quo.

Despite my skepticism, though, the reality was that I was now a professor. Among the classes I was set to teach was a general studies course entitled "The Post-Hip-Hop Generation." Months before, I'd published an article in the *San Francisco Chronicle* entitled "We Are the Post-Hip-Hop Generation," based on conversations I was having with young people around the country who felt that hip hop no longer represented their desire for radical change and wasn't apt to respond to the critical challenges facing our world. A month later, community organizers in Newark put together "Post-Hip-Hop Generation," a panel discussion where music executives, DJs, rappers, and scholars came together to discuss, among other things, the ideas put forth in my article. Despite a lively discussion, nothing could match the promise of a class populated and taught by the post-hip-hop generation.

Zora Neale Hurston, who strolled across the Morgan State University (then Morgan College) campus as a student ninety years before I would begin teaching there, once remarked that "The present was an egg laid by the past that had the future inside its shell." As my first day approached, I grew more and more anxious about my role in helping to hatch the future. And then the day came.

The scene: As I barreled down battered North Avenue on my way to teach my first-ever class at Morgan, I wondered if tomorrow would show up today. Then, just like that, I saw something, something in the way of things, a something that was actually a some*body*—a somebody who nobody else seemed to see. That *body,* stiff and Black, was sprawled on the side of the road, pressed haphazardly against a

filthy curb. Thoughts careened through my mind—*Is he moving?*
Damn, he ain't moving. Maybe he's asleep. Nah, he ain't moving at all.
Why isn't there a crowd huddled around this somebody? How come people
ain't stoppin'? Why aren't cars pulling over? Why ain't I pulling over?—
as I sat at a red light. As the light turned, I snatched a glance at the
clock: 10:40. My class started at eleven and I was about ten minutes
away. *You can't keep going,* I told myself. *You made an observation, now*
you have an obligation.

I pulled over and shimmied out of my car.

With each step toward the body, came a new revelation: Stiff.

Blood.

Damn.

Dead.

Finally, I arrived to find a boy, not a moment older than I, shot to
death on the busiest street in Baltimore, lying in a pool of crimson
and garbage, as cars and people sped past.

"Sorry . . . for . . . being . . . late," I huffed to my new students, out of
breath from sprintin' across campus. When I explained to them that
I'd just seen something terrible and horrifying, something even more
terrible and horrifying happened. My students, all of them Black and
most from Baltimore or Washington, D.C., were completely un-
moved. In matter-of-fact tones they lunged into similar stories about
poor Black men and women killed by the myriad symptoms of urban
poverty and injustice.

"So, that doesn't make y'all upset?" I asked.

"I mean, it's life," one student explained.

"So then, how does life feel?" I asked, which they answered in the frigid language of silence. They had, a long time ago, grown numb to the daily terror of the hellish conditions that were omnipresent. Later, a student explained to me that, for all intents and purposes, this some*body* who I saw was "just anotha nigga dead."

"Where you from, Professor Asante?" a student asked, surprised at my very visible outrage.

"Philly," I responded—proud.

Photo: Ellis Marsalis

"And you never saw a dead body in Philly?" he quizzed.

Quickly, I began to recall my own experiences growing up in the Illadelph. I realized that not only had I seen dead bodies, but I'd seen people shot, stabbed, and brutalized, both by people who looked like them and by people who didn't. However, since going away to fantasyland colleges—first to Lafayette College, then to the University of London, then to UCLA—I'd been removed from so many of the realities of the inner city. It wasn't that I'd forgotten what it looked liked, but rather, I'd forgotten the feeling, forgotten the pain, forgotten forgetting, forgotten forgetting what I forgot to forget in the first place. Feeling it now, after six years or so, was wrenching. Sadly, during my childhood in Philly and my students' childhood in Baltimore and D.C., the violent, unjust, and oppressive conditions, the disregard for Black life, had been normalized and naturalized to such a blunt point that, as one of the students, Shandel, put it, "it's like the rain."

"It just happens and all you can do is try to get inside but at some point, we all get wet, some more than others, though," she proverbed. "I know," she chased, "that things were different back in the day but all people care about now is what's on BET. There's no respect. Nothing. So what can we do?"

Truth is: I didn't know. I was in the classroom, like she was, in search of answers to that same question. I did know, however, that the fact we were having this discussion was a kind of proof that there were small fires beneath the surfaces of apparent apathy.

"Things were bad back then, too," another student offered. "The more things change, the more they seem to stay the same." My goal, as professor—which comes from the Latin "*profitieri*" meaning "to declare openly"—was not only to "declare openly," but to reveal that yesterday, today, and tomorrow are in the same week; to show that injustice, inhumanity, and poverty, conditions of our color rather than our character, are not as natural as the "rain," but instead, were the most unnatural conditions human beings could be subjected to. And, perhaps most important, engage with them in a process that could improve our communities. As bell hooks writes in *Teaching to Transgress: Education as the Practice of Freedom*:

> *The academy is not paradise. But learning is a place where paradise can be created. The classroom with all its limitations remains a location of possibility. In that field of possibility we have the opportunity*

to labour for freedom, to demand of ourselves and our comrades, an
openness of mind and heart that allows us to face reality even as we
collectively imagine ways to move beyond boundaries, to transgress.
This is education as the practice of freedom.

"Never doubt," I told my class, evoking the words of the late an-
thropologist Margaret Mead, "that a small group of thoughtful, committed citizens can change the world. Indeed, it is the only thing that
ever has."

"But it's different now. It's not like it was *backntheday,*" Shandel insisted. She was right.

> The struggle ain't right up in your face, it's more subtle
> But it's still comin' across like the prison tunnel vision.
> —THE ROOTS, "DON'T FEEL RIGHT," *GAME THEORY*

The racism our parents' generation endured—legal segregation,
lynching, hoses, dogs—was certainly more "in your face" than today,
and that is precisely the danger of today. What we are experiencing is
the manifestation of what President Richard Nixon told his chief of
staff H. R. Haldeman, "You have to face the fact that the whole problem is really the blacks. The key is to devise a system that recognizes
this while not appearing to."

One of my students, Ryan, explains the frustration of knowing
something is afflicting you, yet being unable to clearly identify it. "It's
like a huge mosquito," he tells the class. "No, it's a big-ass wasp with
a deadly stinger that you can't see but it is constantly biting you," he
says about invisible institutional oppression. "Eventually, since you
can't see the damn thing, you start to think that there is no big-ass
wasp, that maybe something is wrong with you. But I know, from
reading and just being aware, that the wasps are real!"

Young people are the most dangerous clan of folks to the oppressive power structure, because we are, many of us for the first time in our brief lives, thinking critically about the world we were born into and are outraged. We have always been instrumental, not only in recognizing the flaws in our society, but engaging in corrective action. When Huey Newton founded (along with Bobby Seale) the Black Panthers he was just twenty-four years old. The Panthers were a response to the state-sponsored racism that oppressed the masses of Black people. They asked, as former Black Panther Mumia Abu-Jamal asked the graduating class at Evergreen State College during his historic commencement speech that he delivered from death row, "Why was it right for people to revolt against the British because of 'taxation without representation,' and somehow wrong for truly unrepresented Africans in America to revolt against America?" Furthermore, they understood that "For any oppressed people, revolution, according to the Declaration of Independence, is a right." The Black Panthers created the Ten Point Program that set an agenda to address what they considered to be the most urgent needs of oppressed people.

1. WE WANT FREEDOM. WE WANT POWER TO DETERMINE THE DESTINY OF OUR BLACK AND OPPRESSED COMMUNITIES.

2. WE WANT FULL EMPLOYMENT FOR OUR PEOPLE.

3. WE WANT AN END TO THE ROBBERY BY THE CAPITALISTS OF OUR BLACK AND OPPRESSED COMMUNITIES.

4. WE WANT DECENT HOUSING, FIT FOR THE SHELTER OF HUMAN BEINGS.

5. WE WANT DECENT EDUCATION FOR OUR PEOPLE THAT EXPOSES THE TRUE NATURE OF THIS DECADENT AMERICAN SOCIETY. WE WANT

EDUCATION THAT TEACHES US OUR TRUE HISTORY AND OUR ROLE IN THE PRESENT—DAY SOCIETY.

6. WE WANT COMPLETELY FREE HEALTH CARE FOR ALL BLACK AND OPPRESSED PEOPLE.

7. WE WANT AN IMMEDIATE END TO POLICE BRUTALITY AND MURDER OF BLACK PEOPLE, OTHER PEOPLE OF COLOR, ALL OPPRESSED PEOPLE INSIDE THE UNITED STATES.

8. WE WANT AN IMMEDIATE END TO ALL WARS OF AGGRESSION.

9. WE WANT FREEDOM FOR ALL BLACK AND OPPRESSED PEOPLE NOW HELD IN U.S. FEDERAL, STATE, COUNTY, CITY AND MILITARY PRISONS AND JAILS. WE WANT TRIALS BY A JURY OF PEERS FOR ALL PERSONS CHARGED WITH SO—CALLED CRIMES UNDER THE LAWS OF THIS COUNTRY.

10. WE WANT LAND, BREAD, HOUSING, EDUCATION, CLOTHING, JUSTICE, PEACE AND PEOPLE'S COMMUNITY CONTROL OF MODERN TECHNOLOGY.

What struck my class most as we read the Ten Point Program—which concludes with "We hold these truths to be self-evident, that all men are created equal; that they are endowed by their Creator with certain unalienable rights; that among these are life, liberty, and the pursuit of happiness"—was how many of the issues that the civil rights/Black power generation struggled against are still prevalent today and must be faced by us.

"We don't even have to make a new list," a student remarked. "We still don't have those things—still."

"Okay, so do we have decent housing?" I posed.

A chorus of "nos," "nopes," and "uh-uhns" fluttered back.

"What about health care? We got it? Y'all got it?"

"Nah."

"What about police brutality—is that still happening?"

"Man, I got beat up by the cops yesterday on my own block for no damn reason. See," one student shouted as he pulled up his shirt to reveal a combination of dark smudges—all too familiar marks of the beast.

For the students who thought the Panthers' goals were utopian, we summoned the words of Emma Goldman who told us that "every daring attempt to make a great change in existing conditions, every lofty vision of new possibilities for the human race, has been labeled Utopian." For the students who believed the demands of housing and health care were unrealistic and too radical, we checked out the United Nations' Universal Declaration of Human Rights, which states:

> *Everyone has the right to a standard of living adequate for the health and well-being of himself and of his family, including food, clothing, housing and medical care and necessary social services, and the right to security in the event of unemployment, sickness, disability, widowhood, old age or other lack of livelihood in circumstances beyond his control.*

Human rights should never—must never!—be perceived as too lofty or radical. This occurs, however, because of the incessant onslaught from systems that don't recognize oppressed people as people, generating a sense of undeserving-ness of even basic human rights. Forty years after the Ten Point Program, much has changed and yet, sadly, too much has stayed the same. It was Malcolm X who advised,

> *Policies change, and programs change, according to time. But the objective never changes. You might change your method of achieving the*

objectives but the objective never changes. Our objective is complete
freedom, complete justice, complete equality—by any means necessary.

Indeed, polices have changed. Programs, too. From Vietnam →
Iraq; Nixon → Bush; ghetto → ghetto; and oppressed → oppressed,
the freedom that previous generations fought for still eludes many.
The post-hip-hop generation may be closer to freedom than my
father's generation, but being close to freedom ain't freedom. Just as
one cannot be half-pregnant, half-free is not a reality, either. To recognize this is not a matter of political orientation. Radical, moderate,
or conservative, it's obvious that the status quo, as far as the majority of
young Blacks is concerned, is dysfunctional. If this strange place,
where the lives of Black children are stunted before they ever start
and where ignorance is celebrated, is not dysfunctional, then what is?

Photo: Jamal Thorne

"But today, it comes at us from all angles. Plus, we ain't unified,"
one keen student observed. On one hand, nothing says "let's unify

against this bullshit" like screaming fire hoses, rabid police dogs, and WHITES ONLY signs. However—

"There's definitely the necessary criteria for unity, though," someone called out. "The question is what agenda are we unifying around?" I paused, panning the sea of sepia-colored pupils that formed my class.

One of them stutter-stated: "The . . . first thing is the schools. How many of y'all went to a school in Baltimore city?" he asked. Hands flung skyward. "Okay, so y'all know that our schools are horrible. We're not even supposed to be here—in college—given where we came from. We need textbooks, working bathrooms. The basics."

Another student called out, "What about these Black-people-hating redneck cops from the country who come in and beat the shit out of us in our hoods—and never get tried or punished?"

"Instead they get promotions," someone else threw in.

"Then you got so many people dying and it's because there are absolutely no—I mean *no*—opportunities out here. They want to lock everybody up before they create jobs in Baltimore and I'm sure it's like that in other places."

"It definitely is the case in other areas," I responded, reflecting on my experiences living in Philadelphia, Los Angeles, and Harlem. As the students lunged into more agenda points, I realized that we, part of a new generation, needn't look beyond ourselves to see and set our agenda. Indeed, each of us represented many of the great challenges that face young Blacks in America and beyond.

"The curse of poverty has no justification in our age," declared Dr. Martin Luther King Jr. in his last book *Where Do We Go from Here: Chaos or Community?* Today, exactly forty years later, too many of us suffer, because of our hue, from the ills of poverty and are forced to struggle against the desolation and despair that is pumped "into the spiritual bloodstream" of our lives. The reality that 60 percent of

America's poor youth are Black and that 50 percent of all Black babies are born into the pitiful pits of poverty, in the richest nation in the history of the world, is a national, international, and human tragedy. The post-hip-hop generation faces the challenge of following through on Dr. King's call for the "total, direct and immediate abolition of poverty."

> They vote for us to go to war instantly,
> But none of their kids serve in the infantry.
> —IMMORTAL TECHNIQUE, "HARLEM STREETS,"
> REVOLUTIONARY VOL. 2

In my first semester, one of my students—an Iraq War veteran and an immensely gifted poet who wrote "My generation has been destroyed by guns, drugs and violence"—was shot and killed in the streets of Baltimore. Black-on-Black violence is a symptom of the violence of poverty and should not be looked at in a vacuum. Instead, one must, from a place of love, ask "Why are young brothas killing each other?" In inner cities across America, Black-on-Black violence arises primarily out of the crack-cocaine economy, an economy that not only exists, but flourishes because of the scarcity of sustainable employment options and the reality of inadequate educational facilities available. Consider that gun-related homicides for Black males shot up 79 percent between 1980 and 1990, while unemployment for Black males in inner cities fell to all-time lows and, most poignantly, crack cocaine was introduced (administered) to the ghettos of America. Today, with very few options still available, Black men between fifteen and thirty-four are most likely to be killed at the hands of other young Black men over crumbs. To take it a step further, the gun my student held in Iraq is a reflection of his limited opportunities. Violence against people of color, it seems, is endorsed both directly and indirectly by the state. More funding for schools and training programs, increased access to qualified teachers and educational resources, drug rehab programs, more employment opportunities, as well as an end to the racial discrimination seen in these institutions are essential to putting an end to the unnecessary violence that riddles our communities.

"How many of y'all have immediate family in prison?" I curiously asked my class one day after a student rushed out of class, hurriedly explaining to me that her "brother just got knocked."

"What for?" I let out in a concerned whisper.

"He has a drug problem," she said, shaking her head and drifting away.

Although I shouldn't have been, I was surprised to see one-third of my students' hands spring up. Again, these skyward mahogany hands reflect the reality that on any given day in America, more than a third of Black men in their twenties are in jail, on parole, or on probation. In northern cities like Baltimore and Philadelphia, this number often grows to two-thirds. Although most of the attention is usually given to Black men in prison, Black women are among the fastest growing group to be incarcerated. Most of the imprisoned Black women and men are poor and are in jail for nonviolent drug offenses. However, because of the War on Drugs and mandatory minimum sentencing, they serve cruel and unusually long prison sentences for possessing small amounts of narcotics. In addition, the racism in sentencing has been well documented. Consider the disparity in federal sentencing laws between crack cocaine (primarily used by Blacks) and powder cocaine (primarily used by whites):

5 GRAMS OF CRACK = 5 YEARS IN PRISON

500 GRAMS OF POWDER = 5 YEARS IN PRISON

Despite the fact that crack and powder cocaine are pharmacologically the same, crack cocaine is the only drug that the first offense of simple possession can trigger a federal mandatory minimum sentence of five years. Yet possession of any quantity of any other substance by a first-time offender—including powder cocaine—is a misdemeanor offense punishable by a maximum of one year in prison. Most of America's drug users are white, yet most of those incarcerated for drug use are Black. The injustices surrounding the prison industrial complex represent one of the most urgent motivations for this generation to become engaged with organizing around issues of social justice.

These prison policies have an incestuous relationship with the corporations that use prison labor (tantamount to slave labor) and the private companies who build, maintain, and operate prisons. Prison labor also takes jobs away from poor and working-class communities as corporations will always opt for the cheaper labor. In the next two decades, my students' relatives (and mine!) will be released from prison with no voting rights, no job prospects, no education, and no welfare—a repulsive, premeditated recipe for recidivism.

There is a crisis when the people profiting most from the prison industry are the same people who make the laws that dictate who goes to prison and for how long. It will be up to the new generation to thrust our "bodies upon the gears and upon the wheels, upon the levers, upon all the apparatus," as Mario Savio once proclaimed, and "make it stop." For folks both on the inside and outside to indicate, by any means or medium necessary, to the people who run it, to the people who own it, that without justice, "the machine will be prevented from working at all!"

Although it's still very taboo to discuss in many circles within the African-American community, I had one student inform me that her inconsistent performance in class was because she was battling HIV. We know, of course, from statistics and special reports that she wasn't alone. It's a national crisis that Black teens represent 60 percent of all new HIV cases. For Black men and women ages twenty-five to forty-four, AIDS is the first and second leading causes of death. This, combined with the AIDS epidemic that is ravishing Africa, is the greatest both domestic and international threat to Black health.

The cumulative effect of all the poverty-related challenges, coupled with a racist, pervasive media that tells us we are not beautiful, not intelligent, is often overwhelming enough to cause serious identity issues, depression, anxiety, physical sickness, and suicide. Consider that two of the hip-hop generation's greatest icons—Tupac and Notorious B.I.G. (Biggie)—both rhymed often about "ending it all." The chorus for Biggie's "Everyday Struggle" is: "I don't wanna live no more / Sometimes I see death knockin' at my front door." Similarly, on "So Many Tears," Tupac rhymes: "Now I'm lost and I'm weary, so many tears / I'm suicidal, so don't stand near me." Despite knowing this, I couldn't help feel startled when a student divulged to me, through e-mail, that her "heart was breaking every day," that she was "sick of crying," that her "life has been hell on earth," and asking, "so why not cut out the part about being on earth." She was as certain as Biggie or Tupac that taking her fledgling life would drive away the pain that ran through her frail frame. According to the Centers for Disease Control, suicide is now the third leading cause of death for young Blacks between fifteen and twenty-four. In addition to access to mental health resources, our survival will depend on how well we are able to instill genuine values of love, compassion, and worth in our communities and among our peers.

Since I was a teenager, I've been harassed on numerous occasions, too many to name, by Philadelphia, Baltimore, Los Angeles, New York, and even London police. The vast majority of my students, when I asked them, confirmed that they'd been on the receiving end of some form of police brutality.

One student, after missing several classes, asked me: "Have you seen the lady on the news? The one who was killed by the police? Electrocuted by the police? In her house?"

"Yeah, I did see that," I responded.

"That's my aunt," he informed me. His aunt was Uywanda Peterson, a forty-one-year-old unarmed Black woman who, at five foot one and one hundred pounds, was Tasered to death by the Baltimore police department. This incident, just one out of hundreds that occur daily, is causing a new generation to not only challenge, but find ways to radically transform the current system in which a rural, predominantly white police force, reminiscent of the slave patrols of the nineteenth century, patrol Black inner cities, criminalizing young Black men and women.

> I wouldn't be fightin' for Bush or White America's dream.
> I'd be fightin' for my people's survival and self-esteem.
> —IMMORTAL TECHNIQUE FEATURING KRS-ONE,
> "BIN LADEN (REMIX)," *BIN LADEN 12"*

And finally, despite the enormous domestic problems we face in the inner cities of America, there is an overwhelming opposition to the new strain of American imperialism that is hell-bent on waging war on other nations of color around the world. In fact many make a connection between American imperialism and the oppression they face domestically.

"It's the same shit, 'scuse my language," a student shouted.

"What's the same?" I asked.

"Okay, what they're doing in Iraq, with the occupation, is the same thing that they do over here, in our communities. It's not right. When I see a U.S. soldier in Iraq, I think of the cops, because both the soldier and the cops usually aren't from the community, and they are sent there supposedly to protect or 'liberate' but they really just make things worse," he explained as his classmates nodded.

Due to the Bush administration's overt disregard for international law and human rights, many in the post-hip-hop generation are becoming increasingly aware of the harsh injustices their country is engaged in enforcing overseas. Technology, specifically the Internet, has broadened our worldview and made global information more accessible. As a result, young people, my students and myself among them, can be a part of international movements, not just antiwar efforts, that seek to restore justice and reveal the possibility of another world.

Perhaps the largest consensus among the post-hip-hop generation class was the notion that our lives and, in fact, our unborn children's lives were dependent upon the preservation and nurturing of the earth, our common mother. Environmental issues such as climate change are increasingly becoming a part of our discussion. It is clear to us that the people in power now have not inherited the world from their forefathers, but rather have borrowed it from us and our children. It's time to free her from the toxic grips of corporate greed and callousness.

I anticipated, at some point during the class, a student asking, "Where does hip hop fit in to this?" I anticipated acknowledging the sweeping power of hip hop, particularly rap music, and using it as the spark for ideas to mobilize around. Affixed to that power, however, is great danger. Although artists have traditionally been able to rally masses of people, the reality that hip hoppers don't own or control how the culture is disseminated complicates the efficacy of using hip hop to implement social change. The hope here lies in the underground, as the mainstream has hijacked ideas like Malcolm X's "by any means necessary" and applied it to guerilla capitalism, hence: *Get Rich or Die Tryin'*. This lack of ownership has caused hip hop to be transformed into a consumer movement dictated primarily by an affluent base of whites who purchase and distribute it.

The post-hip-hop generation shouldn't wait for mainstream musicians to say what needs to be said. The most important component is taking what is said—wherever it may come from—and converting that into positive social and political action. At the same time, since we live in a celebrity culture, it's essential to leverage the voices, however few and far between they may be, of those icons willing to place their endorsement deals, record contracts, and status on the line for a greater cause. As the media literacy increases among the new generation, we will begin to realize that leadership and being on TV are not synonymous. That strong leadership is not about fiery rhetoric or nice punch lines, but a commitment to doing the work that needs to be done.

No movement is about beats and rhymes. Beats and rhymes are tools—tools that if held the right way can help articulate the world, a new world, in which we want to live. These tools are important to the post-hip-hop generation; however, more important are the ideas from the people themselves, not the ideas from an elite supposed to represent us. From the streets. From the schools. From you, from me. "People do not always need poets and playwrights to state their case," declared Lorraine Hansberry, a Black playwright whose works included *A Raisin in the Sun* and *To Be Young, Gifted and Black*. "We all cry for freedom." And because we all cry freedom, we must all, then, as Hansberry continues, concern ourselves

With every single means of struggle: legal, illegal, passive, active, violent and non-violent. That they must harass, debate, petition, give money to court struggles, sit-in, lie-down, strike, boycott, sing hymns,

pray on steps—and shoot from their windows when the racists come
cruising through their communities. . . . The acceptance of our present
condition is the only form of extremism which discredits us before
our children.

But the question I anticipated never came.

Instead, students articulated the ideas that we should embrace hip
hop's positive aspects, but it must be bigger than hip hop—bigger
than any one medium and bigger than us. They made clear that rather
than committing ourselves to any one person or medium, it's wiser to
commit ourselves to the promise and potential of tomorrow, employing hip hop and other forms at the service of change.

Over the course of our semester, it was revealed that all of the
sociopolitical components needed for a new movement were in place
and that it was up to us to solder them together. It was revealed that
the struggle today was the struggle of yesterday and tomorrow; revealed that today is what today is because of what yesterday was;
revealed that to change our societies, we must make serious efforts in
understanding how our society works—and why it doesn't work for
so many. It was revealed that it's going to take all of us, mothers,
daughters, sons, fathers, scientists, rappers, painters, filmmakers, nu-
tritionists, entrepreneurs, teachers, et cetera, each one of us, loving
each other, which is only possible by loving ourselves, affirming our
own self-worth, and realizing that we are all connected. It was revealed that I am because you are. It was revealed that all revolutions
are birthed from love and that revolution, in this world, as Assata
Shakur, ex–political prisoner and aunt of Tupac, tells us from Cuba,
"means changing from the inhumane to the humane. It means everybody has a right to live, to eat, to have a house, an education, to be
free from torture, from repression."

On an individual level, we realized that the change we want

doesn't end with us, but rather begins there. Indeed, the best we can do for ourselves is the best we can do for others. Our obligation as human beings, both to ourselves and our fellow sisters and brothers, is to resist and challenge all forces that seek to dominate, oppress, repress, silence, and destroy their spirits. When the weeds of doubt creep into our minds and tell us that we are too small, as individuals, to make a difference, let us remember what the Ghanaian proverb says: Try sleeping in a small room with a mosquito.

chapter 5.

IT'S BIGGER THAN HIP HOP:

Time Line (1965–1991)

People treat hip–hop like an isolated phenomenon.
They don't treat it as a continuum, a history or legacy.
And it really is. And like all mediums or movements,
it came out of a need.

—MOS DEF

Sankofa, symbolized by a mighty and mythic bird that soars forward while looking backward, is an Akan concept that means "go back to your roots in order to move forward." That said, if we want to move forward, it is essential that we understand where we came from. The following time line highlights *some* of the key events—cultural, economic, political, and musical; good, bad, and ugly—that birthed, shaped, and molded hip hop into what we see, hear, and feel (or don't feel) today.

Unlike other hip-hop time lines that focus exclusively on events related to the four elements of hip hop (emceeing, DJing, graffiti, and breakdancing), this time line aims to spray-paint a much larger representation of hip hop in a global context. In some senses, this time line is a loop if one considers, for example, it begins with the Watts rebellion and ends with the spark that ignited the L.A. rebellions. It begins with the Vietnam War and ends with the Gulf War. "Those who don't know their history are doomed to repeat it," proclaimed Marcus Garvey. To that effect, this time line should also serve as a deterrent for the post-hip-hop generation.

Ella Baker, an African-American human rights activist who fought against Jim Crow, rallied against apartheid in South Africa, was a leader in the Puerto Rican independence movement, and witnessed the birth of hip hop, once said, "Give light and the people will find their own way." The events listed in this time line—from Malcolm X's assassination in 1965 to Ice Cube's St. Ides commercial in 1991— function as one of the "lights" that can help our generation part the darkness of our current times.

1965

Don't be scared of Malcolm X Cuz he died for ya.
—DEAD PREZ, "FOOD, CLOTHES & SHELTER,"
TURN OFF THE RADIO

Malcolm X (El—Hajj Malik El—Shabazz), a Black Muslim minister, national spokesman for the Nation of Islam and founder of the Muslim Mosque, Inc., and the Organization of Afro-American Unity, is assassinated while delivering a speech at the Audubon Ballroom in Manhattan on the first day of National Brother Week. Malcolm, like Cuban revolutionary Che Guevara, Indian leader Mahatma Gandhi, quickly becomes an international symbol of liberation for oppressed people.

Affirmative action ain't reverse discrimination
That shit is a pathetic excuse for reparations.
—IMMORTAL TECHNIQUE, FEATURING KRS—ONE,
"BIN LADEN (REMIX)," *BIN LADEN 12"*

President Lyndon Johnson, delivering a speech at Howard University, frames the concept behind affirmative action, asserting that existing civil rights laws alone will not level the playing field. He pronounces:

> *You do not wipe away the scars of centuries by saying: "Now, you are free to go where you want, do as you desire, and choose the leaders you please." You do not take a man who for years has been hobbled by chains, liberate him, bring him to the starting line of a race, saying, "You are free to compete with all the others," and still justly believe you have been completely fair.*

African-Americans lead a race rebellion in Watts sparked by the brutal arrests of Marquette, Ronald, and Rena Frye. Their arrests served as the proverbial straw that broke the camel's back in a Watts community where police brutality, including rape of Black women, use of racial epithets, and excessive force, was rampant. The rebellion, which lasts from August 11 to August 17, results in thirty-five deaths, more than eight hundred injured, and over $35 million in property damage. This rebellion occurs in the midst of a period of rebellions, beginning in Rochester, Philadelphia, and New York City in 1964, and continuing throughout the decade.

On March 8, thirty-five hundred United States Marines are dispatched to South Vietnam, marking the beginning of the American ground war in Vietnam. U.S. public opinion supports the deployment; however, their support is based on the premise that Vietnam is part of a global struggle against communism. Ho Chi Minh, president of the Democratic Republic of Vietnam, warns that if the Americans "want to make war for twenty years then we shall make war for twenty years. If they want to make peace, we shall make peace and invite them to afternoon tea."

1966

The Black Panther Party for Self-Defense is founded by Huey P. Newton and Bobby Seale in Oakland, California. The group was founded
on the principles of its Ten Point Program, a document that called for
"Land, Bread, Housing, Education, Clothing, Justice, and Peace," as
well as exemption from military service that would utilize African-
Americans to "fight and kill other people of color in the world who,
like Black people, are being victimized by the White racist government of America."

And until my people get uplifted
No poppin' shit, just poppin' clips 'stead of
marchin' we gon' rip shit.
—TUPAC SHAKUR, "TRAPPED," 2PACALYPSE NOW

A race rebellion erupts in the predominantly Black community of
Hough in Cleveland, Ohio, spanning a six-night period from July 18
to July 23. The rebellion is sparked when a white store owner told
Black patrons that "Blacks are not served here." By the end of the rebellions, four people will be killed and thirty critically injured.

James Brown, often dubbed the "Godfather of Soul" and the hard-
est working man in show business, wins the Grammy for best R&B
recording for "Papa's Got a Brand New Bag," boosting his international popularity. His call-and-response, dancing, and rhythmic style
would be influential to hip hop a decade later.

On September 27, the second race rebellion of the year breaks out
in San Francisco's Hunters Point, a Black neighborhood, when a
white police officer shoots and kills a sixteen-year-old Black as he flees
the scene of a stolen car.

Maulana Karenga, who founded the Black nationalist US Organization a year earlier, creates the African-American cultural holiday Kwanzaa (celebrated from December 26 to January 1). The first Kwanzaa ceremony is celebrated by members of the US Organization in Los Angeles. The holiday would grow to become an international, pan-African holiday with over 18 million celebrants.

1967

Power to the people, black power, black is beautiful.
—COMMON FEATURING THE LAST POETS, "THE CORNER," BE

Stokely Carmichael/Kwame Ture, a leader of the Student Nonviolent Coordinating Committee (SNCC), popularizes the phrase "Black Power" in a speech delivered to an audience of sixty-five hundred at Garfield High School in Seattle. He defined "Black Power" as "the coming together of black people to fight for their liberation by any means necessary." The concept was immediately endorsed by SNCC and Congress for Racial Equality (CORE), but not the NAACP.

Kool DJ Herc, considered by many to be the father of hip hop and the originator of breakbeat DJing, moves from Jamaica to the Bronx where he, together with Grandmaster Flash, would pioneer hip hop. In a 1989 interview with hip-hop historian Davey D, Herc said, "Hip hop, the whole chemistry of that came from Nigeria, Africa."

Thurgood Marshall, civil rights activist and graduate of the historically Black Lincoln University and Howard University Law School, is nominated for appointment to the Supreme Court of the United States. On August 30, the Senate confirms his appointment, making Marshall the first African-American to serve as a justice of the Supreme Court.

The summer of 1967 is a tumultuous period in American race

relations. Racial confrontations escalate into full-scale race rebellions in Newark, New York City, Cleveland, Washington, D.C., Chicago, Atlanta, and Detroit.

1968

I took a page from the book of Martin Luther,
And decided that it's better to hug you than to shoot you.
—M-1, *"'TIL WE GET THERE," CONFIDENTIAL*

Martin Luther King Jr., the most famous and vocal leader of the Civil Rights Movement, is assassinated in Memphis, Tennessee, on April 4 while on the balcony of the Lorraine Motel. Prior to his assassination, King had become a harsh critic of the Vietnam War, U.S. foreign policy, and capitalism. In the following week, rebellions occur in more than sixty cities throughout the U.S.

The FBI launches COINTELPRO, a covert counterintelligence program aimed at investigating and disrupting dissident political organizations within the United States. With the Black Panther Party as a primary target, the founding document of COINTELPRO directed FBI agents to "expose, disrupt, misdirect, discredit, or otherwise neutralize" the activities of these movements and their leaders. The methods of COINTELPRO included infiltration, psychological warfare, harassment through the legal system, and extralegal violence including murder and assassination.

On October 16, Tommie Smith and John Carlos, African-American sprinters, are suspended from the Olympic Games in Mexico City for holding up their fist in a Black Power salute while receiving their gold and silver medals at the awards ceremony. In addition, they wear no shoes to comment on the poverty endured by the majority of Blacks in America.

1969

On October 29, the U.S. Supreme Court rules that school districts must end segregation "now and hereafter." With clear language, the court, which now had Thurgood Marshall as a member, left little room for misinterpretation or delay.

> *I'm black and I'm a say it loud like James Brown*
> *People be proud 'cause we all up in the game now . . .*
> —STYLES P FEATURING MARSHA AMBROSIUS,
> "I'M BLACK," *TIME IS MONEY*

James Brown records "Say It Loud—I'm Black and I'm Proud!" and "Funky Drummer"; the latter would become one of the most sampled tracks in hip-hop history. Brown would also record "Get on the Good Foot," a song promoting very high-energy, acrobatic dancing that Zulu Nation founder Afrika Bambaataa asserts led to break dancing.

Don Campbell, a young street dancer from Los Angeles, creates the Campbellock, a robotic funk dance style that would evolve into the hip-hop locking and influence the dance styles of popping, break-dancing, and liquiding.

1970

Angela Davis, a Black scholar and political organizer, becomes the third woman to appear on the FBI's Ten Most Wanted Fugitives List after being charged with conspiracy, kidnapping, and homicide, due to her alleged participation in an escape attempt of Black Panthers George Jackson, Fleeta Drumgo, and John Clutchette, known as the Soledad Brothers. She would later be acquitted of all charges.

Niggers always goin' through bullshit change
But when it comes time for real change, niggers are
scared of revolution.
—THE LAST POETS,
"NIGGERS ARE SCARED OF REVOLUTION," *THE LAST POETS*

The Last Poets, a music/poetry group whose members included Abiodun Oyewole, Alafia Pudim, and Omar Bin Hassan, record *The Last Poets,* an LP that combines spoken word with jazz and drum instrumentals and lays the foundation for rap music. Their name is taken from a poem by the South African revolutionary poet Keorapetse Kgositsile, who believed he was in the last era of poetry before guns would take over.

On May 4, the largest student strike in U.S. history takes place and four Kent State University students demonstrating against the Vietnam War are shot dead by the National Guard in Ohio. Ten days later, on May 14, during a student protest at the historically Black Jackson State College, police fire more than 460 rounds of ammunition, killing two African-American students.

1971

I got twenty-five cans in my knapsack crossin' out the
wick-wack
Puttin' up my name with a fat cap.
—KRS-ONE, "OUT FOR FAME," *KRS-ONE*

On July 21, *The New York Times* runs a front-page article on graffiti writer TAKI 183. The article, titled "'Taki 183' Spawns Pen Pals," puts national attention on graffiti writing, one of the four elements of hip hop. The article also ignites competitive tagging among youth across the five boroughs and eventually the world.

On September 13, 1,500 New York State troopers storm Attica prison, killing forty-three prisoners after the inmates led a rebellion. The prison, built to house 1,200 inmates, had over 2,000 inmates, 54 percent of whom were African-American and 9 percent Puerto Rican. All of the 383 correctional officers at Attica were white and frequently abused inmates. The inmates had demanded an improvement in their living conditions, showers, education, and vocational training, as well as reduced censorship of their mail and visitors. Before the uprisings, inmates were given one bucket of water a week as a "shower" and one roll of toilet paper a month.

1972

The Tuskegee Experiments end. Beginning in 1932, the U.S. Public Health Service's forty-year experiment on hundreds of poor, mostly illiterate, Black men was described by one news anchor as using "human beings as laboratory animals in a long and inefficient study of how long it takes syphilis to kill someone."

Soul Train, a Black music TV dance program created by Don Cornelius and backed by Johnson hair products (manufacturers of the Afro Sheen line), moves into syndication and becomes a hit. Tagged by some as the "Black American Bandstand," *Soul Train* would become the longest-running first-run nationally syndicated program in television history.

1973

Passed the Rockefeller laws to make us all state prop
Feds handin' out bids startin' 15 a pop.
—DEAD PREZ FEATURING DIVINE, "BABY FACE," *TURN OFF THE*
RADIO: THE MIXTAPE VOL 2: GET FREE OR DIE TRYIN'

Nelson Rockefeller, Republican governor of New York, introduces and signs the Rockefeller drug laws in his last year in office. Under these extremely harsh laws, the penalty for selling two ounces (approximately fifty-six grams) or more of heroin, morphine, "raw or prepared opium," cocaine, or cannabis, including marijuana, or possessing four ounces (approximately 128 grams) or more of the same substances, was made the same as that for second-degree murder: a minimum of fifteen years to life in prison, and a maximum of twenty-five years to life in prison. As a result New York's prison population jumped from 12,500 in 1971 to 71,000 in 1999, and is now over 150,000.

Jalal Mansur Nuriddin of The Last Poets releases his first solo album, *Hustlers Convention,* under the alias Lightnin' Rod. The album is a poetic narrative exploring a day in the life of two hustlers and would later be remade by rappers Grandmaster Flash & the Furious Five.

Afrika Bambaataa, a student at Adlai E. Stevenson High School in the Bronx, inspired by a trip to Africa, founds the Universal Zulu Nation, an organization of racially and politically conscious rappers, B-boys, graffiti artists, and other people involved in hip-hop culture. The name "Zulu Nation" was inspired by the images of Zulu warriors attacking British colonizers in the Michael Caine film *Zulu.*

1974

President Richard Nixon, who once complained to Assistant to the President for Domestic Affairs John Erlichman that Great Society programs were a waste "because Blacks were genetically inferior to whites," resigns on August 9 due to the firestorm surrounding the Watergate scandal. He becomes the first president to resign from office. His vice president, Gerald Ford, assumes the presidency and pardons Nixon on September 8.

> *Everybody's a rapper but few flow fatal*
> *It's fucked up, it all started from two turntables.*
> —NAS, "CARRY ON TRADITION," *HIP—HOP IS DEAD*

Kool DJ Herc, a year after DJing his first gig at his older sister's birthday party, garners a reputation for his legendary, high-decibel, high-quality mobile sound system and establishes himself as the first hip-hop DJ. Considered the originator of breakbeat DJing, Herc was initially exposed to similar sounds while growing up in Kingston, Jamaica, at dance hall parties.

1975

> *Self—esteem, yo we forgot the dream*
> *On our Jeffersons y'all but we forgot the theme.*
> —COMMON, "IT'S YOUR WORLD," *BE*

The Jeffersons, one of the first sitcoms about an African-American family, premieres on CBS. The show centers around George and Louise Jefferson (played by Sherman Hemsley and Isabel Sanford) and increases ratings for CBS, climbing the Nielsen Rating's top ten in its first season, and is in the top ten again for three consecutive seasons from 1979 through 1982. During its eighth season, *The Jeffersons* becomes the number-three show on network television, behind only *Dallas* and *60 Minutes.*

North Vietnamese forces take Saigon on April 30, reuniting the country. In total, seven million tons of bombs were dropped on Vietnam, more than twice the number dropped in Europe and Asia during World War II. Additionally, the CIA's Operation Phoenix, a covert intelligence operation and assassination program, kills over twenty thousand civilians.

1976

The first three—dimensional graffiti pieces, pioneered by KING 2, show up on subway cars in New York City.

Afrika Bambaataa, considered the founding father of hip hop, plays his first gig at the Bronx River Community Center and is dubbed "Master of Records" by those in attendance. He soon becomes the center's official DJ, spinning records on a sound system given to him by his mother as a graduation present the previous year.

Hundreds of students and protesters in the Black township of Soweto lead a rally against the imposition of the Dutch language Afrikaans in their schools and are killed by the South African apartheid government. African-American rap artists including Melle Mel, RUN-D.M.C., and Kurtis Blow would later condemn the racist system of apartheid in their music.

1977

I'm black like Steve Biko, raised in the ghetto by the people
Fuck the police, you know how we do.
—DEAD PREZ, "I'M A AFRICAN," *LET'S GET FREE*

Steve Biko, a nonviolent, antiapartheid activist famous for proclaiming that "The most potent weapon in the hands of the oppressor is the mind of the oppressed," and "Black is beautiful," is brutally beaten to death by South African police. His death sparks international awareness about the brutal regime of apartheid.

Grandmaster Flash and Grand Wizard Theodore create scratching, a turntable-based technique and instrumental advancement in DJing where scratches are produced by moving a vinyl record back and forth while it plays on the turntable. Flash describes scratching as "nothing but the back-cueing that you hear in your ear before you push it [the recorded sound] out to the crowd."

On February 3, ABC airs the final episode of the miniseries *Roots,* based on Alex Haley's genealogical novel *Roots: The Saga of an American Family.* The final episode of *Roots* achieves the highest-ever ratings for a single program. *Roots,* which stars Maya Angelou, LeVar Burton, O. J. Simpson, and Louis Gossett Jr., would go on to win nine Emmys, a Golden Globe, and a Peabody Award.

1978

But I know y'all wanted that 808
Can you feel that b—a —s—s, bass
But I know y'all wanted that 808
Can you feel that b—a—s—s, bass.
—OUTKAST, "THE WAY YOU MOVE,"
SPEAKERBOXXX/*THE LOVE BELOW*

The Roland Corporation introduces the Roland TR-808 Rhythm Composer, one of the first programmable drum machines. Because of the
808's kick drum sound and deep sub-bass, it provides the basis for
the majority of the early baselines in rap and is still widely utilized
today.

Disco Fever, a small nightclub in the Bronx, crosses over to a hip-hop
club and becomes the first club to play rap music exclusively. Among
the performers at Disco Fever are Grandmaster Flash, Lovebug
Starski, DJ Hollywood, Eddie Cheba, DJ Junebug, Brucie Bee, Sweet
Gee, and Reggie Wells.

1979

"Rapper's Delight" by the Sugar Hill Gang is the first hip-hop hit
single and is released on Sugar Hill Records, a label formed in
New Jersey by former R & B singer Sylvia Robinson. "Rapper's Delight" goes gold and hits number 36 on the U.S. pop charts, number
4 on the U.S. R & B charts, and number 3 on the U.K. singles
chart.

Tanya "Sweet Tee" Winley, the first hip-hop female vocalist to
record on vinyl, releases "Vicious Rap" on her father's label, Paul
Winley Records.

> She untangled the chains and escaped the pain
> How she broke out of prison I could never explain.
> —COMMON, "SONG FOR ASSATA," *LIKE WATER FOR CHOCOLATE*

Assata Shakur, the aunt of Tupac Shakur and a political prisoner,
aided by Tupac's stepfather, Dr. Mutulu Shakur, escapes Clinton Cor-

rectional Facility for Women in New Jersey. No one is injured during the escape; however, Dr. Shakur and Silvia Baraldini would be charged in aiding Assata in her escape.

Kurtis Blow, the first mainstream solo rapper, releases the single "Christmas Rappin'," which goes gold and allows him to start recording the self-titled album *Kurtis Blow* for Mercury Records.

The Metropolitan Transportation Authority (MTA) in New York City introduces Buffen, a machine used to remove the increasing amount of graffiti appearing on subway cars. To the MTA's frustration, the machine ends up further damaging the trains and is quickly discontinued.

The disco group Chic releases "Good Times" on their album *Risqué*. Despite the song's success on Billboard's Hot 100, "Good Times" is the last disco hit record. Months later, DJ Steve Dahl blows up thousands of disco records at an anti-disco party in Chicago, marking the symbolic death of the disco era.

1980

Look what the 80s did
To us Bebe's kids.
—TUPAC SHAKUR FEATURING KASTRO,
"BLACK COTTON," *LOYAL TO THE GAME*

Race rebellions, beginning on May 17, erupt in Miami after the acquittal of four white former police officers on charges that they beat Arthur McDuffie, an unarmed Black businessman, to death. The rebellions end with seventeen deaths and are the bloodiest since Watts and Detroit in 1965.

Mr. Magic (aka Sir Juice) introduces *Rap Attack*, the first radio show devoted to hip hop. Mr. Magic ends each show, which air on

WHBI from 2:00 to 5:00 A.M., with "Get on it, doggone it. 'Cause any fool can learn from his own mistakes, but it takes a wise man, a wise guy like you to learn from the mistakes made by others. Be yourself, 'cause you might find yourself by yourself, and that's no fun."

Dealing with alcoholism and Afrocentricity
A complex man drawn off of simplicity.
—COMMON, "THE 6TH SENSE," *LIKE WATER FOR CHOCOLATE*

Dr. Molefi K. Asante, a professor at Temple University, articulates the theory of Afrocentricity, an idea that challenges Eurocentric notions and urges people of African descent to "see the world through African eyes." Rappers KRS-One, Public Enemy, Dead Prez, and Common would embrace this worldview, infusing Afrocentric themes, images, and ideas into their rhymes.

1981

Instead of a war on poverty they got a war on drugs
So the police can bother me.
—TUPAC SHAKUR, "CHANGES," *GREATEST HITS*

Ronald Reagan, a former Hollywood actor and spokesman for General Electric, becomes the fortieth president of the United States. His policies, mainly Reaganomics and the War on Drugs, which many would call a "War on Blacks," would have a particularly devastating effect on Black people.

ABC's *20/20* newsmagazine airs the first national TV story on hip hop titled "Rappin' to the Beat." Later in the year, ABC News would air snippets of a Rock Steady Crew performance at Lincoln Center. Both television events would help to popularize hip-hop culture with many Americans who were unfamiliar with it.

> *Historically speakin', 'cause people be dissin'*
> *The first graffiti artists in the world were the Egyptians.*
> —KRS—ONE, "OUT FOR FAME," KRS—ONE

New York City mayor Ed Koch declares a "war on graffiti," allotting over $22 million to build double fences with razor edges in eighteen subway yards and employ guard dogs. Despite his efforts, graffiti writers, rather than be deterred, would grow more motivated to tag and intensified their efforts.

Tommy Boy Records is founded in New York City by Tom Silverman. Four years after its inception, Warner Bros. Records would buy 50 percent of the label, which Silverman would later buy back in 1995. Tommy Boy would sign such artists as Queen Latifah, De La Soul, and Naughty by Nature.

1982

> *I don't want no computer chip in my arm*
> *I don't want die by a nuclear bomb.*
> —DEAD PREZ, "PROPAGANDA," LET'S GET FREE

Close to one million activists and concerned citizens rally in New York City's Central Park calling for nuclear disarmament as President Reagan, undeterred by the protests, prepares to unveil Star Wars, a strategic defense initiative to use ground-based and space-based systems to protect the United States from attack by nuclear ballistic missiles.

Grandmaster Flash & the Furious Five release "The Message," one of the first rap songs to address the desolate conditions and hardships of the ghetto. The song's chorus—"Don't push me 'cuz I'm close to the edge"—resonates through the inner cities of America and becomes one of the most cited and well-known choruses in hip hop.

The United States, under President Reagan, floods the inner cities with crack cocaine in an effort to fund the Honduran contras to overthrow the Sandinista government of Nicaragua.

> *Who can be so cruel*
> *We all ignorant to AIDS till it happens to you.*
> —TUPAC SHAKUR, "THE GOOD DIE YOUNG," *STILL I RISE*

The term "AIDS" (Acquired Immune Deficiency Syndrome) is coined by the CDC. The disease claims the lives of 853 U.S. citizens. Thirteen years later, N.W.A. rapper Eazy-E would die of AIDS at just thirty-one years old. From his deathbed, he released the following statement:

> *I'm not religious, but wrong or right, that's me. I'm not saying this because I'm looking for a soft cushion wherever I'm heading, I just feel that I've got thousands and thousands of young fans that have to learn about what's real when it comes to AIDS. Like the others before me, I would like to turn my own problem into something good that will reach out to all my homeboys and their kin. Because I want to save their asses before it's too late.*

Wild Style, the first feature film about hip-hop culture, hits theaters. The film spawns a *Wild Style* tour with artists such as Fab 5 Freddy, Cold Crush Brothers, and Rock Steady Crew performing throughout the United States and Europe, making *Wild Style* the first international hip-hop tour.

Shatter, we on the front lines prepare
I want Mumia out the cage the time for action is here
—THE ROOTS, "MUMIA 911," MUMIA 911

Political activist and journalist Mumia Abu-Jamal, in a trial rife
with injustice, is falsely convicted of the murder of a Philadelphia
police officer. As a result, Mumia, a political prisoner, receives the
death penalty. Mumia says: "At my trial I was denied the right to
defend myself. I had no confidence in my court-appointed attorney, who never even asked me what happened the night I was
shot and the police officer was killed; and I was excluded from
at least half the trial. Since I was denied all my rights at my trial I
did not testify. I would not be used to make it look like I had a
fair trial." His conviction ignites an international movement in his
support.

1983

DJ Red Alert launches his hip—hop show on WRKS in New York, playing
a mix of hip hop and dance hall. Red Alert's show airs on Friday and
Saturday nights, and becomes the first rap show on a commercial station. "That's when I started learning the fundamentals of how to be
in and out without playing certain records around the clock," Red
Alert told *Billboard*.

Watchin' for the beast 'cause many artists they shoot 'em
And beat 'em in the yards, while doin' a top to bottom
—KRS—ONE, "OUT FOR FAME," KRS—ONE

On September 15, Michael Stewart, a twenty-five-year-old Black
man, is arrested for writing graffiti on a subway platform in New

York. While in handcuffs, Stewart is beaten to death by two white NYPD officers.

The Fearless Four, whose members include The Great Peso, Devastating Tito, Mighty Mike C, Krazy Eddie, OC, and DLB, are signed to Elektra Records, making them the first rap group to sign to a major record label.

President Ronald Reagan signs a bill establishing January 20 as a federal holiday in honor of Martin Luther King Jr.

Guion "Guy" Bluford Jr., a NASA astronaut, becomes the first African-American in space as a member of the crew of the space shuttle *Challenger* on mission STS-8. Bluford, a mission specialist, would later be inducted into the International Space Hall of Fame.

The Color Purple, a novel by Alice Walker, receives the Pulitzer Prize for Fiction. The novel, which addresses critical issues facing African-American women in the early twentieth century, would later be adapted into a film directed by Steven Spielberg, as well as a Broadway musical produced by Quincy Jones and Oprah Winfrey.

1984

L worth paper
Ask Def Jam who put 'em up in that skyscraper.
—LL COOL J, "10 MILLION STARS," 10

Russell Simmons and Rick Rubin found Def Jam Records with eight hundred dollars and release sixteen-year-old LL Cool J's "I Need a Beat," which would go on to sell more than 100,000 copies, establishing the label as a force and launching the careers of Simmons, Cool J, and Rubin.

KDAY, the first rap-only radio station in Los Angeles, hits the air-waves. Dr. Dre, a well-known local DJ from Compton, mixes music on Saturday nights. Dre would go on to be instrumental in rap as a producer, rapper, and executive.

Run-D.M.C., founded by Joseph "Rev Run" Simmons, Darryl "D.M.C." McDaniels, and Jason "Jam-Master Jay" Mizell, releases the self-titled album *Run-D.M.C.,* which goes gold, becoming the first hip-hop album to do so.

In support of Jesse Jackson's first presidential run, Grandmaster Flash and Melle Mel release "Jesse," an overtly political rap song in support of Jackson's presidential campaign. Despite hard-hitting, promotional lyrics—"Brothers stand together and let the whole world see / Our brother Jesse Jackson go down in history"—Jesse Jackson did not use the song during his campaign.

1985

Philadelphia's first African-American mayor, Wilson Goode, orders the Philadelphia police to drop a bomb from a helicopter on the head-quarters of MOVE, a Black nationalist, back-to-nature organization founded by John Africa. The bombing leaves eleven people dead, in-cluding five children. Two hundred and fifty people are made homeless and more than sixty-two homes on Osage Avenue in West Philadelphia are destroyed.

Run-D.M.C. releases *King of Rock,* the first rap album to go plat-inum. The following year, their album *Raising Hell* would become the first multiplatinum rap album, thus turning hip hop into a mainstream commodity.

Krush Groove, a feature film about the early days of Def Jam Record-ings and Russell Simmons, directed by African-American film pioneer

Michael Schultz, is released by Warner Bros. In addition to coproducing the film, Simmons makes a cameo as a club owner in the film.

1986

Run—D.M.C. releases "My Adidas" and, as a result, signs an endorsement deal with Adidas. Additionally, Kurtis Blow performs in a Sprite commercial. These events mark the first partnership between hip-hop artists and nonmusic corporations and set the stage for the corporate relationships that would become rampant in hip hop. KRS-One and Scott La Rock release the highly influential album *Criminal Minded,* which posits a sociopolitically conscious viewpoint and boasts samples from James Brown and AC/DC. The next year, Scott La Rock is shot and killed while trying to stop a gang fight in the Bronx.

> *Now, now, now every January on the third Monday*
> *We pay homage to the man who paved the way.*
> —KING DREAM CHORUS AND HOLIDAY CREW,
> "KING HOLIDAY," *KING HOLIDAY*

The first national celebration of the Dr. Martin Luther King Jr. holiday takes place on January 20, eighteen years after it's first introduced by U.S. Congressman John Conyers (D-MI).

1987

> *Human rights violations, we continue the saga*
> *El Salvador and the Contras in Nicaragua.*
> —IMMORTAL TECHNIQUE, "THE 4TH BRANCH,"
> *REVOLUTIONARY VOL. 2*

The Iran—Contra investigation reveals illegal and covert actions by the Reagan administration. Among the revelations are that the U.S. government allowed the inner cities of America to be saturated with crack cocaine in order to fund the Honduran contras to overthrow the Sandinista government of Nicaragua.

The Beastie Boys, the first white rap group, releases *Licensed to Ill* and becomes the first rap group to reach number 1 on the pop charts.

Eric B. and Rakim release *Paid in Full* on Zakia/4th & Broadway Records. Rakim's use of elaborate metaphors, double puns, and paradoxes make it one of the most influential rap albums of all time.

1988

*I think it's too late
Hip hop has never been the same since '88.*
—CANIBUS, "POET LAUREATE," *CANIBUS*

N.W.A. (Niggaz with Attitude), a West Coast group whose members include Ice Cube, Dr. Dre, Eazy-E, DJ Yella, and MC Ren, releases their first album *Straight Outta Compton,* which goes gold and causes the media to dub their hardcore style "gangsta rap."

Yo! MTV Raps premieres on MTV with Fab 5 Freddy as host. The images, language, and styles featured on this show would help to nationalize Black youth culture.

The Omnibus Anti-Drug Abuse Act, designed to make existing laws even harsher and more unjust, is passed. The racism apparent in these laws is blatant. For instance, although crack and powder cocaine are pharmacologically the same drug, possession of only five grams of crack cocaine (predominantly used by Blacks) yields a five-year mandatory minimum sentence; however, it takes five hundred grams of powder cocaine (predominantly used by whites) to prompt the same sentence.

The Source magazine, founded as a newsletter in 1988 by college students David Mays and Jon Shecter, releases its first issue. The magazine will grow to become the premiere hip-hop magazine in the world.

Jesse Jackson makes a second run at the U.S. presidency. Running on a campaign platform that includes reversing Reaganomics; declaring apartheid-era South Africa a rogue nation; issuing reparations to African-Americans; providing universal health care and free community college to all; and supporting the formation of a Palestinian state, Jackson, despite being briefly tagged a front-runner, would lose the Democratic nomination to Michael Dukakis.

Dr. Molefi K. Asante introduces the first Ph.D. in African-American studies at Temple University. Public Enemy and other Afrocentric rappers frequent the department. The department also encourages young scholars to write dissertations on hip-hop culture, advancing the discipline.

Bill Cosby, during the height of the popularity of his sitcom *The Cosby Show,* donates $20 million to Spelman College, the largest donation ever made.

1989

Spike Lee's film *Do the Right Thing,* a story about racial tension in a diverse Bedford-Stuyvesant, Brooklyn, community, is released by Universal Pictures and features a soundtrack from Public Enemy. The film stars Ossie Davis, Ruby Dee, and Samuel L. Jackson and is the debut for Martin Lawrence and Rosie Perez.

Under international pressure, South African president F. W. de Klerk releases eight African National Congress (ANC) leaders from jail, including Walter Sisulu, founder of the ANC Youth League and prominent figure in the formation of the militant MK or Umkhonto we Sizwe ("Spear of the Nation").

1990

The leader of 2 Live Crew, Luther Campbell, gets arrested 'cause of the lyrics on *As Nasty as They Wanna Be*.

On February 11, Nelson Mandela, leader of the ANC, is freed from Victor Verster Prison in Paarl, South Africa, after twenty-seven years in prison. On the day of his release, Mandela spoke to the nation and to the world:

> *Our resort to the armed struggle in 1960 with the formation of the military wing of the ANC (Umkhonto we Sizwe) was a purely defensive action against the violence of apartheid. The factors which necessitated the armed struggle still exist today. We have no option but to continue. We express the hope that a climate conducive to a negotiated settlement would be created soon, so that there may no longer be the need for the armed struggle.*

1991

Now I see her in commercials, she's universal
She used to only swing it with the inner—city circle.
—COMMON, "I USED TO LOVE H.E.R.," *RESURRECTION*

Ice Cube writes and performs an original song for a St. Ides Malt Liquor commercial. In the thirty-second commercial, Cube rhymes: "Get your girl in the mood quicker / Get your jimmy thicker / With St. Ides Malt Liquor."

On January 16, the United States begins an unprecedented bombing campaign on Iraq, primarily targeting civilian life. The bombs, cumulatively, were the equivalent of seven Hiroshimas and resulted in the death of over 100,000 Iraqi citizens.

On March 3, Los Angeles police officers brutally attack and arrest Rodney King after a San Fernando Valley traffic stop. The beating of King is captured on videotape and quickly broadcast. All of the officers, during a trial that would take place the following year, would be acquitted—an event that sparks the second L.A. rebellions.

chapter 6. OLD WHITE MEN
(OR, WHO OWNS HIP HOP?)

It's nothin' black about the head niggas that's running the
industry, they not even niggas.
—JADAKISS

Foreigners, who have not studied economics but have
studied Negroes, take up business and grow rich.
—DR. HAROLD CRUISE

Black culture is too significant in American culture
for blacks to be glorified employees.
—RUSSELL SIMMONS

It has been said that while a wise person learns from his mistakes, an
even wiser person learns from the mistakes of others. Survival for
the post-hip-hop generation means being deeply engaged in the latter
and confronting, challenging, and correcting the issues that have
plagued previous generations and paying special attention to those issues that have maintained a consistent presence throughout our history in America. One such issue is the relationship African-Americans

have had and still have with incredibly lucrative industries that, without us, would not exist as such.

"Old white men is runnin' this rap shit," Mos Def, in his Brooklyn drawl, rhymed through the trembling speakers in the New York studio I sat in.

> *Corporate forces runnin' this rap shit*
> *Some tall Israeli is runnin' this rap shit*
> *We poke out our asses for a chance to cash in.*

My lips parted, not because I was surprised by what *he was saying,* but rather, that *he was saying it.* For so long, critical issues of power, race, and music have been neglected to the point where one wondered if the economic domination of Black music by non-Blacks was normalized beyond question.

The one-and-a-half-minute song continues as a lyrical indictment of an industry that tells Black performers to *get in the line of fire, we get the big-ass checks.* The song ends with a laundry list of culprits: MTV, Viacom, AOL, Time Warner, cocaine, and Hennessey.

A few weeks prior to hearing this song, I was a producer on *Blokhedz,* a short animated film for a digizine that Mos Def did a voice for. *Blokhedz,* a comic book created by Mike and Mark Davis of Imajimation Studios, tells the story of young Blak, an aspiring teenage rapper who is blessed with the mystical gift of turning his rhymes into reality. Living in the Monarch Projects of Empire City, Blak—who sports a red, black, and green wristband—must struggle to survive the violence and temptation of the streets, while also remaining true to himself and his gift. It was while working on this project, as I sat behind an engineer in a recording studio watching legendary movie director Michael Schultz *(Krush Groove, The Last Dragon, Cooley High),* along with his son Brandon (a writer for *Blokhedz*) direct the voice-over artists, that I heard this song playing in another section of the studio. I followed the beat.

Aptly titled "The Rape Over," I learned that this song, which I was hearing a few weeks early, was slated to appear on Mos's album, *The New Danger.* The song, like so many truths that surface in our lives, came to me at an important time. I was a student in college and had, over the course of my senior year, created *Focused Digizine,* an urban digital media enterprise with an estimated worth of $1 million. Part of our ability to raise funds and grow was due to the enormous amount of resources Lafayette College, a small, private liberal arts college with an endowment of more than $780 million, bestowed upon me: offices, interns, equipment, et cetera. In addition, this 94 percent white college located in rural Pennsylvania had resources that would bring me to point-blank range with the crisis.

"I want you to meet some of our board members and alumni in New York who are super successful and can help you. I don't know much about what they do, but I know they are into the whole rap thing," a fifty-something white administrator at the college told me.

Weeks later, I found myself, along with my producing partner, in robust Manhattan high-rises with fancy elevators and views that were surreal, meeting with executives from record labels, cable channels, and radio stations who were "into the whole rap thing." Old white man after old white man, blazer after blazer, gray head after gray head, and striped tie after stripped tie, I was shocked to discover that hip hop's decision makers weren't hip hop at all. I quickly came to the realization that hip hop, this urban Black creation, was something that urban Blacks (or even just Blacks) didn't control at all. The brutal fact is, as Afrika Bambaataa says: "Today a lot of the people who created hip hop, meaning the Blacks and Latinos, do not control it anymore." These meetings symbolized how perhaps African-America's richest cultural capital is outside of African-American hands.

It became clear that the hip-hop community and hip-hop industry were two totally different entities. As Yvonne Bynoe points out in her essay "Money, Power, Respect: A Critique of the Business of Rap Music," the hip-hop industry "is comprised of entities that seek to profit from the marketing and sales of rap music and its ancillary products" and includes "record companies, music publishers, radio stations, record stores, music-video shows, recording studios, talent bookers, performance venues, promoters, managers, disc jockeys, lawyers, accountants, music publications, and music/entertainment websites," most of which are not owned or even operated by the progenitors of the music—Black folks. Peep:

HIP–HOP COMMUNITY = THE STREETS

HIP–HOP INDUSTRY = WALL STREET

HIP–HOP COMMUNITY ≠ HIP–HOP INDUSTRY

Mos Def's "The Rape Over" had validated what I was seeing, verbalized what I was feeling, and aired out what needed to be made public. What's shocking is that he is among a select few to voice this gross disparity; it has been the proverbial elephant in the room. It's easy to see why most rap artists would be deterred from challenging the institution that feeds them, but what about the critics, fans, and scholars? Most writers and critics who have written about hip hop have not approached the topic from a perspective rooted in history, making it difficult for them to fully assess the function of Black music in American life or to put forth a serious analysis of how hip hop and R & B undergird the entire music business. The most in-depth analysis usually arrives in the form of a moral objection to the content of the rappers' lyrics rather than an analysis or scrutiny of the corporations that profit most from such "immoralities." By focusing on the content, they unskillfully avoid the tough questions: Who sponsors rap? Who buys the most rap? Who promotes death and violence? Who backs ignorance? Who exploits rappers? Who profits from Black-on-Black violence? Who owns the radio stations? Who owns TV? Who owns who, you and your crew? Who runs the media? Who runs radio? Who, who, who? Norman Kelley, one of the few writers to seriously address these disparities, reminds us in his essay "The Political Economy of Black Music," "Never has one people created so much music and been so woefully kept in the dark about the economic consequences of their labor and talent by their intellectuals and politicos."

However, all of that was about to change. Mos's song, *I just knew*, would ignite all of our minds, pens, voices, and feet. It would spark new strategies about community control as well as expand upon discussions that needed to be had—discussions like Passage to Peace held at the 2004 Congressional Black Caucus in D.C., where Congresswoman Maxine Waters told the crowd:

> *Something is going on in hip hop today. . . . We have been the creators of a tremendous art and it gets imitated, it gets redefined, it gets repackaged. . . . It is time to take the economic riches and divert some of the benefits and resources of hip hop to our struggling communities. . . . It's time to open up this discussion about who owns hip hop.*

At this same conference, something strange, something emblematic of the problem occurred. David Mays, a white Jewish Harvard graduate and founder of *The Source* magazine, stood up and added:

> *This union with Congresswoman Waters and CSDI [Community Self-Determination Institute] is a way to educate our people on the real issues affecting our 'hoods and help bring hip hop back to the streets.*

Hip hop culture was born and became a voice for this country's most powerless and endangered demographic group. It is the responsibility of hip hop artists, executives, and true fans to reclaim control of this multi-billion-dollar industry from racist corporations and reap the rewards of hip hop's success for our disenfranchised communities. We must not silently participate in the overall exploitation of our culture.

Our hoods? Back to the streets? Our culture? Listening to Mays was like listening to George W. Bush tell us that "we cannot allow terrorists to rule the world." This was way beyond chutzpah. Mays, who allowed *The Source* to be overrun with ads by the same "exploitative" corporations he's denouncing, reveals the incredible amount of control white corporations have over hip hop—not just the music, but the publications, fashion, et cetera.

As the release date for *The New Danger* approached, I told everyone I knew to cop it, especially Black folks in "the industry," hoping that it would spark a dialogue that was long overdue.

"Yo, you gotta cop Mos's new album . . . if only to hear one track: 'The Rape Over,'" I told one childhood friend and emcee from Philly.

I was sure, too, that because of the "tall Israeli" line, the song would probably generate a mountain of controversy. A year earlier, the state of New Jersey abolished the position of poet laureate after its first appointee, Amiri Baraka, asked, "Who told 4,000 Israeli workers to stay home that day? / Why did Sharon stay away?" This despite the fact that in the same poem, Baraka asks, "Who killed the most Jews . . . who put the Jews in the oven? And who helped them do it? Who backed Hitler? . . ." Sadly, many people perceive criticism of the governmental policies of the Israeli state as criticism of Jews, and hence, anti-Semitic. We see this same tactic used against Americans who are critical of the government when they are tagged "unpatriotic." Mos's comment that "some tall Israeli is runnin' this rap shit" certainly had the same potential to push some of those same buttons, despite the fact that he was not making a broad statement about Jewish domination, but rather a specific shot at Lyor Cohen, president of Warner Music Group, who is, indeed a tall Israeli whose tremendous influence in hip hop has often been criticized. In any event, I was hopeful that any controversy would be good because it would push other issues—mainly, who runs rap, who controls our music, et cetera—to the surface.

October 19, 2004: *The New Danger* is released. I got a call from the emcee who I specifically told to get the album.

"What's the track on the Mos jawn called?" he asked.

" 'The Rape Over.' "

"All right, hold up," he said, as he checked the album cover.

"I don't see it," he broke to me. "Are you sure that's the name?"

"Positive."

Hmm.

Silence occupied our line.

"All right, I'll call you back," I said.

I went to the store, bought the album, and—

Hmm transformed into *damn.*

"The Rape Over" was indeed missing. Gone. Vamoosed.

And "missing" because, interestingly enough, according to Mos Def's label Geffen Records, the LP was initially shipped with "The Rape Over" on it. However, the album hit stores with that particular song missing and with no public explanation from Geffen. Without "The Rape Over," *The New Danger* debuted at number 5 on the *Billboard* charts. When word began to spread about the missing track and corporate censorship, Jim Merlis, head of publicity at Geffen, released a statement claiming that although the album was initially shipped with "The Rape Over" on it, the company realized shortly before the album's release date that a musical sample on the song by The Doors had not been properly cleared. So, rather than push the album's release date back (a common practice among record labels) Geffen decided to remove the controversial song and release the album as scheduled. " 'The Rape Over' was never removed from the album for any reason other than the clearance of the sample," Merlis said.

Are we to believe that the removal of one of the only songs, and certainly the first song by a mainstream artist, to challenge the corporate sharecropping in hip hop was purely coincidental? A song that didn't challenge "hatin'-ass niggas," "bitch-ass niggas," or "lame-ass niggas," but rather "old white men," "corporate forces," and "some tall Israeli"? The overt omission of this song was a testament to Mos's track, a validation of his words, a real-life example of the white corporate domination he rhymed about. A music executive at a major label, who chose to remain anonymous, summed it up to me as "nothing more than a routine instance of censorship—corporate censorship by the labels. It's unfortunate but it happens. It's effective because it sends a message to all artists on the label about what the label will tolerate."

The First Amendment—which states: "Congress shall make no law respecting an establishment of religion, or prohibiting the free exercise thereof; or abridging the freedom of speech, or of the press; or the right of the people peaceably to assemble, and to petition the Government for a redress of grievances"—gives people the right to free speech, a right that historically has been called upon to protect otherwise marginalized voices. However, the rise in corporate censorship—censorship through intimidation, budget-cutting, refusing to advertise or allow airtime, and via other legal channels—has been used to restrict the sociopolitical voices of commercially viable artists.

Radical rap group Dead Prez knows all too much about corporate censorship. Rawkus Records deleted their verse on the *Hip Hop for Respect* LP and Loud Records placed a huge sticker on the case of their first album, *Let's Get Free,* censoring a photo of South African youths with guns celebrating victory over the police.

"Censorship by omission is worse, because, in effect, it's a way of leaving the door open, letting you think freedom of expression is possible in certain instances, when really the [corporate executives who control radio, TV, and the record industry] have made up their minds to make that impossible," explains the rapper Paris, who has also battled against corporate censorship. Ultimately, corporate censorship works because, as the industry adage goes, distribution is king. Since they control the distribution of a product, they ultimately have the power to gag artists by fumbling the paperwork needed for the "clearance of the sample."

Just a few weeks later, it was all revealed to me. The whole *thing*.

The next segment I was producing for the digizine took me back—*way back*—to the Motherland. Accra, the capital city of Ghana in West Africa, is a colorful compilation of African greatness. Warm charcoal faces, with even warmer smiles, welcomed me back. As I stood in the Doorway of No Return, the door through which my ancestors passed before being forced to board slave ships headed for the Americas, I contemplated beauty and tragedy. Beautiful because it was the Motherland; and tragic because of the brutal history of slavery and colonialism. I was there to produce a segment about an emerging music genre called "hiplife."

Highlife is a West African musical genre that emerged in the 1920s and has an up-tempo, synth-driven sound. As hip hop spread across the globe, it infused itself into much of the continental African music, including highlife.

"Hiplife is just highlife plus hip hop," one Ghanaian teenager told me. Hiplife takes imported hip-hop beats and rhymes over them using local Ghanaian languages and dialects.

Under the shade of a wooden storefront, weed smoke sashays through the air as Lil' Kwesi, a local hiplife emcee, takes control of a cipher. After he finished his rhyme, which he spit in the Ghanaian language Twi, I asked if he could explain to me what his rhyme was about.

"Our country and our people were colonized by the British."

"Yeah, I know. Y'all gained independence in the sixties right, under Nkrumah?" I said, to which Lil' Kwesi slid out a chuckle.

"We are still not independent. That's what my song is about. The British still control our country in many ways," he explained to me. "They come here, take our goods, pay us nothing, than sell our stuff in Britain, the so-called mother country, so we don't even benefit, as a country, from the fruits of our own labor. We have not won independence!"

"Neocolonialism" describes the economic arrangements by which former colonial powers maintain control over their former colonies and create new dependencies. This is twenty-first-century colonialism where the same countries continue to economically exploit their former colonies while maintaining that this exploitation is beneficial for the former colony. I realized that Mos Def's "The Rape Over" was ultimately about neocolonialism, a topic seldom discussed but that sucks the life out of Black music.

"Colonialism," as Immortal Technique points out, "is sponsored by corporations." Similarly, just as there were four dominant colonial powers (England, Portugal, France, and Spain) that raped and maimed Africa, Latin America, and Asia, there are four corporations who are not only "runnin' this rap shit," but as Mos says, "run Black music." Appropriately dubbed the "big four," Universal Music Group, Sony BMG, EMI Group, and Warner Music Group, according to Nielsen SoundScan, account for 81.87 percent of the U.S. music market and supply "retailers with 90 percent of the music" that the public purchases, according to New York's *Daily News*.

Consider that the colonial powers were/are called "mother" countries. Although formerly colonized countries like Ghana, Jamaica, and Senegal may appear to be independent, their economies are still controlled by the old colonial powers—mother countries. Ironically, the "big four" of the music industry are called "parent" companies. Despite the perception that Black entrepreneurs like P. Diddy, Russell Simmons, Jay-Z, Cash Money are moguls, they are, in actuality, the children of their respective parent companies. P. Diddy's Bad Boy Records is owned by Warner Music Group; Suge Knight's Death Row by Interscope is owned by Universal Music Group; Def Jam is also owned by Universal. They are, as Norman Kelley writes in his article on Black music, "Black gnats." What's worse is that, despite popular perception, there are no Blacks—*none*—in top executive positions of the parent companies. What the parent companies, as well as the Black moguls, would like us to believe is that "the R.O.C. is runnin' this rap shit." This is why Jay-Z is touted as the "CEO of Hip-Hop." Russell Simmons once said that Blacks are too valuable to be "glorified employees of American Culture, Inc.," yet this is precisely what has occurred. Where is the outrage?

> *We so confuse you*
> *We front rap music.*
> —MOS DEF, "THE RAPE OVER," *THE NEW DANGER*

Simmons, discussing perception management, explains that "It is how you develop an image for companies. So in other words, you give out false statements to mislead the public so they will then increase in their mind the value of your company." In the same way, we have been given a false impression of Black control in hip hop.

Simmons's statements are reminiscent of the brilliance displayed in August Wilson's 1984 *Ma Rainey's Black Bottom,* a play that, like this essay and Mos's "The Rape Over," explores white corporate exploitation. Set in Chicago in 1927, *Ma Rainey* focuses on the exploitation of blues musicians. Wilson's character notes reveal that the white execs—Sturdyvant and Irwin—are completely "preoccupied with money," are "insensitive to black performers," and thus "deal with them at arm's length." The brilliance of Wilson's piece illustrates Simmons's comments, because although Sturdyvant and Irvin are not on stage much, they circumscribe and dictate the lives of the Black performers who are constantly *seen* on stage. They are both nowhere and everywhere at once.

Under the classic colonial model, raw materials like rubber, cocoa, and gold were extracted from the colonies and sent to the mother country to be finished and commodified for the marketplaces of the mother country. Additionally, these products were often sold back to the same colonies from which the raw materials were extracted in the first place. In other words, the colonies—because of regulations that prevented them from manufacturing their own products—were forced to buy back their own goods. Under this system, which Kwesi correctly insisted "is still in place under neocolonialism," raw materials are taken from places like Ghana and sold to the citizens of the mother country. Similarly, in hip hop's case, the citizens of the parent companies are, according to Forbes, "45 million Hip-Hop consumers between the ages of 13 and 34, 80% of whom are white and has $1 trillion in spending power."

Blacks in the inner cities share many of the characteristics of the colonized. As Norman Kelley, who has also elaborated on this colonial connection, describes in his essay "The Political Economy of Black Music":

> *Blacks in the inner cities, if not as an aggregate, share some of the classic characteristics of a colony: lower per capita income; high birth rate; high infant mortality rate; a small or weak middle class; low rate of capital formation and domestic savings; economic dependence on external markets; labor as a major export; a tremendous demand for commodities produced by the colony but consumed by wealthier nations; most of the land and business are owned by foreigners.*

So essentially, the ghetto—with poverty, poor schools, drugs, police terrorism, et cetera—provides the raw materials needed to produce rap. Then, just as the gold and diamonds that are taken from Africa are primarily sold in the mother countries (Europe and the United States), rap is mainly purchased by a white audience, the parent companies' citizens, if you will. "Economically, colonialism programmed African countries to consume what they do not produce and to produce what they do not consume," writes Nigerian Bade Onimode in *A Future for Africa*. This fact has deadly ramifications.

The middle—aged, wealthy white executives that I met with in Manhattan—the decision makers of hip hop—I'd initially perceived to be very ignorant with regards to hip-hop culture, history, and ideology. I realized, however, that they were very knowledgeable, we just had different knowledge(s). They may have not understood the ghetto, or the Black experience, or the current struggle, or even Black music, but they had a rich—*rich!*—understanding of the tastes and values of white consumers. That is to say, by default, they understood white racism on an intrinsic level, which meant that they understood how to sell products to young white males. As Chuck D noted in his essay "Death of a Nation": "It's hard for me to support an 85% white teenage audience screamin' 'smoke that nigger' and call it the shit."

The idea of selling Black violence, misogyny, and sexuality to a white teenage audience conjures up the image of blues musician Tommy Johnson, who in the film *O Brother, Where Art Thou?* sells his soul to the devil. He has a photograph, titled "Tommy and fans," where Tommy, a chocolate-colored brother, stands surrounded by a group of whites in KKK outfits. It is this reality that prompts M-1 of Dead Prez to explain:

Hip hop today is programmed by the ruling class. It is not the voice of African or Latino or oppressed youth. It is a puppet voice for the ruling class that tells us to act like those people who are oppressing us. The schools, the media, capitalism, and colonialism are totally responsible for what hip hop is and what it has become. But we didn't intend on that—hip hop was a voice just like the drum, the oral tradition of our people.

Allowing white executives, not from the hip-hop culture, to control and dictate the culture is tragic because the music, and ultimately the culture, as we can see today, has not only lost its edge, but its sense of rebellion and Black improvement—the very principles upon which it was founded. In Byron Hurt's groundbreaking documentary, *Hip-Hop: Beyond Beats & Rhymes,* former Def Jam president Carmen Ashhurst-Watson recalls:

> *At the time where we switched to gangster music was the same time the majors brought up all the [hip-hop] labels and I don't think that's a coincidence. At the time we were able to get a place in the record store and a bigger presence because of this major marketing capacity, the music became less and less conscious. We went to Columbia, and the next thing I know we went from Public Enemy to pushing a group called Bitches with Problems.*

As rap music began to show serious economic promise in the 1980s, major record labels, alien to the culture and unsure what would sell, began signing up a wide variety of artists—from Public Enemy to LL Cool J. However, soon after the acquisition of these artists, it became evident—through lyrics like "Better you than me / I'm a cop killer, fuck police brutality! / Cop killer, I know your family's grievin' (fuck 'em) / Cop killer, but tonight we get even"—that many of the recently signed artists had a political agenda that was in direct conflict not only with the label's politics but with their bottom line as well. The result, as Ashhurst-Watson remembers firsthand, was a mass dismissal of artists who insisted upon challenging the status quo. Put another way, the labels were saying, "We want to make money off your art and culture, but we don't want you to truly express yourselves if that means rage or challenging the politics of the status quo."

Tragically, the history of African-American music has been one of white corporate exploitation and outright theft of Black artists and music. Even in the midst of the most virulent and vehement racism, whites still figured out "how to grow rich off of Black fun," as one minstrel performer notes. And the main way to "grow rich" was from blatant theft. This stealing is a part of a system of theft that dates back to the immensely popular minstrel shows of the nineteenth century where whites would blacken their faces and imitate and pervert Black dance and music forms before white audiences. The evolution of this theft can be observed in the subtle historic categorizations of Black music and to more outright and blatant forms of larceny.

Blues artists responsible for countless gold and platinum records were constantly cheated. Many were paid as little as fifty dollars for an album and were denied royalties, even while their songs stayed on the hit charts for months at a time. To make matters worse, the lawyers who represented the artists were assigned by the labels—a clear conflict of interests. In the end, Black artists, like the sharecroppers who worked plantations after enslavement, always ended up owing the labels. Artists like Bo Diddley, who was cheated by Chess Records and stayed broke despite recording hits, has recently come out to speak up. When asked about why he chose to challenge his former label, he says, "I decided to tell it like it is. They're the ones who should be ashamed, not me." Diddley's label, Chess Records, thought of its artists as childlike men who were interested only in Cadillacs and beautiful women, and who needed "plantation owners" to look after their affairs, as Marshall Chess, son and nephew of the founders of Chess Records, recalled. Through exploitation and a plantation-owner mentality, white businessmen were able to spin the blues into gold.

The jazz era was no different. Trumpeter Rex Stewart, who joined Duke Ellington's band in 1934, echoed Mos Def when he asked, "Where the control is, the money is. Do you see any of us [Black musicians] running any record companies, booking agencies, radio stations, music magazines?"

Black saxophonist and composer Ornette Coleman, who won the Pulitzer Prize for Music in 2007, has been a consistent voice against this exploitation:

> *The problem in this business is that you don't own your own product.*
> *If you record, it's the record company that owns it; if you play at a*
> *club, it's the nightclub owners who charge people to listen to you, and*
> *then they tell you your music is not catching on. . . . This has been my*
> *greatest problem—being short-changed because I'm a Negro, not be-*
> *cause I can't produce. Here I am being used as a Negro who can play*
> *jazz, and all the people I recorded for and worked for act as if they*
> *own me and my product. They have been guilty of making me believe*
> *I shouldn't have the profits from my product simply because they own*
> *the channels of productions. They act like I owe them something for*
> *letting me express myself with my music, like the artist is supposed to*
> *suffer and not live in clean, comfortable situations. The insanity of*
> *living in America is that ownership is really strength. It's who owns*
> *who's strongest in America . . . that's why it's so hard to lend your*
> *music to that kind of existence.*

The "existence" Coleman reflects upon is, in part, a classical component of capitalistic relationships. The term for this relationship, where the fruits of an artist's labor are controlled by the employer, is "alienation." Then and now, this alienation is the result of the employer owning and controlling both the means of production and the manufactured products that are the end result of the workers' labor.

To complicate matters and to add insult to rape, many of the jazz executives despised the musicians and the music. Consider John Hammond, a descendant of the Vanderbilt family and a top executive at

Columbia Records, who signed Billie Holiday and Bessie Smith to a series of contracts where they were given a small flat fee for each recording and no royalties. Holiday, for example, was paid thirty dollars for six recordings—recordings that went on to sell hundreds of thousands of copies. What's worse, Columbia designated Hammond as the "sole recipient of all royalties" from sales of a 1970s reissue of Smith's albums. Hammond, if we adjust for inflation, made roughly $360,000 off that album alone.

The exploitation of artists continues even after their deaths. Recordings withheld from the market are often released with much publicity after the artist has died. Smith, for example, came out with an album after she had passed that was much talked about and acclaimed. Columbia made a fortune off of this, all while Smith lay dead in an unmarked grave. After a campaign by rock singer Janis Joplin and Juanita Green, a Black nurse, a few hundred dollars was raised for a headstone and a scholarship in Smith's name. Columbia Records finally saw fit to put a measly thousand dollars toward the fund. Hammond, who had exploited Smith for so long, reluctantly contributed fifty dollars for a headstone.

The theft of Black music has been so rampant and pungent that a group of major record labels, overcome by guilt, founded the Rhythm and Blues Foundation in 1994 in an effort to help "victims of poor business practices, bad management and unscrupulous record companies," wrote *The New York Times*. Kick-started with a $1.5 million endowment from Atlantic and $450,000 from Time Warner, the Washington, D.C.–based foundation promotes the importance of past musicians and gives annual awards; however, nothing is being done about the redistribution of the enormous wealth gained off the original exploitation. The R & B Foundation may be a step in the right direction, but it fails miserably at seriously addressing the gross theft that occurred.

The attempt by Atlantic Records is, at best, thoughtful, but it isn't nearly enough. Consider, for example, Ruth Brown, who received as little as sixty-nine dollars per song, with no royalties for a series that enabled the then-fledgling Atlantic Records to become an industry giant. Brown was one of the highest-selling recording artists of the fifties and was so instrumental in the success of Atlantic Records, it was often referred to as "the house that Ruth built."

Similarly, today, with the billions of dollars that hip hop generates annually, the modern music industry is a house, a mansion, built by Black youths. And within that mansion, the same exploitation continues to take place. Norman Kelley writes:

> *Contracts are structured in such a way that the odds are against musical neophytes remaining in the business for very long. They see the likes of Michael Jackson, Prince, Tupac, Snoop Doggy Dogg or Quincy Jones, dazzled by the big money makers but don't understand how the music industry depends on a fresh crop of naive, young and talented artists—black, white, and Latino—to grease the industry's wheels. Most of those who sign contracts will not enjoy long careers and the industry has ways to recoup the money that it spends on producing and promoting what they call "talent," but viewed as either disposable or exploitable.*

What makes this even more troubling is the lion's share of music industry profits that hip hop generates. With all other genres losing music, the music industry, for years now, has relied almost exclusively upon hip hop to stay afloat. "What is keeping some labels solvent, many executives agree, is hip hop and contemporary rhythm-and-blues," writes Neil Strauss of *The New York Times*. According to *Forbes*, hip hop generates over $15 billion per year and "has moved beyond its musical roots, transforming into a dominant and increasingly lucrative lifestyle."

There's an image in John Gabriel Stedman's 1790 book, *Narrative of a Five Years' Expedition Against the Revolted Negroes of Surinam*, that is called "Europe supported by Africa and America." The image depicts three nude women: an African, a European, and a Native American. The African and Native American women, both wearing shackles, are holding up a shackle-less European woman draped in pearls. This is the best way to think about colonialism and indeed the rap industry. More than that, though, Stedman also leads us to some of the answers.

Stedman, who was a soldier in a Dutch military unit, found himself in Surinam, a small country sharing its southern border with Brazil. In his book, Stedman describes the many abuses the Dutch inflicted upon the enslaved Africans in Surinam until something monumental happened: The enslaved Africans realized that their labor was supporting the entire Dutch economy and, led by the Surinam Maroons, resisted, rebelled, and revolted.

Blacks, not just in the hip-hop community and industry, but in all areas, need to realize the incredible power we yield over markets. Before we can even seriously discuss the content of the music, we have to own it. The "old white men" that I met with in New York, hip hop's decision makers, don't have the interest of the Black community at heart. We must also not make the mistake of believing that all Blacks have the best interests of Black folks. That's why a consciousness that values the collective interests of the people is vital. Consider, for example, that Ossie Davis in 1971 said, "Cable TV is a new opportunity for those seeking their fair share of power, and the black man must do, at the beginning, what he has failed to do in the past—get in at the beginning." Bob Johnson, founder of BET, followed through on Davis's advice; however, because of a lack of collective consciousness, turned it over to Viacom, who, as Mos rhymed, "is runnin' this rap shit."

Clarence Avant, music industry veteran and former president of

Motown, crystallizes this point and reinforces the notion that we must take seriously what scholar Harold Cruise called a "community point of view":

> *We have always been entertainers, but we have never really owned anything. Based on the number of Black artists who are successful, we should have more ownership. We are not owners because we have a combination of the wrong attitude and no money. For instance, our artists become famous, and they want to be known as pop stars. How can we own anything when our best assets want to be stop being Black when they are successful? . . . Whoever controls the talent is going to be in the best position, but we do not. . . .*

Today that wrong attitude can and must be *righted.* "The Black economy is a myth only because a truly viable Black economy does not exist," writes Cruise.

Chuck D warned, "If we don't get up on the good foot—I'm talking to my people—then we're going to be behind the eight-ball again. . . . White businesses have built themselves up and blacks are still working for the white businesses." When Nas rhymes "Hip-hop been dead, we the reason it died / Wasn't Sylvia's fault or 'cause MC's skills are lost / It's 'cause we can't see ourselves as the boss," he follows up with an even more astute analysis of Black pathology:

> *Deep-rooted through slavery, self-hatred*
> *The Jewish stick together, friends in high places*
> *We on some low-level shit*
> *We don't want niggas to ever win . . .*

Despite criticism of white, corporate, or Jewish influence in hip hop, the Jewish model, with respect to Hollywood, is one African-Americans can learn a great deal from. As Neal Gabler writes in *An Empire of Their Own*:

> *Within the studios and on the screen, the Jews could simply create a new country—an empire of their own, so to speak—one where they would not only be admitted, but would govern as well. They would fabricate their empire in the image of America as they would fabricate themselves in the image of prosperous Americans. They would create its values and myths, its traditions and archetypes. It would be an America where fathers were strong, families stable, people attractive, resilient, resourceful, and decent. This was their America, and its invention may be their most enduring legacy.*

Our history is filled with African-Americans overcoming a great number of obstacles and achieving what was thought to be impossible. The logical, necessary, and vital next step for the post-hip-hop generation is simple: ownership over its cultural creations.

chapter 7.
BEYOND JENA: FREE 'EM ALL

I believe that all African American prisoners are political
prisoners, whether or not they label themselves as such.
Because of the circumstances that got them into jail as
well as the harshness of sentencing applied only to them.
—EVELYN WILLIAMS

The courts have become a universal device
for re—enslaving blacks.
—W. E. B. DUBOIS

Trying to solve the crime problem by building
more prison cells is like trying to solve the problem of
AIDS by building more hospitals.
—JAMES AUSTIN

"No justice, no peace!" a sparkling crowd of hundreds chanted in front
of Morgan State University's Soper Library in a student-led rally to
support the Jena Six. With students clad in varying tones of black, the
scene at Morgan mirrored scores of similar events across the country

123

including in Jena, Louisiana, where tens of thousands of people, also dressed in black, gathered to participate in the biggest civil rights demonstration since the 1960s. In many ways, the coordinated protocol to wear black clothing symbolized not only solidarity, but a kind of funeral—one that marked the death of an apathy that had become emblematic of this generation. And with that memorial "a new movement was born," as one student reflected.

I recalled Jordan, the young man in prison who explained to me that although there was a mattress in his cell, he didn't sleep on it, because the comfort of a bed would numb him to the brutal reality of where he really was. Just as the frigid floor reminded him of where he was, the six Black teenagers sentenced to a total of more than one hundred years in prison for a schoolyard fight revealed to the post-hip-hop generation where we are today: a day, born yesterday, grayed with the evidence of things unseen.

Thirty years ago, a rash of posters began smothering the brick and mortar of walls throughout Brooklyn. The posters pictured a young woman whose face, which was the color of the earth, was crowned by a spectacular wheel of black wool. Just below her high cheekbones WANTED screamed out in violent typeface. The posters claimed that the woman, whom they called "Joanne Chesimard," was a "murderer" and was "armed and dangerous"—assertions that not only stood in stark contrast to the radiant figure who floated above the brazen words, but to the woman who was loved by her community, the woman whom they called Assata.

"They made her sound like a super-villain, like something out of a comic book," rapper and actor Mos Def remembers of the posters that tattered his Bed-Stuy neighborhood. "But even then, as a child, I couldn't believe what I was being told," he adds. Mos Def's position was reflected in the actions of his Brooklyn community when, time after time, the WANTED posters were yanked down as fast as they were put up and replaced with colorful posters that read: ASSATA IS WELCOME HERE.

The community, unremitting in their support despite what outside forces may have thought, remembered that the same external forces have dubbed most of their heroes and sheroes, at one point in time, as criminals. Assata's community remembered what the "authorities" said about Dr. Martin Luther King Jr., about Fannie Lou Hamer, about Paul Robeson, about Rosa Parks, even 'bout Jesus. As a result, they were (and still are) skeptical about what the authorities say. That is why when the authorities called Assata a criminal, her community—who often mentioned her in the same breath as Harriet Tubman—was unfazed because, after all, Harriet Tubman was a "criminal," too. So instead of turning Assata in, they honored her as they did Harriet, knowing that by honoring these women, they were honoring the best in themselves, ourselves.

Assata was a—

Perhaps it is most appropriate for her to introduce herself, in her voice, with her words:

My name is Assata ("she who struggles") Shakur ("the thankful one"), and I am a twentieth-century escaped slave. Because of government persecution, I was left with no other choice than to flee from the political repression, racism, and violence that dominate the U.S. government's policy toward people of color. I am an ex–political prisoner, and I have been living in exile in Cuba since 1984. I have been a political activist most of my life, and although the U.S. government has done everything in its power to criminalize me, I am not a criminal, nor have I ever been one. In the 1960s, I participated in various struggles: the black liberation movement, the student rights movement, and the movement to end the war in Vietnam. I joined the Black Panther

Party. By 1969 the Black Panther Party had become the number one organization targeted by the FBI's COINTELPRO program. Because the Black Panther Party demanded the total liberation of Black people, J. Edgar Hoover called it the "greatest threat to the internal security of the country" and vowed to destroy it and its leaders and activists.

On May 2, 1973, Assata was pulled over by the New Jersey State Police, shot twice, and then charged with murder of a police officer. After spending nearly seven years in prison under torturous conditions, she escaped in 1979 and moved to Cuba.

Even with political asylum in Cuba, Assata's struggle still persists. In September 1998, the U.S. House of Representatives bloodthirstily passed a resolution that called upon Cuba to extradite Assata—a call that Cuba ignored. Then, in the summer of 2005, thirty-two years later, the FBI classified Assata as a "domestic terrorist" and increased the reward for her capture to an unprecedented $1 million.

"She is now 120 pounds of money," snarled New Jersey State Police superintendent Rick Fuentes. In echo, Colonel Williams of the New Jersey State Police announced that his department, in desperation, "would do everything we could to get her off the island of Cuba, and if that includes kidnapping, we would do it." All of this despite an overwhelming mass of evidence that demonstrated Assata's innocence.

In the same spirit demonstrated thirty years ago, Assata's community came out in full support, launching several initiatives dedicated to protecting their courageous Black rose. Most visible among these campaigns is the Hands Off Assata Coalition, a "collective comprised of activists, artists, scholars, elected officials, students, parents, attorneys, workers, clerics, and concerned community members who are standing against the latest attack upon Assata Shakur." The hip-hop community, whose interest in her was heightened upon the discovery that she was Tupac Shakur's aunt, praised her on T-shirts, Web sites, and in rap lyrics. Common retells her story in "Song for Assata," which he prefaces with a soulful libation:

In the Spirit of Assata Shakur.
We make this movement towards freedom.
I'm thinkin' of Assata, yes, listen to my Love, Assata, yes
Your Power and Pride is beautiful, may God bless your Soul.

In Havana, President Fidel Castro reminded Cuban citizens that "They [the U.S. government] wanted to portray her as a terrorist, something that was an injustice, a brutality, an infamous lie," and that Assata had been "a true political prisoner."

Amnesty International, the nongovernmental organization that campaigns for internationally recognized human rights, defines a political prisoner as "any prisoner whose case has a significant political element: whether the motivation of the prisoner's acts, the acts themselves, or the motivation of the authorities." Political prisoners are often arrested and tried beneath a veneer of legality, where false charges, manufactured evidence, and unfair trials are used to disguise the fact that an individual is a political prisoner. Assata was a political prisoner, joining a long legacy of African-American political prisoners whose "acts" have had a "significant political element." In 1927, scholar, activist, and Black Star Line founder Marcus Garvey was imprisoned and deported after being criminalized on a bogus charge of mail fraud. In 1951, scholar and activist W. E. B. DuBois, who was Garvey's rival during the 1920s, was imprisoned during the height of the Cold War for advocating world peace. He was officially charged with "failure to register as an agent of a foreign principle." While imprisoned, DuBois realized that he was connected to all African-American prisoners, writing, "We protect and defend sensational cases where negroes are involved. But the great mass of arrested or accused Black folk have no defense."

The events in Jena demonstrated to young people that fifty-six years after DuBois was falsely imprisoned, "the great mass of arrested or accused Black folk" still "have no defense" and that the racism our parents and grandparents fought against is still alive and well. Since many of our parents have long put away their marching shoes, the marches to support the Jena Six and to stand up against injustice, orchestrated primarily by this new generation, represented a passing of the mantle.

This new generation of concerned citizens, diverse in race, gender, orientation, and class, understands that while methods and programs change with time, the objectives that the previous generation struggled to achieve—freedom, justice, and equality—remain the same. While there is no doubt that the Jena rallies illustrated this generation's commitment to social justice, a fundamental question arose: Where do we go from Jena?

"This is bigger than Jena—much, much bigger," a high school student, who left his school to attend various Jena rallies in Baltimore, tells me as he exits a rally held at Coppin State University. "Jena is happening everywhere," he adds. "And that's why I'm here." He tells me that his cousin is imprisoned at a federal correctional institution (FCI) in Fairton, New Jersey, where he joined thousands of Black men who represent a fraction of the more than 1.5 million imprisoned Black men and women. To fully understand what 1.5 million means, consider the horrifying reality that no other society in the history of the world has ever incarcerated so many of its citizens—not even the Soviet Union at the height of the Gulag or South Africa during the brutal regime of apartheid.

Let us carry with us Amnesty's internationally recognized definition of a political prisoner in our minds as I spray-paint a picture of the right here, right now, and illustrate the idea, expressed by young people throughout the country at the Jena rallies, that a great majority of the 1.5 million African-Americans in prison today are political prisoners. "Free 'em all, free 'em all," were the chants that cascaded through the crowds.

As a teenager in Philadelphia, whenever I traveled—whether to the store, a party, or just wandered aimlessly—it was always with all of my friends . . . all at once. Ten of us, sometimes more, mahogany-colored saplings, hiking across concrete, exploring the gritty labyrinth of the city.

"All a y'all not go'n make it," a woman who resembled my grand-mother, all of our grandmothers, once told us as we congregated at a bus stop on Market Street in West Philadelphia. Tight coils of muted silver peeked out from beneath her brightly colored head wrap as she warned us, both with her squinting purple-black eyes and soothing singsong soprano, about our futures.

"Y'all be careful, now. They lookin' for y'all: young Black boys. Y'all gotta know that. Avoid the traps," she grimaced, knowing what we were up against. Roughly a decade later, at twenty-five, with most of my team of ten depleted (jailed, killed, et cetera), I find myself on similar streets, echoing sister elder, trying to find the words, if there are words, that might prevent today's youth from becoming part of the third (or even two-thirds in some northern cities) of African-American men in their twenties that are in jail, on parole, or on probation.

The prison industrial complex, as it has come to be known, is the frigid, mechanical name for the ferocious combination of government institutions, private corporations, national policies, and cultural atti-tudes that have created what scholar Manning Marable dubs the "new leviathan of racial inequality that has been constructed across our country." "New" because unlike the old leviathans of chattel slavery and Jim Crow, this new one, as Marable observes, "presents itself to the world as a system that is truly color-blind."

Consider Marable's observation with what H. R. Haldeman, White House chief of staff under President Richard Nixon, wrote in his diary about his former boss's approach to law and order:

> *President Nixon emphasized that you have to face the fact that the whole problem is really the blacks. They key is to devise a system that recognizes this while appearing not to.*

Haldeman's recollection of Nixon's agenda is immensely important if we wish to understand the challenges that the post-hip-hop generation must confront. For it is Nixon's rabidly racist "system" that is at the foothills of today's mountain of racial injustice.

The African-American experience, since we were enslaved for longer than free, could easily be categorized as one of resistance and rebellion. The late sixties were no different. African-Americans, fed up with the decimation and exploitation of their communities, took to the streets in national protests that were often given the misnomer of "riots" by the mainstream press. The front-page images of Black rage, of course, terrified a white America for whom fear has been among its core characteristics, then and now. Harris polls conducted in the sixties reveal that 81 percent of white Americans believed that "Negroes who start riots" were to blame for the perceived collapse of law and order in the cities of America. Politicians like Barry Goldwater, an influential senator from Arizona, used this fear in his 1964 presidential run. "Law and order has broken down, mob violence has engulfed great American cities, and our wives feel unsafe in the streets."

If politicians failed to react to the growing sense of fear they would lose their white voters, some of whom were arming themselves. During the 1967 uprisings in Newark, for example, a group of whites led by future New Jersey assemblyman Anthony Imperiale armed themselves and patrolled Black neighborhoods in what they called "jungle cruisers." When asked about the Black Panther Party for Self-Defense, Imperiale declared that "when the [Black] Panther comes, the white hunter will be ready." As would Nixon, who had an idea of how to capitalize on white fear while simultaneously eliminating what he dubbed as "the Black problem." Nixon's logic: "Crime meant urban, urban meant Black, and the war on crime meant a bulwark built against the increasingly political and vocal racial other by the predominately white state," as Christian Parenti writes in *Lockdown America: Police and Prisons in the Age of Crisis*. Additionally, the administration "linked street crime to the civil disobedience of the civil rights movement."

James Reston, in his 1968 *New York Times* op-ed, "Political Pollution," foresaw that Nixon, during his campaign, "undoubtedly will emphasize order in the cities, for that is his best issue . . . he thinks he can tame the ghettos and then reconstruct them, and he may very well make reconciliation with the Negro community impossible in the process."

Reston's analysis was correct. To Nixon and his cronies, running a successful campaign meant appeasing white fear by promising to enforce law and order by any means, thus creating the illusion of security. As journalist and political prisoner Mumia Abu-Jamal writes, "promise death, and the election is yours. A vote for Hell in the Land of Liberty, with its over one million prisoners, is the ticket to victory."

Nixon—who once told Secretary of State Henry Kissinger, "Henry, leave the niggers to Bill and we'll take care of the rest of the world," and complained to Assistant to the President for Domestic Affairs John Ehrlichman that Great Society programs were a waste "because blacks were genetically inferior to whites"—would take office in January 1969, immediately setting in motion a vicious system responsible for much of what we see today.

Before Nixon could "tame the ghetto," he would first have to prepare the troops. As president, he immediately allocated millions of dollars to local police forces and heightened the federal government's role in local policing. In addition, police departments across the country drastically changed their training policies. Prior to this period, about half of the states in the United States didn't have literacy requirements for their officers and, on average, barbers and hairstylists spent triple the amount of time training than cops did. As Daryl Gates, who would be the chief of the LAPD during the Rodney King beating and uprising that followed the trial, noted in a 1968 article, "the police of America have not been overwhelmingly successful in their control of riots," and he even acknowledged that their initial efforts to "tame the ghettos" were "pretty awful."

Nixon would respond with a plan to not only control, but to profit, as well. Nixon's presidential crime commission found that most police departments "were not organized in accordance with well-established principles of modern business management." Police departments around the country, starting with the LAPD, sent high-ranking officers to study business management at Ford, Rockwell, IBM, and Union Oil. Funded by the LEAA (Law Enforcement Alliance of America), police departments set up management development centers and began to embark on a campaign against the ghettos of America—one that would be gross, robust, and, because it was now in tune with "business management," highly profitable.

Nixon's system, in which he was able to target blacks while appearing not to, was the War on Drugs, a phrase he coined to describe his new design to enhance drug prohibition. Nixon characterized the abuse of illicit substances as "America's public enemy number one." However, this war didn't target whites who statistically used drugs at a much more alarming rate, but rather Blacks in the ghettos. Instead of fighting the causes of crime or drug use, they made sentences abnormally long and mandatory and transformed correctional institutions into punishment warehouses for the poor and Black. This Molotov cocktail of fear, brutality, and power ignited a prison boom unmatched in the history of the world. When the late Tupac Shakur rhymes in "Changes," "Instead of a war on poverty / They got a war on drugs so the police can bother me," he is, some twenty-five years later, responding to Nixon who declared, "I say that doubling the conviction rate in this country would do more to cure crime in America than quadrupling the funds for Humphrey's war on poverty." And with that brutal logic, the onslaught began.

> *Passed the Rockefeller laws to make us all State Prop*
> *Feds handin' out bids startin' 15 a pop.*
> —DEAD PREZ FEATURING DIVINE, "BABY FACE,"
> *TURN OFF THE RADIO: THE MIXTAPE VOL. 2*

In 1973, New York governor Nelson Rockefeller would follow Nixon's lead by introducing the Rockefeller drug laws, which would prescribe a mandatory fifteen-year prison sentence for possessing small amounts of narcotics. To understand the effects of a law like this on the Black community, consider that in New York State between 1817 and 1981, a total of thirty-three prisons were erected. And then from 1982 to 1999, thirty-eight more prisons were constructed. New York's prison population during the Attica rebellions in 1971 was 12,500. By 1999, there were over 71,000 incarcerated and today that number has almost doubled.

The introduction of crack into Black neighborhoods in the eighties was accompanied by a series of new legislation—The Omnibus

Crime Bill (1984), Anti-Drug Abuse Act (1986), and the Omnibus Anti-Drug Abuse Act (1988)—designed to make existing laws even harsher and more unjust. The racism apparent in these laws, which are still in place, troubles the soul. For instance, although crack and powder cocaine are pharmacologically the same drug, possession of only five grams of crack cocaine yields a five-year mandatory minimum sentence; however, it takes five hundred grams of powder cocaine to prompt the same sentence. Moreover, crack cocaine is the only drug for which the first offense of simple possession can trigger a federal mandatory minimum sentence. Yet simple possession of any quantity of any other substance by a first-time offender—including powder cocaine—is a misdemeanor offense punishable by a maximum of one year in prison. With 90 percent of those convicted in federal court for crack cocaine being Black, these laws were targeted at our communities. As Holly Sklar writes in "Reinforcing Racism with War on Drugs," "By government count, more than 24 million Americans, mostly White, have used marijuana, cocaine or some other illicit drug in the past year. Imagine if the war on drugs targeted Whites in the suburbs instead of Blacks and Latinos in inner-city neighborhoods. Imagine if undercover cops were routinely sent to predominantly White schools and colleges to sell drugs."

> *Niggaz ain't scrappin', they bangin' ya*
> *The judge don't need a tree branch when they hangin' ya.*
> —STYLES P FEATURING J—HOOD, "G—JOINT," *TIME IS MONEY*

Even as the national crime rate declined, these racist policies were ratcheted up during the Clinton era and can be seen in legislation like the Violent Crime Control and Law Enforcement Act in 1994, which appropriated $10 billion solely for prison construction. In addition, mandatory minimums grew harsher. Although politicians argued that the extended prison sentences were set aside for the worst-of-the-worst criminals, the reality is dramatically different. In 1980, there were 40,000 drug offenders in prison. Today that number has ballooned to over 500,000. The vast majority of these offenders, African-Americans and Latinos, are drug users who simply need rehab rather than punishment. Many others, who may have been caught selling drugs, are petty pawns, "not the kingpins of the drug trade," but rather impoverished "low-level sellers who are incarcerated and rapidly replaced on the streets by others seeking economic gain," says Mark Mauer of the Sentencing Project, a national organization working for a fair and effective criminal justice by promoting both reforms and alternatives to incarceration.

> *Every crime I did was petty*
> *Every criminal is rich already.*
> —THE COUP, "EVERYTHANG," *PARTY MUSIC*

Although it is often made to appear on the fringes, the observation and analysis of the gross injustices that riddle the current system have maintained a steady presence in the mainstream. In the mid-nineties, a *USA Today* special report on the War on Drugs acknowledged, among a myriad of other injustices, that:

> *The War on Drugs has, in many places, been fought mainly against blacks. . . . Tens of thousands of arrests—mostly in the inner-city— resulted from dragnets with paramilitary names. Operation Pressure Point in New York City. Operation Thunderbolt in Memphis. Operation Hammer in Los Angeles . . . "We don't have whites on corners selling drugs . . . They're in houses and offices," says police chief John Dale of Albany, N.Y., where blacks are eight times as likely as whites*

to be arrested for drugs. . . . "We're locking up kids who are scram-
bling for crumbs, not the people who make big money."

Or, perhaps Nino Brown (played by Wesley Snipes), the leader of the
Cash Money Brothers in the 1991 Mario Van Peebles film *New Jack
City,* said it best:

> *I'm not guilty. You're the one that's guilty. The lawmakers, the politi-*
> *cians, the Colombian drug lords, all you who lobby against making*
> *drugs legal. Just like you did with alcohol during the prohibition.*
> *You're the one who's guilty. I mean, c'mon, let's kick the ballistics*
> *here: Ain't no Uzis made in Harlem. Not one of us in here owns a*
> *poppy field. This thing is bigger than Nino Brown. This is big busi-*
> *ness. This is the American way.*

Nino was right. Historically, it has been the "American way" to
subjugate, murder, and oppress people of color. The War on Drugs,
often fittingly described as the "War on Us," proves no different.
Chilling evidence of this can be seen if we look at New York, where
African-Americans and Latinos comprise 25 percent of the total
population, but 83 percent of all state prisoners and 94 percent of all
those convicted of drug offenses.

It's crucial to understand that "the typical cocaine user is white,
male, a high school graduate employed full time and living in a small
metropolitan area or suburb," admits former drug czar William Bennett. The U.S. Commission on Civil Rights concluded that African-
Americans constitute about 14 percent of the drug-using population,
35 percent of drug arrests, 55 percent of all drug convictions, and 75
percent of all prison admissions on drug offenses. As the *Los Angeles
Times* concluded, "Although it is clear that whites sell most of the nation's cocaine and account for 80% of its consumers, it is Blacks and

other minorities who continue to fill up America's courtrooms and jails."

> *Got a law for raw niggaz now, playa what it be like?*
> *When will niggaz see they got us bleedin' with three strikes.*
> —TUPAC SHAKUR, "MILITARY MINDS," *BETTER DAYZ*

In the early 1990s, with crack drenching deep into the ghettos of America, the federal government and twenty-three states ratcheted up the mandatory-minimum concept another notch by passing "three strikes" laws dictating prison sentences of twenty-five years to life for third felonies. These laws have undoubtedly taken some violent offenders out of circulation—but they have also handed out life sentences to thousands of people for petty crimes such as possession or stealing a spare tire.

Not only did the War on Drugs lock up an inhumane amount of Blacks, but it ensured that they would stay in jail for abnormally long periods of time. Now, "it's less about more people going in than about people staying longer," says Allen Beck, chief of the Corrections Statistics Program at the federal Bureau of Justice Statistics. Take, for example, California's three-strikes law, which eliminates the possibility of parole for repeat offenders and mandates life in prison for persons found guilty of three felony convictions. The Sentencing Project reports that one out of every eleven people imprisoned are serving life, 25 percent of them without parole. Many of these people are in jail for nonviolent drug crimes, minor robberies or thefts, or are found guilty by association. In California, for example, more people are serving life in prison under the three-strikes law for simple marijuana possession than for kidnapping, murder, and rape combined. Further, under three strikes, more people have been sentenced for drug possession than for violent offenses. To give a personal example, when I was a

graduate student at UCLA, I was the editor-in-chief for *Nommo*.
Nommo, a newsmagazine founded in 1968 at the height of the Black
liberation struggle, is a historic institution and the first non-HBCU
newsmagazine for Black students. Every day, without fail, at least two
dozen letters like this one would arrive:

READ ME READ ME READ ME!

*In 1994, I was convicted and sentenced to serve a (40) year to life
prison term, pursuant to the then (new) "Three Strike Law." I received
this sentence for the theft of a bicycle.*

*I am guilty of the theft of the bicycle, but not to the tune of a (40)
year to life prison term.*

*In all my years I have never hurt any one, there are white prisoners
here to whom have killed two or three people, yet they do not suffer the
sentence that I must.*

READ ME READ ME READ ME!

Tragically, stories like this were/are common. Moreover, these stories are not exclusive to adults.

> *They put kids in jail, for a life they ain't even get to start*
> *That's murder too, and it's breaking my heart,*
> *It's breaking our nation apart.*
> —TALIB KWELI, "JOY," QUALITY

Even more tragic, more horrifying, is that the onslaught on poor
African-Americans and Latinos begins early. According to the Justice
Department, African-American youths are six times more likely to be
sentenced to prison than white youths. For youths charged with drug
offenses, African-Americans are forty-eight times more likely than

whites to be sentenced to juvenile prison and serve more time once there. Consider, for example, the unconscionable case of fourteen-year-old Shaquanda Cotton. She explains:

> *I am a 14-year-old black freshman who shoved a hall monitor at Paris High School in a dispute over entering the building before the school day had officially begun and was sentenced to 7 years in prison. I have no prior arrest record, and the hall monitor—a 58-year-old teacher's aide—was not seriously injured. I was tried in March 2006 in the town's juvenile court, convicted of "assault on a public servant" and sentenced by Lamar County Judge Chuck Superville to prison for up to 7 years, until I turn 21.*

To illustrate how deeply entrenched judicial racism is, consider the fact that just three months before Cotton's sentencing, Judge Superville sentenced a fourteen-year-old white girl who was convicted of arson to probation. Fortunately, a national campaign led by Cotton's mother generated media interest and after a year, after support from the NAACP and other groups, Cotton was released after serving one year. For every Cotton, and she is still a victim, there are hundreds of thousands of others who, despite unfair trials and sentences, are never released.

Cases like Michael Lewis, an African-American from a ghetto in Atlanta, who at thirteen years old was arrested for a murder that a mountain of evidence suggests he did not commit. At the time of his arrest he was a ward of the state, but Michael was never assisted by Child Protection Services or even read his Miranda rights.

"We are going to try this boy like a man," declared D.A. Paul Howard at the onset of the trial. Tried as an adult under Georgia Senate Bill 440, which allows children aged thirteen to seventeen to be prosecuted and sentenced as adults for certain offenses, Michael was sentenced, after a mere three-day trial, to life in prison at the age of fourteen. This, despite the fact that the only evidence against Michael was the testimony of an admitted drug dealer and murder suspect; despite the lack of forensic evidence; despite not interviewing or subpoenaing any of Michael's alibi witnesses; and despite the fact that Michael's public defender was facing his own criminal charges. Despite all of this, Michael, at fourteen years old, was taken to Lee Arrendale State Prison, a maximum security adult prison. Michael's case is not unique. Since Bill 440 was passed, 94 percent of the children tried and convicted under this law have been African-American. Michael rhymes in reflection: "The streets raised me / jail enslaved me."

The enslavement that Michael speaks of is a keen observation and one of the critical components to this crisis. Many have been writing, saying, singing, speaking, and hollering that the current crisis is a form of enslavement. You cannot have any real discussion of the modern-day prison industrial complex without addressing the economic component. Dr. Tukufu Zuberi, director of Africana Studies at the University of Pennsylvania, told me that "when you lock up millions of brothers, you have reinstituted the institution of slavery."

Although most people believe that slavery was abolished in the United States after the Civil War by the passage of the Thirteenth Amendment, it wasn't. The Thirteenth Amendment reads:

> *Neither slavery nor involuntary servitude, except as punishment for crimes whereof the party shall have been duly convicted, shall exist within the United States, or any place subject to their jurisdiction.*

Clearly, the Thirteenth Amendment was not about abolishing slavery, but rather limiting it to prisoners. After the Civil War, many freshly "free" Africans found themselves enslaved once again as prisoners leased out to plantation owners to work fields of cotton for free.

> *We used to run around tryna' get money and power*
> *Look at us now, gettin' fuckin' twelve cents a hour.*
> —OSCHINO, "JAIL LETTERS," *BEST OF OSCHINO*

"Prison labor is like a pot of gold. No strikes. No union organizing. No health benefits, unemployment insurance, or workers' compensation or pay," explains Linda Evans, a prisoner in California. Since the Supreme Court's 1993 ruling that inmates did not have the right to minimum wage, corporations such as American Airlines, McDonald's, Microsoft, Victoria's Secret, and Toys "R" Us have exploited and continue to exploit prisoners to meet their bottom line. Prison labor allows corporations to boast "Made in the U.S.A." while paying paltry wages that are even lower than the slave wages doled out in Southeast Asia, the Pacific Rim, and Latin America. This has made prison labor a cost-effective alternative to relocation. And because of this fact, the number of prison inmates working in prison industries between 1972 and 1992 shot up by 300 percent, from 169,000 to 523,000. Put another way, the prison industry hires more people than any Fortune 500 company, with the exception of General Motors. Prisons profit so much from leasing out their prisoners to corporations that they've even begun ad campaigns like the following one from Wisconsin:

CAN'T FIND WORKERS?

A willing workforce waits . . .

We're looking for businesses in need of a willing and productive workforce. New legislation has created an exciting new opportunity for private businesses to work in partnership with Wisconsin's prison inmate work program. Consider low risk expansion of your business with the help of the Department of Corrections' labor, management support and quality control resources.

New legislation permits ". . . three private businesses to employ prison inmates to manufacture products or components or to provide services for sale on the open market." Companies establishing operations within a correctional institution can now create inmate jobs to help build private businesses—not compete with them or organized labor. In October, the department will issue a request for proposal to any business interested in these opportunities. All proposals will be considered. Call Today!

The prison crisis is exacerbated even further by media corporations who further politicize the issues surrounding African-American prisoners. Television, especially with the rise in competition from twenty-four-hour news channels, has a vested interest in perpetuating the idea that crime is rampant. Consider the Center for Media and Public Affairs study that showed crime was the number one topic on the nightly news for more than a decade. As the homicide rate dropped by half nationwide, homicide stories on the news quadrupled. This media saturation has a direct impact on public perception, which has a direct impact on political campaigns and policy. It's "impossible to run an election campaign without advocating more jails, harsher punishment, more executions, all the things that have never worked to reduce crime but have always worked to get votes," concludes George Gerbner, former dean of the University of Pennsylvania's Annenberg School for Communication and one of the nation's foremost experts on the media. "It's driven largely, although not exclusively, by television-cultivated insecurity."

The images shown by the mass media of Blacks being arrested, detained, or imprisoned have a serious impact on our psyches. We begin to think of Blacks, and this is true for all races, as perpetual criminals. During the early eighties, as America's drug epidemic hit all-time highs, news crews became increasingly fixated on drug stories. However, they were not able to gain access to elite yacht clubs, high-rises, and gated suburban neighborhoods where most of America's drugs are consumed, and they found poor Black communities extremely accessible. As a result, impoverished Black communities became fertile ground for reporters to show the "dark" face to America's "drug war." Consider that researchers at the University of Michigan discovered that starting in 1985, the number of whites shown on TV using cocaine dropped by 60 percent, and the number of Blacks using jumped up by 60 percent.

All of this is reinforced and justified through a sensationalized media that present images of Blacks as "violent," "aggressive," and "hostile," influencing everyone's notions about race, crime, and punishment. There exists a psychological connection between perception and conviction. This is why time and time again, racial bias can be clearly seen in capital cases where juries are more likely to execute the killers of white victims than Black victims. Writer, activist, and death-row inmate Mumia Abu-Jamal explains, "Perhaps we can shrug off and shred some of the dangerous myths laid on our minds like a second skin—such as . . . the 'right[s] to a fair trial,' even. They're not rights—they're privileges of the powerful and rich. . . . Don't expect the media networks to tell you, for they can't, because of their incestuousness . . . with government and big business."

America was founded on the exploitation of African labor during slavery, which lasted more than two hundred years. Even after the Civil War, imprisoned Africans were leased out to plantation owners to work fields of cotton. The current crisis is just as political as slavery, the Civil War, or Jim Crow.

Most of the African-Americans in prison today are political prisoners. The War on Drugs and mandatory sentencing, responsible for the explosion of incarceration we see today, takes the power of release from parole authorities and discretion from judges and allows for legislatures to set sentencing policies. Franklin Zimring, a criminologist at the University of California, Berkeley, says, "Punishment became a political decision." Even conservative Supreme Court Justice William Rehnquist acknowledges that sentencing is politically motivated, remarking that "mandatory minimums are frequently the result of floor amendments to demonstrate emphatically that legislators want to get tough on crime."

The result of this politicization leads to an increasing number of people, organizations, and institutions that benefit significantly from the policies that not only mass-police, but mass-incarcerate and keep people in prison for lengthy amounts of time.

The prison industrial complex, in subtle ways and in overt ways, is political. Consider for example that Corrections Corporation of America (CCA), the largest private prison operator, was started by a major investment from Honey Alexander, the wife of then Tennessee governor Lamar Alexander, and Ned McWherter, then speaker of the Tennessee house, and later governor.

"CCA has been one of the most successful companies on Wall Street," says Harmon Wray of Restorative Justice. CCA now builds prisons based on speculation. This intimacy between prison and politics means that there are many with great financial stakes in the current structure—interest groups that have incentives to ensure their prisons can stay full. On top of that, you have other companies that reap hundreds of millions of dollars annually by providing health care, phones, food, and other services to the new prisons. Many small white rural towns depend on the influx of imprisoned Black urbanites to survive economically. And private prison companies, including CCA, contribute huge sums of money to the American Legislative Exchange Council, a policy group that has helped draft tougher sentencing laws, and the California prison guards union doles out millions every election to tough-on-crime candidates—or, put another way, candidates who will ensure their livelihoods at the expense of entire communities.

Political elements not only determine who goes in, but who comes back. Former prison inmates are punished even after they have served time. "Laws deny welfare payments, veterans benefits and food stamps to anyone in detention for more than 60 days," writes Berkeley sociologist Loïc Wacquant. "The Work Opportunity and Personal Responsibility Act of 1996 further banishes most ex-convicts from Medicaid, public housing, Section 8 vouchers and related forms of assistance." Bill Clinton, in particular, "proudly launched 'unprecedented federal, state, and local cooperation as well as new, innovative incentive programs' . . . to weed out any inmate who still received benefits," writes Wacquant. In addition, convicted felons are further disenfranchised because they cannot vote or participate in political elections. It should be noted that the only states that allow prisoners convicted of felonies to vote after their release are Maine, Vermont, Massachusetts, and Rhode Island—states with very small African-American populations.

While recognizing the institutional racism that creates and maintains these laws, the new generation does not simply treat this as a Black issue. Rather, they see it "as a challenge for all of us, for humanity," Ahmed Artis tells me as he relaxes on a charter bus that motors him back home to Los Angeles after a monumental day in Jena, Louisiana. "This is something that affects all of us, and you could feel that

today; Black people, Latino, white, Asian, Pacific Islander, everybody
was united."

Photo: Jamal Thorne

James Baldwin once reminded us that "We live in an age in which
silence is not only criminal but suicidal . . . for if they take you in the
morning, they will be coming for us that night." And indeed they already have. Alisa Solomon writes in *The Village Voice* that "the only incarcerated populations sustaining reliable growth now are INS
detainees and federal prisoners, many of them noncitizens." Starting
in 2001, the Federal Bureau of Prisons began directing prison contrac-
tors to "build prisons that meet a new category called Criminal Alien
Requirements." According to the Justice Department, between 1995
and 2003, convictions for immigration offenses rose by 394 percent.
Additionally, between 1980 and 2005, the number of women in state
and federal prisons jumped by 873 percent—from 12,300 to 107,500.

Poverty has always been the defining feature of who is imprisoned
in the richest country on earth. Today is no exception. As of 2005,
approximately 37 percent of women and 28 percent of men in prison

had monthly incomes of less than six hundred dollars prior to their arrest. The law—a political institution in itself—provides the frame-

Photo: Maya Freelon Asante

work for the war of social control against oppressed people, working classes, and noncompliant women. The vast majority of prisoners are not imprisoned because they are "criminals," but rather because they have been criminalized. Although challenging, this great dilemma represents, for the post-hip-hop generation, a way to unify. What is increasingly clear is that the racialized and politicized prison industrial complex is one of the great moral and political challenges of our time. Indeed, it is our cultural assignment.

Assata Shakur was sentenced to spend the rest of her life rotting in a super-maximum-security prison. However, her spirit and the spirit of her community wouldn't allow that to happen. "Love is the acid that eats away bars," she reflects on her great escape, adding, "I have been locked by the lawless. Handcuffed by the haters. Gagged by the greedy. And, if I know anything at all, it's that a wall is just a wall and nothing more at all. It can be broken down."

Following the marches in Jena, young people began the process of breaking down those walls. Not satisfied with a single day of protests, students, once again taking the lead, organized a post-Jena meeting where they not only explored the problems that create and foster Jenas around the county, but identified solutions as well. They came up with a plan to put pressure on local, state, and national officials to end mandatory minimum sentencing and revise federal sentencing guidelines. They also recognized that the current War on Drugs spends the bulk of its resources locking up users. A year of treatment costs much less than a year of incarceration and it would allow a person to work and support a family. Pushing for drug rehabilitation, thus changing the approach to the War on Drugs, was a vital part of the discussion. Also, they proposed to radically change the structure of probation. Two-thirds of people on probation are rearrested, mostly on technical violations. Probation policies should provide resources to help people stay out of jail, not be a force to put them back in. In Baltimore, where they've seen unemployment rates soar as ex-offenders are released, they knew it was essential to put an end to the legal discrimination of people who have served time. We can do this by restoring full access to public housing, welfare, food stamps, student financial aid, driver's licenses, state-licensed professions, and voting rights.

It is important for the new generation to understand that there is nothing inherently unique about the situation in Jena. Around the country, in each state, one can find an abundance of equally unjust cases involving young African-Americans. Jena is important; however, it is only because young people have made it important. It is news because young people have made it news. This new generation, spurred by innovative grassroots organizations like Color of Change, which utilize "the organizing power of the internet" to call to action, has shone a spotlight on Jena—one whose gleam has been effective both in raising national awareness and in amending the case itself.

"The walls, the bars, the guns and the guards can never hold down the idea of the people," Huey P. Newton, cofounder of the Black Panthers, once said. The idea of the people, today, is the same as it was yesterday. The idea is, has always been, freedom. Simple.

George Jackson, one of the most well-known political prisoners, who published a collection of letters entitled *Soledad Brother* while incarcerated at Soledad Prison, remembered that,

> *Down here we hear relaxed, matter-of-fact conversations centering around how best to kill all the nation's niggers and in what order. It's not the fact that they consider killing me that upsets . . . The upsetting thing is that they never take into consideration the fact that I am going to resist.*

The only sane thing we can do, given the situation we all find ourselves in today, is resist. According to Amnesty International's definition, the vast majority of African-Americans imprisoned today are political prisoners. If our government refuses to recognize this fact, then we must take it to the international level. Following World War II, the Nuremberg Trials, and in fact the world, agreed that:

> *Individuals have international duties which transcend the national obligations of obedience. Therefore [individual citizens] have the duty to violate domestic laws to prevent crimes against peace and humanity from occurring.*

Contrary to popular belief, the most terrible occurrences (slavery, war, genocide) occur only when there is no resistance; when we, in essence, allow them to. What is happening today is only happening because we are allowing it to. The time has never been more just, the hour never more right to act, than now.

Regardless of the outcome in Jena, it is imperative that we claim no easy victories. The injustice in Jena must be looked upon as a symbol of the problem, but not the problem. If this generation is to truly be successful in making America live up to its promise of freedom and equality, we cannot simply move from here to the next Jena. Instead we must use this momentum to educate each other about the systemic issues that allow Jenas to happen and then do what each generation is called to do: change the world.

chapter 8

FTP*

If you try to tell the people in most Negro communities
that the police are their friends, they just laugh at you.
—DR. MARTIN LUTHER KING, JR.

Fuck the police.
—TRADITIONAL SAYING

SAMO was the graffiti name artist and pop icon Jean-Michel Basquiat
spray-painted on lower Manhattan walls in the early eighties. When
asked what his tag meant, he'd sigh, "same ol' shit." Regardless of
the time period or generation, from the iron shackles of bondage to
the platinum ones of today, African-Americans' relationship to the
police has been nothing short of the SAMO—a consistent, involuntary arrangement of fear, hostility, violence, and overall distrust. It is
this relationship, built upon centuries of unspeakable acts, that gives
a grassroots campaign like "stop snitchin'," a national code of silence

---

*Fight the Power; Fuck the Police; Free the Prisoners; Free the People; For the People; Feed the
People.

among young Blacks, its proper context. The questions we must concern ourselves with now, however, revolve around our ability to trek beyond the usual castigations and FTP rhetoric, and instead, employ our collective imaginations to achieving something new, if for no other reason than because our very lives depend on doing so. While the hip-hop generation has been steady at voicing our frustration with the current system of policing, it has failed in its ability to imagine anything that might supplant it. If the next generation—us—is to be successful, we must, as one young man told me after he'd witnessed his friend assaulted by the police, "stop talking about it and be about it." Or, as it goes, be subject to the SAMO.

The scene: A calm, star-spangled sky suspended above Philadelphia like the snatch of silence before a great storm. This moment of clarity was fitting because, just hours earlier, on Flatbush Avenue in Brooklyn, I interviewed rappers Dead Prez about their altercation with and subsequent civil suit against the notorious NYPD. Even amid a hip-hop landscape overrun with toxic waste, Dead Prez has been an unflinching beacon of light, critically exposing, among a myriad of other contributions, the police brutality that occurs routinely in Black and Latino communities. In their song "Police State," they rap:

> *The average Black male*
> *Lives a third of his life in a jail cell.*

Instead of *protecting and serving* the community, these cops *served* Dead Prez (etc.) with nightsticks and handcuffs. Dead Prez responded, in part, by retaining the legal services of Brooklyn-based activist and attorney Karl Kamau Franklin in hopes of using the System against itself. One wonders, though, as I did driving through "the city of brotherly love" on my way home, if this could really be done. Wasn't this a case of running to the wolf to tell on the fox? Wasn't it Audre Lorde who proclaimed, "The master's tools will never dismantle the master's house"? That while "they may allow us temporarily to beat him at his own game, they will never enable us to bring about genuine change"? Or, perhaps like the work of all great artists, there was something else—something greater, something deeper, something more knotty—at work here. And I began to see, as I drove up the battered blocks of North Philadelphia, the black face of Caliban, the slave from Shakespeare's *The Tempest* who was taught, by brute force, the bloody language of Prospero, his oppressor. Caliban, in turn, used Prospero's language to curse him, just as Dead Prez sought to do now.

M.K.A.: What do you hope to accomplish with your lawsuit against the NYPD?

Dead Prez: Our legal representation right now is in Karl Kamau Franklin, who has been very gracious to us and who has been one of the movement lawyers. He donates a lot of his time, pro bono. Knowing that we suffer so much economically, financially, and legally in the hood we need resuscitation. We're in an emergency, we're dippin' in the red zone. We need an IV and he is there to administer. He is leading our legal campaign and has been working with [us] for years and years on some of the same issues, since three years ago when we were attacked and before then. A huge civil suit is being piled up against the state of New York and NYPD by many, many people, who were terrorized by the police here including ourselves, which he hopes to lead along with the Center for Constitutional Rights. That's a major part of our campaign. However, our campaign cannot simply be legal, there also needs to be people campaigns that put the pressure on Doomberg or Bloomberg to make decisions he wouldn't normally

have to make. We have to use the legal aspect to provide an out for
any community pressure that he might face and he may get a rock
thrown at him at a press conference, and he may not be able to open
up the stadium that he wanna open up over here for the Brooklyn
Nets in the middle of our community in Brooklyn so easily. If the
community provides pressure and legally Karl Franklin can point toward a strategy that relieves some of that pressure for him, i.e., free-
ing political prisoners and prisoners of war, stopping the unjust police
practices and so on and so forth.

I was almost home when I, too, was blinded by Prospero's bloodred and cold, blue flashing lights and deafened by his high-pitched
gulp of a cry—*Woop-woop! Woop-woop!* I pulled my car over and
came to a full stop in front of a check cashing spot and a thin storefront with a handwritten sign that read OFF THE CHAIN BAIL BONDS.

Possible (not probable) causes cascaded through my mind—*Maybe
my brake lights are out . . . Maybe my tag's expired . . . Damn, maybe I
didn't pay those parking tickets . . . Nah, I paid them*—as a cop approached my car, crushing gravel beneath his bulky boots.

"Problem?" I asked, as a pale, paunchy man whose eyes were veiled
with tinted shades arrived at my door.

"Where you coming from?" the officer questioned.

"Brooklyn," I told him as I scanned his tag—L. CLARK— into my
memory.

"Brooklyn?" he said, surprised. "What's in Brooklyn?" I knew that,
because of the Fifth and Sixth Amendments, I wasn't obliged to answer his questions, but because I wanted to get home as soon as possible, I did.

"I was conducting an interview," I said plainly.

"License and registration," he requested as his eyes, chasing the orb
of his flashlight, searched through my car.

"It's in the glove compartment," I stated.

"Slowly," he warned.

My hands, moving in calculated slow motion, floated toward the glove compartment when—

"I said slow," the cop screeched as he grabbed the handle of his Glock. "Unless you want to get shot!" His voice harshened.

At that moment, I came to the pungent realization—just as so many, too many, before me have—that this already tragic encounter could very easily conclude with that gun, which his pink hand was now molesting, tugged out of its dark nest, aimed at me, and fired multiple times into my Black body. What's worse is that this outcome, which was not at all uncommon, was beyond my control. If I followed his instructions, he might, overwhelmed by an unwarranted but very real fear, imagine my wallet or cell phone to be a gun and shoot me. If I didn't follow his instructions, then he would certainly send shots my way. Either way, because of my hue and, indeed, his, he had carte blanche. With my back against the wall, I knew, as James Baldwin did when he inked *A Dialogue,* that "he's got a uniform and a gun and I have to relate to him that way. That's the only way to relate to him because one of us may have to die."

My fingertips and palms, moist with the anxiety of sudden death, handed him my license and registration.

"Why was I stopped?" I asked.

"Hold tight," he said, as he took my papers and turned around.

"Why was I stopped?" I repeated as he wobbled back to his squad car.

I watched him, through the sharp panorama of my mirror, as he ran my papers. I was reminded of the armed white men, dubbed "pattie rollers" by African-Americans, who were deployed throughout the South to patrol and prevent slave rebellions. These pattie rollers, which white men in the South were required to serve in, patrolled

exclusively at night, traveling on horseback from plantation to plantation, harassing Black people, looking for contraband (weapons, liquor,
books, et cetera) that might indicate a plan to flee. Pattie rollers were
instructed to viciously lash any enslaved African without a written
pass. In North Carolina, a law ordered pattie rollers to whip on the
spot any "loose, disorderly or suspected person" found among enslaved Africans. It was from these pattie rollers, funded by local taxes,
that many modern policing concepts were derived. For example, pattie rollers, like modern police, referred to patrollers' designated areas
of operation as "beats."

M.K.A.: Why did the cops start harassing y'all?

Dead Prez: There's nothing we did wrong except for being Africans in
our community and standing up for what we believe in. This ain't a
new struggle, it happens to thousands and thousands of Africans each
day. Our comrades had been accosted by the police, who came up
and asked, I guess suspiciously, that they show ID. There is no law on
the books that states that in New York City you have to walk around
with your ID in your pocket nor do you have to show it to the police.
We had the right to ask "why." Because we know our rights and also
because we are always aware that there is this constant engagement
going on between the people in the community and the occupying
army, which to us, comes to us in the form of the police department.
We knew that we had rights and our rights were that we ask, "Why?
Why do we have to show ID?" Not that we were resisting showing ID
but we have the right to ask why. Why? Why were we even being
questioned at all? When that was asked there was no reasonable response by the pigs, or the police, as some of y'all call them. Since they
couldn't come up with any reason why they were asking for ID and
because we were firm with the fact that we knew we had rights, they
began to call for help in that situation, because the community was

around. It's a Saturday, in the middle of the day, we're shining, re-silient Black soldiers, RBG [revolutionary but gangsta] in the broad daylight, you know. I believe that they saw this as a position that they didn't really want to back down from. I think they wanted to be seen as the people who run the block. But we know that it's the people who run the block. So, they called for backup and so some more pigs came. These pigs came in white shirts, I guess this means that they are special kinda pigs, 'cause those other pigs were in blue.

I think that not knowing what to do, because we knew our rights and we insisted to know why, we never backed down on why. We never said no, but we insisted on why. I think the pigs then gave the order that they move in on us and start handcuffing brothas. They started to try to handcuff each and every one of us. They began to try to move forward, handcuff us, harass us. Some of us were handcuffed. Dedan, one of my comrades, wouldn't be handcuffed easily, because we don't back down easily. We just don't. There is no reason to, espe-cially because we've only been criminalized; we're not criminals. At that, they began to show excessive force, at that point we began to show more force. And that's when, to me, the brutalization began. My partner Nes was beaten so bad his eyes became swollen. Dedan was slammed onto the hood of the police car, the pigs' car, and four of our comrades were consequently taken to the seventy-seventh precinct where they were given no due process for twenty-four hours in a cold cell, with no rights to medical treatment, and no rights to phone calls—pretty much the standard arrest procedures for brothas.

M.K.A: What happened next?

Dead Prez: We ended up inside the central booking, in Brooklyn, Brooklyn Central Booking, Brooklyn House, about thirty-six hours later. Then from there some of the comrades sat inside the holding cell until this kangaroo court thing happened. The pigs grabbed them up, called their names, and like some old back-in-the-days Mississippi shit, opened the back door and booted them out the back door. Like, "Don't say nothing. Y'all just go." And they kept one of them, without any reason at all. So, three of the comrades were released, through the back door, with no due process, still no due process, not even speaking to anybody who would have any semblance of leadership in this whole thing, including the judge or any pigs. But one of my comrades was still held hostage, held kidnapped, 'cause that's what it was, he was kidnapped, not arrested—kidnapped. He remained kidnapped until we freed him. We freed him and he faces charges of aggravated assault, assaulting an officer, and resisting arrest. And one of them is a felony charge. A felony resisting arrest charge, I mean what is that? Really, his hands were handcuffed. So, right now we're still facing court dates.

M.K.A.: Has the community been supportive of you and your comrades?

Dead Prez: On the first court date we held a conference, which was basically for our community to know that when the pigs jive us like this, there are things that we can do: there is community action and legal action to be taken. Our intent by holding the press conference, which was held at the House of the Lower Church, Reverend Herbert Daugherty's church, which is a historical place for struggle, and right around the corner from the courthouse. We held the press conference to announce to the community that not only would we be a part of the people's self-defense campaign which has been administered and run by the Malcolm X Grassroots Movement, which is similar to a cop-watch program, but also that we would be suing the New York Police Department and the state of New York for its crimes against us. We've had words of support from people like Charles Barron and Mos Def, and from the National Hip-Hop Action Network and from the ACLU, believe it or not, and community organizations like Black Arts Collective. Because it was just well supported, we were able to get it out into the broadstream media about what had gone down and that was on the first day of court. And me being in a leadership role, at that point, as the president of the Uhuru Movement, we planned demonstrations that really rocked the courthouse. Pumped in thousands and thousands of leaflets, probably fifty thousand leaflets. So all these people who were going into court the same day we had to go to court . . . were all victims, too, so they felt the same way we did.

Everything came back clean. No tickets. No warrants. No nothing. "Do you have any drugs or weapons in the car?" the officer asked.

"You still haven't told me why I was stopped," I stressed.

"One more time. Do you have any drugs or weapons," he repeated, resting his hand on his gun (again).

"I've got a registered handgun and a permit to carry it," I stated.

I felt his demeanor morph and I could see from the involuntary breach between his cold lips that he wanted to say something. I anticipated him asking me, "Why are you brandishing a firearm?" And I anticipated telling him that although I hated guns—and never have liked them, not even as toys!—I was overcome just a few weeks prior with the awful feeling of not being able to save my own life. The trigger for me was when Sean Bell, twenty-three, an unarmed Black man and father of three children, was shot in a vicious hail of fifty bullets on the night before his wedding.

I'd made up my mind that I was not going out like Patrick Bailey, the twenty-two-year-old unarmed Black man shot and killed by twenty-seven NYPD bullets. Or Amadou Diallo, the twenty-three-year-old unarmed Black man who was shot forty-one times and killed by four plain-clothes NYPD officers. Or Abner Louima, another unarmed Black man who was beaten by the NYPD, and then sodomized by Officer Justin Volpe with the filthy handle of a toilet plunger, severely rupturing his colon and bladder, before Volpe jammed the excrement-soiled stick down his throat, damaging his teeth, gums, and mouth. Mos Def, during the Diallo trial, asked, "At this rate, can we expect the hail of fifty-five bullets to be unloaded on another New Yorker by next fall?" He reminded folks that "this is not a Black issue, it's a human issue."

I thought about the family of Artrell Dickerson, the eighteen-year-old boy who was gunned down by Detroit police during a funeral, just a few weeks after Bell's murder. Dickerson's family, in a passionate statement that is a challenge to all of us, wrote:

> *I charge you to prove that the actions of this officer (who still remains anonymous) were justified. I charge you to prove that Artrell's death was not over-kill that he did not die face down on the ground with as many as six bullets in him on a cold Monday afternoon, in broad daylight with up to a hundred men, women, and children as witnesses to murder. I charge you to prove to this community that black men are not being killed indiscriminately in the city of Detroit at the hands of police officers whose crimes are being covered. Until then we will not be silenced because we are empowered in our belief that Artrell's death is characteristic of many other killings of African American men in inner cities across the United States at the hands of police officers. And we wish to inform and empower the public to demand the respect and protection of the lives of our brothers, cousins, fathers, uncles, and friends. Artrell Dickerson will not have died in vain.*

I decided that unlike Bailey, Diallo, Louima, Bell, Dickerson, and countless others too numerous to name, I would not be unarmed, and that if they shot at me, I would shoot back with everything I had. The logic: If white police officers love their families as much as we love our Black units, then knowing we are armed as well, perhaps they will think twice before they shoot at us. "As the racist police es-

calate the war in our communities against black people, we reserve the right to self-defense and maximum retaliation," former Black Panther leader Huey Newton said while incarcerated on bogus charges. And this wasn't just rhetoric, Newton saved his own life by firing back at Oakland police officers when they attempted to assassinate him in 1967. Similarly, Tupac Shakur, in 1993, shot two off-duty police officers who were harassing him and a Black motorist. When it was discovered that the cops were drunk and in possession of stolen weapons, all charges against Tupac were dismissed.

We must never mistake the self-defense of the victim for the violence of the attacker. Self-defense is not an act of violence, but rather an act of self-love and self-preservation. In 1919, when a thick brush of race riots swept across the country like wildfire, Harlem Renaissance poet Claude McKay responded with "If We Must Die," a poem urging Blacks to fight back. McKay's poem, written nearly a century ago, spoke to me now:

> If we must die, let it not be like hogs
> Hunted and penned in an inglorious spot,
> While round us bark the mad and hungry dogs,
> Making their mock at our accursed lot.
> If we must die, O let us nobly die,
> So that our precious blood may not be shed
> In vain; then even the monsters we defy
> Shall be constrained to honor us though dead!
> O kinsmen we must meet the common foe!
> Though far outnumbered let us show us brave,
> And for their thousand blows deal one deathblow!
> What though before us lies the open grave?
> Like men we'll face the murderous, cowardly pack,
> Pressed to the wall, dying, but fighting back!

M.K.A.: Do you believe your experience was an isolated incident or symbolic of a larger national problem?

Dead Prez: New York is no different than Florida, no different than California, no different than Cincinnati, no different than Philadelphia. So that shows you what we're dealing with. It's the same pigs, the same pig mentality, and the same enforcement that's going down, the only thing that is changing is the people that they're arresting. They're arresting more and more of us and they're getting to the babies now. It's the same blue steel ring around our community, which attempts only in criminalizing us with no social justice, we get no justice at all. At the end of the day we are still locked out economically, so it's the same war around the hood. You know the only thing they leave us with is dope to sell and a basic demoralization in the hood. We're here to provide, to say that we won't be demoralized and that we're gonna stand up and that there's something that you can do, you can organize to fight for your damn rights and don't punk out. Let's do it for the babies so the babies don't have to come up and live in terror 'cause that's what it is: it's police terror inside our communities. It's terrorism and it's been long before that. I really believe that there's a syndrome that we need to be aware of that happens inside of our community. It happens to me all the time where I don't even drive a car because I know if the police pull up behind me, chances are I probably will go to jail. It's not because I'm doing anything illegal, it's because we are made criminal just by where we live and the profiling that happens when we're doing what we do. Once again, the U.S. law, you know, that's Amerikkkan justice with a triple "k."

The officer didn't ask me why I had a gun; he had something else in mind.

"You don't mind if I take a look around, *do ya?*" The officer slurred as he opened my door.

"Actually, officer, I don't consent to a search of my private property," I informed him, myself informed by a fairly good understanding of my Fourth Amendment rights, which state:

The right of the people to be secure in their persons, houses, papers, and effects against unreasonable searches and seizures shall not be violated, and no warrants shall issue, but upon probable cause, supported by Oath or affirmation and particularly describing the place to be searched and the persons or things to be seized.

"You hiding something?" the officer pried.

"No," I said flatly, "I'm exercising my Fourth Amendment right against unreasonable searches and seizures." I knew that according to the Plain View Doctrine, he could only initiate a search if an illegal item was in plain view and that the only reason he was asking me to consent to a warrantless search was because he didn't have enough evidence to search without my consent. I also knew, from both common sense and previous experiences, that just because a law is on the books, its application is much less clear, especially where race is concerned. After all, in 1857, the U.S. Supreme Court ruled in *Dred Scott vs. Sandford* that Blacks "had no rights that a white man was bound to respect." But this didn't deter me from asserting my rights because in that same year, Frederick Douglass warned:

Find out just what the people will submit to and you have found out the exact amount of injustice and wrong, which will be imposed upon them; and these will continue until they are resisted with either words or blows, or with both. The limits of tyrants are prescribed by the endurance of those whom they oppress.

So, in an attempt to limit his tyrannical oppression, I refused to submit. As Ras Baraka explained on The Fugees sophomore album *The Score*, "Cuz if you let a mothafucka kick you five times, they gonna kick you five times. But if you break off da mothafucka's foot, won't be no more kickin'."

M.K.A.: Can you speak on the importance of knowing your rights?

Dead Prez: Coming out into these U.S. streets, prison streets, prison states, police states without knowing your rights is like a soldier without a weapon. You almost have no defense for the bullshit. And believe me they come at you with X amount of it. A lot of times if we knew our rights a lot of things that happen with the police wouldn't have happened. Illegal searches and even some arrests wouldn't even go down the same way. Knowing your rights is almost like turning your lights on with the roaches because they scatter and with the lights on there is your protection. I also believe that our protection is with the people because the people define what rights are you know what I mean. Getting pulled over for making an illegal right turn is grounds for being murdered in St. Petersburg, Florida. Tyrone Lewis was murdered for being a motorist. Often it happens to us, we're tried and delivered a sentence of death so many times in our community by these terrorist police officers, so knowing your rights is one of the chief ways that you can defend yourself. But the struggle continues, the resistance is hot. The resistance is still hot.

We have always been resistant towards police brutality and treatment in Brownsville, Brooklyn, where these secret underground teams basically crawl the streets at night and abrogate brothers' and sisters' rights, patting us down looking for the gun knowing we got the gun, looking for everything else—you know all kind of unjust treatment in our community. We've always been resistant to it. It's nothing new. We know that our first job is to be soldiers and be defenders of our rights so we began organizing ourselves. We organize with many community organizations and structures including people like the December 12th Movement or The National People's Democratic Uhuru Movement, The Malcolm X Grassroots Movement, student organizations like Fisk.

"Step out of the car," the officer ordered as he opened my door.

"You *still* haven't told me what I was pulled over for? What was I pulled over for?" I insisted.

Completely ignoring my question, he says, "What are you hiding, boy?"

"Boy?"

"Fuckin' nigger," he vomited.

At that moment, I was faced with two distinct choices: life or death.

This is exactly his plan, I chuckled to myself as I chose life. *He wants me to flip. He wants me to flip. Nope, I'm not givin' in. Not givin' in,* I told myself, attempting to prevent my blood from bubbling, desperately trying to prevent the death, which was waiting above the scene like a vulture, from occurring.

"I know my rights," I insisted, to which he threw my license and registration into my car and stalked off, frustrated at his impotence.

In France, the Black and Arab youth scream *"Police partout, justice nulle part!"* meaning "Police everywhere, justice nowhere." So long as officers like L. Clark patrol neighborhoods in a predatory manner, there will be no justice—can be no justice.

M.K.A.: So, what does this experience prove or confirm to Dead Prez?

Dead Prez: More than anything it confirms, it supports the fact that we're at war. And to me that was the most glaring thing that I probably learned out of that experience is that three years later we still don't have an apparatus in place that can truly defend the people's rights. We need some courageous soldiers, some really courageous soldiers to step up. Those of us who don't have a whole lot of records, who ain't gon' face three strikes, those of us who feel like we know we have nothing to lose but our chains, just step up and take leadership. And I got to say if you see it you go get it, RBG means be "revolutionary but gangsta" but it also means "reading 'bout Garvey" and "ready to bust gats."

M.K.A.: Do events like this one shape your lyrics?

Dead Prez: Let me tell you something, as an emcee you know, is only one part of the person that is M-1, I'm not just a rapper. Now it's time for me to use the propagandist in me to be able to put it into our culture as part of our resistance. You need that experience because people will ask what will you do when somebody robs your house or when the big bad wolf comes. But in these situations we need to know not to advocate the police at any point. And only in that experience do you learn the treachery of dealing with that man's arm of his protection of capitalism, which is his army: the pigs. So that experience helped me know exactly what to do. It informed me as to what to say to people in my rhymes and in my life. We're in a war and people automatically put your agenda up for you when you're a rapper, like you get a car and a mansion and you're good, you're pretty much good, you go to jail for having a vest or some weed or hope that you don't get caught up with a weed charge but that's the life of a rapper. Now we put a new face on a rapper, we say to the members of the community when you fuck with me now I know how to organize, I know how to activate my community with the words that we say instead of a lot of times walking into the agenda that was put here before us and just doing the normal thing and cop a plea, which is what rappers normally do. So that's what helps inform me, to act from experience to make it be part of our culture to be resistant. I don't want to preach and Dead Prez doesn't want to preach; I mean I can't tell anyone right from wrong and what to do. All I can talk about is based off of my experience and I can tell you how to avoid traps, some of those traps. And I think with hip hop the general problem that we have, besides the fact that we don't own hip hop as a property, is that we don't even own it as an intellectual property. We don't provide the agenda by which success is gained and most of the time we don't achieve it. Zero percent of rappers don't even got what rappers are supposed to have. So with that agenda being caught up in that way we find ourselves being caught up in a lot of meaningless discussions. At Morehouse a brother stood up and said, "What are we gonna do with all the twenty-four-inch rims and what are we gonna do with all the women with the tight-ass clothes?" I said, "Well brother, what are you gonna do?" I said you should "ignore it, you should organize in your community so that when people have the choice between twenty-inch rims and some semblance of freedom or justice they will choose justice." So it's my job to bring it back 'cause don't forget that our biggest enemy is the red, white, and blue. George Bush is laying down more laws than any brotha that ever dissed you, I understand the game and so this is what I'm here to do.

M.K.A.: Do you have a message to the youth, perhaps, that you'd like to express?

Dead Prez: If I had to deliver a message to the youth I'd say to keep your eyes open and your fist clenched. I'd say they can try to kill the messenger but they can't kill the message, they can try to jail the revolutionary but not the revolution.

M.K.A.: Peace.

Dead Prez: Peace.

Although the racist, hostile, and violent attitudes police officers display in cities across America present a real problem, the new generation mustn't be shortsighted in analyzing and solving this age-old conflict. Just as we cannot blame the teachers who are put in crumbling, overcrowded schools for the education problem or the soldiers on the ground in Iraq for the war, we must be committed to working our way up the ladder of power. It is there—among the decision makers—that the problems that plague all of us are preserved and maintained. Despite the anger that we may feel toward police, it is not guns that will save our collective lives, for they never have and never will. Instead, it is organizing in such a way to attack the injustice at its root and save the lives of our unborn children and grandchildren. Most important, it is up to us to imagine a new system—a system not rooted in the past of America's slavery days, but in the freedom of tomorrow.

chapter 9

UNIVERSAL LANGUAGE

The only thing worse than fighting with your allies
is fighting without them.
— TRADITIONAL SAYING

Take sides. Neutrality helps the oppressor,
never the victim. Silence encourages the tormentor,
never the tormented.
— ELIE WIESEL

"El pueblo unido jamás será vencido. El pueblo unido jamás será vencido," I
soul-shouted from the center of my heart as I marched through the haze
of downtown L.A. with a half million brown brothers and sisters behind
me. Another half million in front. Across the United States—in Houston, Philadelphia, Lexington, Boston, New York, Washington, D.C.,
Las Vegas, Miami, Chicago, San Francisco, Atlanta, Denver, Phoenix,
New Orleans, Milwaukee, and everywhere in between—similar spirits

were stomping, sweating, and singing songs of freedom and resistance—songs arranged with courage, inspired by revolution, organized peacefully, and played loudly before the whole wide world.

> Unify with others who have also been denied
> their existence to discover the magnitude of
> our collective resistance.
> —WELFARE POETS, "IN THE SHADOW OF DEATH,"
> RHYMES FOR TREASON

I would have marched that day, May 1, 2006, even if I wasn't in production on *Super Imigrante,* a documentary film about Latino immigration/migration in America. Even if I hadn't spent months in the homes of undocumented citizens and in predominantly Latino schools, recording their struggles. Even if I couldn't speak or understand Spanish, which, for the most part, I couldn't. In fact, that day—which came to be known as "a day without immigrants"—was the first time in my life that I'd said more than *"hola"* in Spanish.

My voice grew louder as my ebony fist, in unison with all of the other fists, thrust toward the heavens.

"El pueblo unido, jamás será vencido!"

The massive demonstrations were sparked by the racist attitudes and policies aimed primarily at Latino immigrants. Specifically, the Border Protection, Antiterrorism, and Illegal Immigration Control Act (HR 4437), a bill introduced by House Judiciary Committee Chairman James Sensenbrenner (R-WI). Rather than provide a comprehensive, rational, and effective approach to immigration issues, Sensenbrenner's bill vilified immigrants. Among its many provision, HR 4437 would make it extremely difficult for *legal* immigrants to become U.S. citizens; would make it a felony to aid or transport any undocumented worker including family members and relatives; would make all immigrant workers subject not only to deportation but also imprisonment; and would drastically disrupt the U.S. economy by instituting an overly broad and retroactive employment verification system without creating the legal channels for workers to acquire verification.

"*El pueblo unido, jamás será vencido!*"

My comrade and codirector, Abraham, whose dad had left Mexico, his country of birth, in the tattered trunk of a battered Buick, knew that I didn't speak or understand Spanish, his native language.

"Yo, want me to tell you what that means?" he asked me as we filmed the shimmering sea of tan faces that transformed L.A.'s smoggy landscape into a cloudless one; both the vision and the focus was clear.

"I already know what it means," I told him as our wide eyes met and our heavy heads nodded to the invisible rhythm of common understanding.

At that moment, he knew that *I knew without knowing.*

I didn't know the linguistic translation into English, but I knew the emotional translation. I didn't know that the lines I sang were from a song written by Chilean composer Sergio Ortega, but I knew that they were written for those of us who were, at that moment, writing history with the boiling ink that surged through our bodies. I knew that human beings weren't "illegal." That, actually, employers who exploit vulnerable workers are the criminals. That Chicano children—like African, Native American, Asian children, et cetera—need to learn about their history and their people's contribution to the world. That wrenching apart families is wrong. And that searching for a better life, just as the heroic, green card–less immigrant Superman did when he fled Krypton, is a human right.

"*El pueblo unido, jamás será vencido!*"

Photo: José Alamillo

When the rain falls
It don't fall on one man's house.
—LAURYN HILL, "SO MUCH THINGS TO SAY,"
MTV UNPLUGGED

When Mexico welcomed Africans who'd escaped the shackles of slavery in the nineteenth century, they were doing the same thing I was doing: recognizing the connectedness of struggles against oppression and domination. Historically, it has been the failure to recognize this connectedness, combined with strategic campaigns by those in power to ensure disunity, that have kept the oppressed *oppressed*. As raptivist Immortal Technique explains:

> *Black and Latino people don't realize that America can't exist without*
> *separating them from their identities, because if we had some sense of*
> *who we really are, there's no way in hell we'd allow this country to*
> *push its genocidal consensus on our homelands.*

Blacks and Latinos in America are both suffering under the same oppressive system of structural racism and domination. As Latina activist Elizabeth Martinez points out in her "Open Letter to African-American Sisters and Brothers": "We're both being screwed, so let's get together!"

It is because we are "both being screwed" that we need to resist those people who seek to divide. Those poor Blacks and whites who scream that "the Mexicans are taking our jobs!" "No," we must explain to them, "rich white men are giving away your jobs to workers who they can not only pay less, but also workers who are more vulnerable. Workers whom they feel they don't have to pay at all. Workers who can be threatened with deportation."

The river of resistance to oppression flows far beyond African-American or Mexican struggles. The resistance is, indeed, a river. And that river, although it may pass through many countries that claim it as their own, is just one river. This hit me, on a spiritual level, when a Salvadoran friend of mine called me from Malcolm X Park in Chicago where thousands of people from different neighborhoods and ethnicities had formed a human chain as a symbol of their togetherness. The fact that this chain of solidarity was happening in Malcolm X Park couldn't be more fitting. For it was Malcolm who knew, toward the end of his life, that the fundamental problem is not between Blacks, whites, browns, yellows, reds, or any other racial category, but rather, between the oppressed and those who do the oppressing, the exploited and those who do the exploiting—regardless of skin color.

Malcolm realized that the only way to fight oppression is to unite with people who share the same spirit of resistance against inhumanity and injustice—and those spirits may, and in fact should, have different colors, genders, religions, et cetera. We may not always agree on the fine points, but those who are fighting against oppression must unite. Malcolm, for example, just before his death, visited Dr. King in Selma. Although for years they'd publicly disagreed on many issues, Malcolm offered his hand in friendship to Dr. King, explaining, "We may differ, Martin King, on tactics, we may differ on philosophy, we may differ on many things, but you are black, and I am black, and let's not forget that, and let's stand together on that basis!" This fraternal act had a contagious effect as Dr. King, just weeks after he won the Nobel Prize, went to Newark, New Jersey, to see Amiri Baraka (then LeRoi Jones) to extend the same statement of brotherhood that Malcolm made to him. They believed that being Black was enough to establish unity. Today, we must take that brotherhood and make sure it is motherhood, sisterhood, and simply hood. We must unite not simply around color, for we know now that oppression comes in many colors, and we must simply be against it in all of its colors.

What unites me with my Latino/a brothers and sisters, now, again, is the struggle—not for civil rights but to the higher level of human rights. It is important that we never fall into the trap of demoting human rights issues to civil rights struggles. When we do that, we limit the involvement and influence that the international community can have. Let us never forget that the Latino struggle in the United States is not one that is solely under the jurisdiction of the Untied States, but it is an international issue of human rights. For when we elevate our causes to the level of human rights, the world hears us—as they heard Paul Robeson's deep baritone. "You are our children," he told us, "but the peoples of the whole world rightly claim you, too. They have seen your faces, and the faces of those who hate you, and they are on your side."

We see this idea of solidarity and unity in the late Tupac's art gallery of a tattooed chest. Directly in the center is a charcoal-colored AK-47 with the words "50 Niggaz" hovering above it. The idea behind the tat is that if "niggaz" in all fifty states united, we could bring about radical change. I say it's time to take Tupac's idea to that next level: 50 Nationz.

There's a button displayed in the window of Red Emma's, a collectively owned radical bookstore in Baltimore named after Lithuanian-American revolutionary Emma Goldman, that reads: I AM PALESTINIAN. And in that one button, we can see thousands more that have yet to be made and worn: I am a Zapatista. I am Tibetan. I am Bosnian. I am South African. I am African-American. I am Chicano. I am Indian. I am Iraqi. I am Oppressed. My future is in progress.

If we want to fully understand what is happening in Baghdad, we must understand what's happening in Soweto and North Philadelphia, et cetera. They are, like the rivers, not just connected, but one. Malcolm concludes:

> *You cannot understand what is going on in Mississippi if you don't understand what is going on in the Congo, and you cannot really be interested in what's going on in Mississippi if you are not also interested in what's going on in the Congo. They're both the same. The same interests are at stake. The same ideas are drawn up. The same schemes are at work in the Congo that are at work in Mississippi. The same stake—no difference whatsoever.*

It's important for the new generation to keep in the forefront of our minds that all struggles against oppression and exploitation are connected. We cannot take a position of spectator or watch from the sidelines. Imagine yourself stumbling upon an innocent person being brutally beaten. Would you try to stop the beating? Run? Call for help? Or be neutral in the matter? In this situation, which is happening now, anything less than full commitment to the victim is aiding the oppressor. We must listen to Elie Wiesel, the Romanian Holocaust survivor, when he demands, "Take sides. Neutrality helps the oppressor, never the victim. Silence encourages the tormentor, never the tormented."

> Take a look around and be for or against
> but you can't do shit If you ridin' the fence.
> —THE COUP, "RIDE THE FENCE," PARTY MUSIC

Oppressed peoples of the world: I have seen your face in the mirror and so have my brothers and sisters. For we know, as James Baldwin told us, "We must fight for your life as though it were our own—which it is—and render impassable with our bodies the corridor to the gas chamber. For, if they take you in the morning, they will be coming for us that night."

To you, we shout:

El pueblo unido jamás será vencido.
El pueblo unido jamás será vencido.

chapter 10.
TWO SETS OF NOTES

As long as someone controls your history,
the truth shall remain just a mystery.
—BEN HARPER

When you control a man's thinking you do not
have to worry about his actions. You do not have to tell
him not to stand here or go yonder. He will find his "proper
place" and will stay in it. You do not need to send him to
the back door, he will cut one for his special benefit.
His education makes it necessary.
—CARTER G. WOODSON

The only thing about the future we don't already
know is the history we haven't already read.
—HARRY S. TRUMAN

King Drew Magnet High School, located in the heart of Compton, was known as one of the better schools in the Los Angeles Unified School District. Founded in 1982 to address the underrepresentation of Blacks and Latinos in the health care professions, King Drew had a reputation for providing students from the Watts community with hands-on experience in the fields of science and medicine. Given King Drew's brief yet propitious history, I was more than happy to accept an invitation to speak to the entire school about my work as an artivist. A series of dramatic, disturbing events, however, would drastically change our collective agendas.

> *Then they tellin y'all lies on the news, the white people*
> *smiling like everythin' cool*
> *But I know people that died in that pool, I know people*
> *that died in them schools.*
> —LIL' WAYNE, "GEORGIA BUSH," DJ DRAMA

The voyeuristic images of downtrodden, displaced, and disillusioned Black folks in New Orleans coupled with impromptu comments like Kanye West's "George Bush doesn't care about Black people" were, albeit temporarily, news items. So much so that I received a call the morning I was scheduled to speak at King Drew from a reporter at BET.

"I'm working on a story about the Katrina aftermath and wanted to ask you a few questions," the reporter queried in a bare baritone.

Time itself is neutral and can either be used in a constructive or destructive manner. I decided to use time as constructively as possible by agreeing to be interviewed about two hours before my talk at King Drew High School. We'd meet at 5th Street Dick's Coffeehouse, a Black-owned community staple just off Crenshaw Boulevard.

Because of the clogged commuter chaos that is L.A. traffic, I arrived for the interview about forty-five minutes late. This meant, unfortunately, I could only afford to rap for a *minute*.

"I'm speaking at a high school in about an hour," I told the genial reporter as I joined him at a table that was pressed against a colorful wall that held a sun-tinged poster, cornered in a wiry black frame, of a preaching Malcolm X. Below his fiery figure, the searing adage *Only a fool would let an enemy educate his children* rested like the limestone base of a Nubian step pyramid.

"No problem," he replied hastily before diving in: "Okay. What, if anything, has the whole Katrina* aftermath showed you?"

"What has it showed me?" I repeated as I thought about a New Orleans woman who exclaimed that she was "one sunrise from being consumed by flies and maggots."

"It showed us, in gross reality, that the U.S. government *still* doesn't value Black life at all and, in fact, has been one of the greatest threats to Black life. It showed us that what our ancestors—Truth and Tubman, DuBois and Douglass, Huey and Hampton—fought and died for: freedom and human rights, are things we *still* don't have today. And, perhaps most of all, it showed us why we cannot fully depend on the U.S. government for our well-being. And still more, why we must look after each other. We are a great and noble people and the price of our greatness and nobility is that we have to be responsible for each other, because clearly we can't depend on them."

"Who is them?" he challenged.

"*Them* is the individuals and institutions that can fight a war abroad, spending billions daily, but can't get my people food and water after six days; the individuals and institutions that degrade and dehumanize Black life; the individuals and institutions that locked my people in the Superdome; that shot Black boys on bridges; that dubbed survival 'looting'; that profit from our loss. They know who they are and so do we." And with that, I was out.

---

*It should be noted that I use the term "Katrina"; however, most of the damage down in New Orleans was caused by the breaching (or blowing up) of the levees after the hurricane, and not by Katrina itself.

These blocks are a jungle, and the police are the beast!
The school system is tall trees, designed
to keep the fruit out of reach.
—EM SEA WATER, "BALTIMORE," *L.I.V.E: THE LOVE LIFE*

King Drew High School, sprawled on the corner of 120th and
Compton Boulevard, was a modern mix of terra-cotta bricks, glass
slits, alabaster cylinders, and tiny prisonlike windows. A sign boasted
to passersby:

KING/DREW MAGNET HIGH SCHOOL
OF MEDICINE AND SCIENCE

Both the American and the California Republic flags trembled on stiff
poles high above the school's capstone. I wondered if the sizable Mexican student population knew that the California Republic flag (or bear
flag) was designed by American settlers on a piece of fresh southern cotton when they were in a revolt against Mexico. That, in essence, this
blazing flag, hoisted high above their heads, was a symbol of Mexican
defeat. *Guess it's the same as the American flag for me, though,* I reasoned.

Jews don't salute the fuckin' swastika
But niggaz pledge allegiance to the flag that accosted ya.
—RAS KASS, "NATURED OF THE THREAT," *SOUL ON ICE*

I was a few minutes early and decided to take a seat in the hallway and
get my notes together. Moments later, I was joined by Lisa, an eleventh-
grader whose skin was as dark and smooth as the glossy shells of Spanish
chestnuts. She sat across from me and I noticed that her eyes, masked in
blue contacts, wouldn't lift high enough to meet mine so I spoke first:
"'Sup."
Her face, one half hidden behind tracks of strawberry-blond
weave, rose.

"Hi," she whispered, her eyes wandering before finally landing on the book in my hand.

"You reading that?" she chased.

"Yeah," I said, glancing at the cover—*The Wretched of the Earth*—and offering her a look at the book. "Here, wanna check it out." She didn't budge, then finally—

"I don't read nothin'."

"Nothin'?" I asked to be sure.

"Nope, nothin', 'less it's for school," she confirmed.

"That's not cool, you know," I said, not really knowing what to say. "See, this book I'm reading right here is interesting because it breaks down a lot of information—information we should know as African-Americans," I said, to which she sprung a chuckle.

"What?" I questioned. "What's funny?"

"African?" she quizzed.

"Yeah. African," I said with a curious authority.

"I ain't African," she swore.

"Where are your ancestors from, then?" I pushed back.

"*I dunno,* Europe or somewhere," she said, straight-faced.

I scanned her face, searching for signs she was just joking.

She wasn't.

"African refers to our ethnic origin, American refers to our nationality, that's why I called you 'African-American.'"

"I told you I ain't African," she snapped.

I breathed as deeply as my lungs would allow.

"Marcus Garvey said people who don't know their history are like trees without roots."

"Who?"

"Marcus Garvey was a very influential and important Black man."

"*Umph.* I hate Black people," she said spitefully.

"Hate?" I said, shocked.

"Yeah, 'cause they ignorant. Not like white people—they sophisticated," she explained to me.

As I looked into the windows of Lisa's soul, I saw the eyes of Pecola Breedlove, the main character in Toni Morrison's 1970 novel *The Bluest Eye. The Bluest Eye,* Morrison's first novel, is set in her hometown of Lorain, Ohio, and focuses on Pecola's hostile childhood. What's painfully clear throughout the novel, as we watch little Pecola fall in love with the ivory image of Shirley Temple and hear her nightly prayers to God for blue eyes, is that Pecola's world has been molded by the narrow and unattainable standards of white American culture.

> *Each night Pecola prayed for blue eyes. In her eleven years, no one had ever noticed Pecola. But with blue eyes, she thought, everything would be different. She would be so pretty that her parents would stop fighting. Her father would stop drinking. Her brother would stop running away. If only she could be beautiful. If only people would look at her.*

Morrison's ideas were undoubtedly influenced by Malcolm X who warned us that "black people will never value themselves as long as they subscribe to a standard of valuation that devalues them." Afrocentrists followed this up with the idea that Africans should view the world through their own eyes and certainly not through the spectacles of people who view them as inferior.

I thought of the BET interview I'd just done and I realized that Lisa, a victim of the American school system, was no different than the victims of Katrina. The government had failed her, just as it had failed the people of New Orleans (before and after the storm hit). We must ask ourselves: If we can't depend on the local, state, or federal governments to provide water and food to the Black victims of Katrina, can we—should we—depend on *them* to fully educate us?

The answer, as I thought back on my experiences in the public, private, and alternative school systems in Philadelphia, in college and graduate school, and now as a professor, is absolutely not—especially if one wishes to come out alive.

If no historian, as Roxanne Dunbar-Ortiz points out, "would accept accounts of Nazi officials as to what happened in Nazi Germany because those accounts were written to justify that regime," why in the world are Black children, Latino children, Asian children being taught their history from accounts written by those who enslaved them, committed acts of genocide against them, tortured them, and put them in interment camps?

And it is in this question that we begin to realize the power of education, the power of how and why we learn what we learned. We be-

Photo: Chris Metzger

gin to understand why David Walker, who was born to an enslaved African, quizzed, "For colored people to acquire learning in this country, makes tyrants quake and tremble on their sandy foundation. Why, what is the matter? Why, they know that their infernal deeds of cruelty will be known to the world." And why Elijah Muhammad, more than a century later, responded, "The slave master will not teach you knowledge of self, as there would not be a master-slave relationship any longer." In this, we also see that we cannot leave the educational process up to those whose purposes and objectives are different from ours and expect us to walk in the footsteps of our ancestors. How can we follow the examples of Ella Baker or Robert Williams if we don't learn about them?

While writing and producing the film *500 Years Later,* a documentary directed by Owen Alik Shahadah exploring the psychocultural effects of slavery and colonialism on the African Diaspora, I was able to jaunt around the world to Jamaica, London, Paris, Ghana, Senegal, Barbados, and throughout America. At the time, I was a junior in college, struggling for my mind in a predominantly white (socially, culturally, historically, academically) institution. As I filmed Black folks all around the globe, I made it a point to talk to students and teachers alike about their educational experiences and how they kept keepin' on. I was surprised by how similar our experiences were and how they, too, were searching for ways to fill an educational void. Here's some of what came back when I asked them about their formal education:

JASON TERRY, STUDENT—KINGSTON, JAMAICA
There's a lot of Black heroes that I've never learned about, but I can tell you a lot about Henry VIII! Or one of the queen Elizabeths! Can't tell you nothin' about Marcus Garvey though.

JUNKUNG JOBAREH, STUDENT—BANJUL, GAMBIA
Unfortunately the kind of education that we get here enslaves our minds, makes us believe we are inferior. Education should

liberate, not enslave. And eventually, in the long run, liberate the whole world.

AFRAR AFRIYA, STUDENT—LONDON, UNITED KINGDOM
Education for me has to be looked upon on two levels. The first one: the so-called training that we receive in school and we understand that it is indeed training because all it's about is regurgitating a curriculum or regurgitating a set of rules to then pass an exam. But we must also understand that education is also about getting self-confidence, so being proud of who you are. So we must also study the history of our past, meaning African history. However this isn't taught.

TANYA MORRIS, TEACHER—PHILADELPHIA, PENNSYLVANIA
The mainstream educational system has proven that it's not able to meet our educational needs. Just look at the youth today and that's evident.

KHALEEL MUHAMMAD, TEACHER—LONDON, UNITED KINGDOM
This is indicative of why we need to be connected to our past, why we need to *know* what happened to us as people because if we can't tell our students that you actually achieved something why would they feel a sense of achievement? Why would they feel a sense of identity? They have to know what happened before and they have to be able to relate to it and say, "I did that. My people did this. We *are* somebody, we *can* do something!"

DR. SAMUEL HAY, PROFESSOR—EASTON, PENNSYLVANIA
Public education, unfortunately, does not anchor African-Americans in the tradition of Africa. So consequently people float.

KOHAIN HALEVI, TEACHER—ACCRA, GHANA

What institution today teaches the ideology and philosophy of the prophet Nat Turner? What you realize today that with the death of George Washington, Thomas Jefferson, John Adams, James Madison; that even with their deaths no matter what charisma they had, the institutionalization of their ideas into the Constitution of America, into the institutions of America, the universities and schools, that today you have to go to school and learn about these individuals and the principles that they believed in . . . What universities, what elementary schools, what high schools and middle schools do we have that you can come out knowing who Gabriel Prosser was? Who Denmark Vessey was? Who Nat Turner was? Who Booker T. Washington was? Who Malcolm X El-Hajj Malik El-Shabazz was? Who LeRoi Jones was? Is it mandatory reading, are their ideals and their philosophy mandatory reading?

DONTE HARRIS, STUDENT—COMPTON, CALIFORNIA

I feel that [the school system] is not properly designed to educate us in any way, shape, or form. People can say it's not working, but it is working, just not for us.

How could it be that Black students and teachers around the world, at nearly every level, were feeling the same sense of despair in regards to the educational system? Dr. Zak Kondo, in his *Black Student's Guide to Positive Education,* provides a bleak list of what the average Black student will believe upon graduation from high school:

1. BLACKS ARE INFERIOR, LAZY AND DUMB.

2. WHITES ARE SUPERIOR, HARDWORKING AND INTELLIGENT.

3. BLACKS HAVE NO HISTORY AND SHOULD BE THANKFUL WHITES RESCUED THEM FROM SAVAGERY.

4. EUROPE IS THE MOTHER OF CIVILIZATION, AFRICA IS THE MOTHER OF PRIMITIVISM.

5. BLACKS CAN DO NOTHING FOR THEMSELVES.

6. BLACK FEATURES (NOSE, HAIR, SKIN COLOR . . .) ARE UGLY.

7. BLACKS SHOULD STRIVE TO BE LIKE WHITES.

8. EVERY MAN OR WOMAN HAS A PRICE.

9. SUCCESS IS MEASURED BY HOW THICK YOUR WALLET IS.

10. BLACK PEOPLE HOLD BLACK PEOPLE DOWN.

11. BLACKS CAN NEVER UNIFY.

12. BLACKS IN AMERICA HAVE NOTHING IN COMMON WITH BLACKS IN AFRICA.

13. BLACKS MUST DEPEND ON WHITES TO HELP THEM.

14. BLACKS ARE CUT—THROATS, THUGS AND WELFARE CHEATS.

With this picture, it is clear to see why young people, if we look at the numbers of dropouts, have been reluctant to embrace school. This, of course, isn't the only factor for high dropout rates, but studies have shown, time and time again, that what is being taught is directly connected to focus, enthusiasm, and participation. As Dead Prez remembered:

> *Get your lessons, that's why my moms kept stressin'*
> *I tried to pay attention but they classes wasn't interestin'*
> *They seemed to only glorify the Europeans*
> *Claimin' Africans were only three—fifths a human being.*
> —DEAD PREZ, "THEY SCHOOLS," *LET'S GET FREE*

It's important to understand that challenging the mainstream school system is not antieducational, but actually, the contrary. This challenge reveals our deep concern with the educational process, forcing us to examine the social, political, and cultural role that curricula have on students of color. Additionally, it scrutinizes an educational tradition that is more invested in training a workforce of menials to follow instructions rather than teaching the critical-thinking skills necessary for individuals to empower their lives and communities. The tragic reality is that we have been disconnected from emancipatory education. We have been—in the United States and abroad—trapped in an educational system that has, by estranging us from our own culture and history, prepared us primarily for a subservient role in society. Whether you're in Baltimore or Compton, Philadelphia or Accra, Ghana, this tragic phenomenon can be observed both in the actual schools and in the menial job markets graduates are forced into. As a result, many young people conclude that mainstream education is, like so many other things in society, designed, maintained, and controlled by another class/racial group to serve that group's own socioeconomic interests.

I'm not suggesting that we should drop out of school. It's a difficult and competitive world and it's common knowledge that the farther one climbs educationally, the farther away one moves from poverty. My concern is psychocultural. How do we keep our minds? Carter G. Woodson, who wrote *The Mis-education of the Negro,* once remarked, "I went to Harvard for four years, and it took forty years to get Harvard out of me." How do we avoid the Carter G. Woodson fate? This question ran through my mind as—

"It is my pleasure to welcome our guest, M. K. Asante, Jr.," Eric Sanabria, senior class president and recipient of the Princeton Prize for Race Relations, introduced me to his fidgety classmates. Amid a light flutter of applause, I approached the microphone, disturbed by what Lisa had told me and unsure of what I would tell them.

I looked out into the audience and a thousand eyes, sunk in the beaming sockets of Black and brown boys and girls, looked back.

"Thanks for that, Eric. It's an honor to be here," I said, still searching for substance. In the front row, I saw the hungry blue eyes of Lisa. Then it hit me:

"I want to talk with y'all today about something I call 'Two Sets of Notes,'" I announced as I pulled my first book out of my back pocket and opened it to the poem by the same name. I lunged my voice and body into the apropos stanzas:

TWO SETS OF NOTES FOR BLACK STUDENTS
I find myself feeling
As if I am 'pon the ground & ceiling,
In institutions that disengage from healing
Instead, they simply warp open wounds
& Entrap me in rooms
where I am consumed by hypocrisy
& It occurs to me:
Greek philosophers didn't author their own philosophy

& The statues on campus be watchin' me,
Washington . . . Jefferson . . . Williams,
Clockin' me—
As if to say 'time's up'
But I don't run laps on tracks
I run laps around the scholars of tomorrow
Because new schools of thought
Are merely our histories borrowed

& They label me militant, and black national radical,
trying to put my learning process on sabbatical.
I don't apologize,
Instead I spit truth into the whites of eyes infected by
white lies.

They even try to get me to see—
Their point of view from a brother that looks like me,
but that brother don't—
walk like me
       talk like me
                  or
            act like me,
and that brother turned his head
when I asked if he was
black like me.

Mastering their thoughts
and forgetting our own
and we wonder why we always feel alone,
from the media to academia—
hanging brothers like coats
and in their schools. . . .

I always take two sets of notes,
one set to ace the test
        and
one set I call the truth,
and when I find historical contradictions
I use the first set as proof—
proof that black youths'

minds are being—
polluted,
    convoluted,
           diluted,
not culturally rooted.

In anything
except the Western massacre
and most of us are scared of Africa,
we view our mother's land
Through the eyes of David Hume and Immanuel Kant
well
Immanuel kan't tell me anything about a land he's never
seen
a land rich with history
beautiful kings and queens.

They'll have you believe otherwise
their history is built on high-rise lies
the pyramids were completed
before Greece or Rome were conceptualized,
then they'll claim the Egyptians' race was a mystery
you tell them to read Herodotus Book II of the histories
it cannot be any clearer. . . .

Black children
look in the mirror
you are the reflection of divinity
don't let them fool you with selective memory
walk high,
listen to the elders who spoke

Black Students,
Always take two sets of notes.

"Two Sets of Notes" grew out of my experiences in school systems
that neglected to teach me crucial clusters of information connected
to my identity. A system that made African-Americans and all non-
whites an ethnic footnote in American and world history. This is no
light matter as one's identity is often forged through what we learn in
school. This is what Baldwin meant when he said that white American identity "is a series of myths about one's heroic ancestors." But
we—African-Americans, Asian Americans, Latinos, et cetera—don't
learn about our "heroic ancestors" apart from a context of white
subjugation. For example, as students we learn that enslaved Africans
were acquiescent to slavery. We are not taught, for instance, that in
1526, enslaved Africans and Spaniards founded a town near the Pee
Dee River in South Carolina, and that, just months later, the Africans
rebelled, killed many of their masters, and escaped to live with the
Indians while the rest of the Spaniards fled to Haiti. Omissions such
as these not only paint an inaccurate image of history, but adversely
affect the way we view our ancestors and, in turn, ourselves. As Gen.
Petro G. Grigorenko said in "Letter to a History Journal," "Concealment of the historical truth is a crime against the people."

Consider what Kwame Ture remembers about "concealment of
historical truth" when he was a student in the West Indies:

> *The first one is that the history books tell you that nothing happens*
> *until a white man comes along. If you ask any white person who dis-*
> *covered America, they'll tell you "Christopher Columbus." And if you*
> *ask them who discovered China, they'll tell you "Marco Polo." And if*
> *you ask them, as I used to be told in the West Indies, I was not discov-*
> *ered until Sir Walter Raleigh needed pitch lake for his ship, and he*

came along and found me and said "Whup—I have discovered you,"
and my history began.

We must begin to see why Ture never learned, for instance, the rhyme "In 1493 / Columbus stole all he could see."

It is this kind of gross "concealment" that historically has led to events like the 1960s Ocean Hill-Brownsville conflict in New York City, where African-American parents and other community members sought local control of the public schools in their neighborhoods. One of their major grievances was that the curriculum then, just like now, was not culturally relevant. This has also sparked a rise in African-centered schools like the Lotus Academy in Philadelphia whose mission is:

> *To provide an educational opportunity for our children that is*
> *founded on the basis of culture that is steeped in African culture, his-*
> *tory and tradition. We feel that it is important for our students to be*
> *grounded and have a good understanding of who they are. The ac-*
> *complishments of our ancestors and those who walked before us and*
> *all of the subject areas this particular foundation is reinforced,*
> *whether we're teaching math or history, science or social studies, we*
> *infuse the African perspective. So Lotus provides an opportunity for*
> *students to learn, to think, communicate, and problem solve within a*
> *framework of an African perspective.*

Schools like these recognize, as environmentalist Baba Dioum does, that, "In the end, we conserve only what we love. We will love only what we understand. We will understand only what we are taught." If we want to continue the mighty contributions that we've made in art, culture, medicine, and science, it's essential that we know our history.

"I want to show y'all how to survive in this system," I told the students.

Some years ago, singer Lauryn Hill, speaking to a small crowd at the MTV studios in Manhattan, said "I had to be a living example . . . I've become one of those mad scientists who does the test on themselves first." Similarly, "Two Sets of Notes" was something I'd applied at the high school, college, and graduate levels, so I knew it worked.

"As students of color, we have to take initiative with regards to our education, especially in classes like history. It may be presented to you through your history books that history is a fact. No, history is a debate. Napoleon said that 'history is a lie agreed upon'—*Agreed upon by whom?* you must ask. Question, question, question. Challenge. Hit the library, the Internet, the bookstores, the elders, and find out who Garvey was, who Asantewaa was, who Rodney was. Then, once you find out, ask yourself and your teachers why you weren't taught about these African giants." Of course, however, you must pass the test. This kind of double note-taking is reminiscent of freethinking Soviet students who learned one set of facts at home but knew the facts they were required to regurgitate in school.

I explained to them that to take two sets of notes is not easy or fair. It requires reading books, articles, and documents that aren't assigned in class; watching films that aren't in movie theaters; and listening to music that's not on the radio. One must become an active agent in one's educational process.

"You should not depend upon school exclusively for your education," I informed them. "Self-education is just as, if not more, important." School can never be the be-all and end-all. At any level of formal school, self-education is also vital. In many ways, self-education moves against what we've been taught "education" is. Consider that self-education implies self-motivation as opposed to grade-motivation and careerism; it implies a willingness to engage in new activities and experiences as opposed to rote learning and uniformity; it allows one to recognize the teachers and lessons that are omnipresent rather than the hierarchy that assumes the teacher is all-knowing; it suggests acting on what is learned rather than simply memorizing and regurgitating information for quizzes and tests; it also implies the asking and reasking of questions, rather than the suppression of questions.

I reminded the students at King Drew that although self-educating might sound a bit daunting at first, the alternative is far worse.

"And remember what Felix Okoye, founder of the African and Afro-American Studies department at SUNY Brockport, said, 'It would be better not to know so many things than to know so many things that are not so.'"

Students of color—any color—it is imperative that we take two sets of notes, if we wish to gain a clear and healthy understanding of the world. We must understand that, as James Baldwin told his students, "American history is longer, larger, more various, more beautiful, and more terrible than anything anyone has ever said about it."

Before I exited the stage, I left the students with a message from Buddha that I couldn't agree with more:

Make the effort to obtain information that will allow you to best guide your destiny. Make your voice heard in the world through your life and works and do not be cowered into inaction by status, tradition, race, ethnicity, gender or affiliation. Do not believe in anything simply because you have heard it. Do not believe in anything simply because it is spoken and rumored by many. Do not believe in anything merely on the authority of your teachers and elders. Do not believe in traditions because they have been handed down to many generations. But after observation and analysis, when you find that anything agrees with reason and is conducive to the good and benefit of one and all, then accept it and live up to it.

As you move through the dense wilderness of formal education, trying, with all of your soul to retain your sanity, remember to always TAKE TWO SETS OF NOTES!

chapter 11

BY ANY *MEDIUM* NECESSARY

The function of art is to do more than tell it like it is—it's
to imagine what is possible.
—BELL HOOKS

The scene: A group of young men, hoodies hovering over their nodding heads, huddle to form a cipher in East Baltimore.

> X: *Yo, niggaz in my hood sell crack*
> *Move weight, and clap back*
> *I stay strapped . . .*
>
> X: *Yo, yo, I know niggaz that kill for nothin'*
> *Here, take these cracks and move somethin'*
> *Take this gat, and body somethin'*
>
> X: *I walk around with big guns*
> *Niggaz in my crew'll kill for funds*
> *For fun, fuck bitches and run . . .*

I used "X" not because I don't know their names, but because by sounding so similar, they misplaced their identities. If I had simply shut my eyes at any given moment during their frenetic flows, their rhymes would have been indistinguishable.

After the cipher, I stuck around to dialogue with the aspiring rappers about their roles as Black artists in America.

"Do y'all consider yourselves artists?" I put out.

"I do," one of the rappers declared.

"Okay, so as an artist, then, and especially as a Black artist, do you feel that you have a duty to use your art to uplift?" I asked him.

"I mean, I don't know. The rhymes I spit, that's reality, *nahmean,*" he shrugged.

"It's like a mirror, man," another rapper chimed in. "What you see is what you get."

"That's real," another added, nodding his dome in confirmation.

Just as their rhymes were analog replicas, so were their justifications for spittin' them. They were echoing not just an ideology that can be found in mainstream rap, but throughout the greater art landscape: film, visual arts, dance, literature.

I shared with them an edict that Paul Robeson once made: "The role of the artist is not simply to show the world as it is, but as it ought to be." The idea that the filmmakers, rappers, painters, collagists, photographers, choreographers, and other artists of today—amid the arid abundance of desolation and despair— can simply show the ills of the world and then avoid personal responsibility behind the thin veneer of "I'm just a mirror" no longer holds weight.

> Yo, anybody can tell you how it is
> What we putting down right here is
> how it is and how it could be.
> —TALIB KWELI, "AFRICAN DREAM,"
> TRAIN OF THOUGHT

"Yes, the mirror does reflect reality," I concurred, "but the mirror is no passive instrument. It's not as uninvolved as 'what you see is what you get.' No, the mirror gives us instructions about our appearance and offers us a chance to improve it—that's what the mirror does."

"At least a good mirror," said one of the rappers in the trio as he gave me a pound and repeated, "Improvement." And as the four of us, on the bitterly cold four-year anniversary of President Bush's "Mission Accomplished" speech, stood on a battered Baltimore block in a section of the city dubbed "Baghdad," it became harshly seeable that there was no greater call for improvement than right now.

Here it is spelled out: *We are at war.*

America, a country that comprises less than 5 percent of the global population, consumes (and wastes) most of the world's food, resources, and energy. It is a nation fraught with a vulgar material excess that flaunts itself amid sheer poverty and utter desolation. A nation that destroys the most people, animals, plants, habitats, forests, ecosystems, and other *nations* in the pursuit of more . . . *more everything.* A nation that incarcerates and kills millions of its poor Black and brown citizens. A nation built on and maintained by the burglary of other people's land and slave labor. A nation of which we are citizens.

> How could this be, the land of the free, home of the brave
> Indigenous holocaust, and the home of the slaves?
> —IMMORTAL TECHNIQUE, "CAUSE OF DEATH,"
> REVOLUTIONARY VOLUME 2

America is a nation of contradictions. Freedom, on one hand, and slavery on the other. Consider that these words—"All men are created equal, that they are endowed by their Creator with certain unalienable Rights, that among these are Life, Liberty and the pursuit of Happiness"—were written, signed, and agreed upon by men who captured, bought, sold, and tortured my ancestors. Today America launches attacks on nations, killing hundreds of thousands of innocent people in the name of "freedom and liberation." As Indian novelist and activist Arundhati Roy writes, "free speech," "free market," and the "free world" in America have little to do with actual freedom. On the contrary, these terms grant America:

> *The freedom to murder, annihilate, and dominate other people. The freedom to finance and sponsor despots and dictators across the world. The freedom to train, arm, and shelter terrorists. The freedom to topple democratically elected governments. The freedom to amass and use weapons of mass destruction—chemical, biological, and nuclear. The freedom to go to war against any country whose government it disagrees with. And, most terrible of all, the freedom to commit these crimes against humanity in the name of "justice," in the name of "righteousness," in the name of "freedom."*

In an atmosphere rife with grotesque, state-sponsored contradictions, the fundamental question arises: Who will contradict the state?

[enter the artivist]

Who will stage a colorful resistance against the oppression and domination our government imposes on its Black and brown citizens? On the world? Who will promote self, sisterly, and brotherly love? Who will demand justice? Who will be the voice for the voiceless? Who will not only speak, but dance, paint, film, and sing truth to power? Who will contradict war and death? If not us—*artivists*—than who?

German dramatist and poet Bertolt Brecht, in his poem, "When

Evil-Doing Comes Like Falling Rain," gives us the tragic answer if we fail to adhere to these essential task:

> *The first time it was reported that our friends were being butchered there was a cry of horror. Then a hundred were butchered. But when a thousand were butchered and there was no end to the butchery, a blanket of silence spread. When evil-doing comes like falling rain, nobody calls out "stop!"*

The artivist must challenge, confront, and resist this otherwise inescapable fate of torture, injustice, and inhumanity.

Synergy is the interaction or cooperation of two or more agents to produce a combined effect greater than the sum of their separate effects. This is the idea that drives the artivist (artist + activist) to spend her days and nights feverishly creating in the face of ferocious destruction. It is this force that compels the artivist to encourage others to create as well; for the artivist knows that creativity is not reserved for the elite and therefore, as they often say in my birth country Zimbabwe, "If you can walk, you can dance, if you can talk, you can sing." And it is this synergy that urges the artivist to *make* love in wartime.

The artivist uses her artistic talents to fight and struggle against injustice and oppression—by any *medium* necessary. The artivist merges commitment to freedom and justice with the pen, the lens, the brush, the voice, the body, and the imagination. The artivist knows that to make an *observation* is to have an *obligation*.

The artivist, having examined his role throughout history, is aware that the arts have always occupied a crucial and critical space in society and that "Even the worst picture," as Goethe said, "can speak to our emotions and imaginations by setting them in motion, releasing them and letting them run free." The artivist, then, as Ngugi wa Thiong'o points out in *Barrel of a Pen*, "tries to make us not only see and understand the world of man and nature, apprehend it, but to see and understand it in a certain way."

The artivist is Paul Robeson who proclaimed to the world, at the height of his international stardom, in that commanding baritone, "I am today giving up my concerts to enter into this struggle which I call getting to the rank and file struggle of my people for full citizenship in these United States. So I won't be singing, except for the rights of my people. No more pretty songs, no pretty songs. Time for some full citizenship."

The artivist is Billie Holiday who, despite the very real threats on her life, insisted on telling the world that

> *Southern trees bear strange fruit*
> *Blood on the leaves, blood at the root.*

For Lady Day understood that socially cognizant art has the potential to not only inform, but transform our reality by raising awareness and exposing inhumanity wherever it dwells.

"The Negro in this country has to write protest, because he is a protestant," declared Ossie Davis in his 1966 essay "The Wonderful World of Law and Order," in which he spoke about the need for merging art with activism. Ossie bellows:

> *He can't help but be [a protestant]. He cannot accept the situation in*
> *which he finds himself, so, therefore, he is driven to scream out*
> *against the oppression that surrounds him, that suffocates him. . . . It*
> *must irritate, it must shake. It must disturb. It must move the very*
> *bowels of compassion. It must be angry. It must be aimed at corrective*
> *action and now.*

Indeed, there has been a rich history of artivism in African-American culture. This is partly due to the fact that the only sane answer to oppression is resistance. The Black artist, then, has to try very hard (by clenching one's eyes tight and for as long as possible) not to be an artivist. Because of this outspoken artivism and the incessant exportation of American cultural products, Black artivists are looked upon for inspiration internationally. I can recall, while studying in London at the School of Oriental and African Studies, a Muslim student group that, during political discussions, quoted African-American artivists just as much as they quoted Muslim intellectuals.

The African-American tradition of artivism reaches back to the djeli tradition of West Africa. Known in French as "griots," djelis were traveling poets and artists who not only included, but focused on the politics of the day and the condition of the people as a primary function in their work. When artivist Amiri Baraka says, "We learned that Osiris, the djeli, raised the sun each day with song and verse," he's commenting on the role of the artivist; to shed light, to encourage all life-forms, to promote growth, to provide warmth, to let us imagine and dream, but most important: to create and to have a palpable impact in the real world.

How will history, and our children's children, look upon the arts of this dark era? An era where we are under attack by those who degrade life. This war—between those individuals and institutions who seek to destroy humanity and those individuals and institutions who resist that destruction—places all of us in a crucial position in which we must choose between obliteration and restoration, life and death.

African-Americans, of course, are not in any way, shape, or form alone in this. For around two-thirds of the entire world doesn't have enough food to eat! It is fundamental for all who care to identify themselves with other struggles for justice. When this is done, the

stronger we all become. Artivist painter Elizabeth Catlett reminds us
that we can't

> *wrap ourselves in "blackness," ignoring the rest of exploited humanity*
> *for we are an integral part of it. Blackness is important as a part of*
> *the struggle—it is our part—not only of blacks in the U.S., Africa,*
> *and the Caribbean, but of Chicanos and Puerto Ricans in the U.S.,*
> *and the peoples of Asia and Latin America exemplified at the moment*
> *by the Chileans and Vietnamese. Through art we can bring under-*
> *standing to black America, Chicano America, Puerto Rican Ameri-*
> *can, etc. of the character of racism, the need for its elimination, our*
> *mutual problems and our differences. The graphic and plastic image is*
> *invaluable, more so because of the extended illiteracy and semi-*
> *illiteracy among us.*

Regardless of the race of an artist, what needs to be understood,
first and foremost, is that all art and artists—ALL—are political, even
if their politics are disguised as indifference. It is silence—on the critical issues of our day—that supports the system of oppression and injustice. Artistic silence, in times like these, is the same as approval. As
Ngugi warns, "the arts, through the use of images, function as a form
of knowledge about our reality, but never are we to assume that these
images are neutral."

If our art does not challenge and confront, fight and tussle, wrestle,
grapple and stand up against oppression, then our art is actually aiding
that oppression. Neutrality, or the perception of neutrality, only helps
the oppressor, never the oppressed. In a world where human beings are
denied their humanity, the artivists must—by depicting the humanity
of the oppressed—bring value back to human life. If we are oppressed
and our art doesn't counter this oppression and challenge this oppression, then it is, by default, supporting the oppression.

We cannot afford, nor could we ever, to make art just to be makin' it. This is what Black Panther artivist Emory Douglas meant when he said, "In order to create accurate images of awareness we must participate in the changing of society and understand the political nature of art, because there is no such thing as art for art's sake." The idea of art for art's sake, now and in past times, has been a luxury that all of those who seek to fight oppression simply do not have. We, on the contrary, are engaged with art for the people's sake. How can one entertain the idea of art for art's sake in a world that cries out for the artist to save it? When the late Max Roach, the great jazz drummer, took the stage, people knew that he was with them and when they listened, they heard themselves—the mass of Black voices that screamed *We Insist*. It was impossible for people to think that Max Roach was drumming just to be drumming, for the sake of drumming. Today, with so much the same, it should be unfathomable for artists to squander the great opportunity to make a statement, and from that statement evoke the emotion needed for positive action. For nothing is worse than the artist, through inaction, to be a silent partner in his continued oppression.

Throughout history, it has been the inaction of those who could have, should have acted; the indifference from those who knew better; the silence from those who had a voice; and the indifference when the stakes were highest, that made it possible for slavery, oppression, and exploitation to thrive. The artivist "acts" through the page, screen, city walls, subway cars, stage, or whatever else we can express ourselves on . . . and against! And now.

Artivism is about time—and the times we find ourselves in. Poet Asha Bandele, in her poem "No Turn Backs," writes:

Oooh—
And if I cld

I wld write luvpoems all day
Burn incense
Watch my candle glow
And tell u stories of only beauty
But such choices r not mine 2 make
When the times demand of me this ritual

The times, as Bandele illustrates, have demanded that the ritual become the voice of the voiceless. Again, the motivation of the artivist in the context of time can be seen when a CBS reporter asked James Baldwin: "Mr. Baldwin, do you think you'll ever write something that doesn't have a message?" Baldwin responded:

I don't quite know what that means. In my view, no writer who has ever lived, could have written a line without a message, you know. It depends on, what you're asking me, I think, is to what extent do I intend to become a polemicist or a propagandist. Well, I can't answer that because the nature of our situation has imposed on everybody involved in it things that one wouldn't ordinarily do, you take risks which you wouldn't ordinarily take. I don't think of myself as a public speaker or a civil rights leader or any of that, but I'm not about to sit in some tower somewhere cultivating my talent.

Baldwin spoke of "the nature of our situation." It's essential that we realize that we, the budding artivists of today, are bound by the times we find ourselves in. Indeed, this time is not all that different from Baldwin's time. "We must not fall into the age-old cliché that the artist is always ahead of his/her time," as Chicano artivist Malaquias Montoya warns. "No, it is most urgent that we be on time."

Additionally, we must recognize that the arts, like spoken languages, can vary in form, tone, and medium. Indeed, one can think of each artistic genre as a language used to communicate with a group that understands that language. To give a personal example, when my first book, *Like Water Running Off My Back,* was published, I found myself in the Bronx talking with one of my cousins.

"So, I heard you got a book out?" he asked.

"Yeah, man. It's out, my first book," I told him as I nodded, proud.

"Shit, I don't know why the hood don't read," he stated bluntly, deflating my energy. "I mean, no disrespect," he clarified. "They watch TV and movies and shit, but a lot of the niggas I know, including me, don't read at all," he told me.

My cousin's statement was not a dis. He was simply stating the reality that there are a vast number of people who have great difficulty comprehending the language I choose to communicate in. Rather than be deterred from writing books, I confronted the reality that if I wanted to reach my cousin, I was going to have to learn a new language—a language that could speak to him in a way he'd understand. That language or medium was filmmaking and I realized through making films that I could in fact reach him and others whom I'd previously been unable to reach. Different people. People who might not pick up a book, but who have become well-versed in sitting in front of screens. This is the power of art as language. There are some who understand the language of poetry, others who do not. Some who understand the language of hip hop, others who do not. The artivist must not be afraid to learn a new language in order to inspire and empower new people—by any medium necessary.

To artivists throughout the world, write—because you can't not write; paint—because you can't not paint; film—because you can't not film; and create because you can't accept what not creating means. Let us unfold our arms out of the fragile stance of spectators. Let us use our tools, sometimes like a scalpel and other times like a sledgehammer, in the service of the oppressed—liberation through imagination. Let us be courageous and without fear as we know, from the Kenyan freedom song, that "too much fear encourages oppression." If Picasso said "Art is a lie that makes us realize the truth," I say art is the emotional truth that makes us realize who's lying.

As the late Palestinian poet Tawfiq Zayyad reminded us, all we have is "a flute's melody," "a brush to paint my dreams, a bottle of ink," and "an infinite love for my people in pain."

chapter 12

CHANGE CLOTHES (STATE PROPERTY)

The ghetto is a prison with invisible bars.
Politicans know the problems, but they never get solved.
—DEAD PREZ

No matter how they confine your body,
they can't imprison your soul.
—TRADITIONAL SAYING

When comedian Chris Rock told a packed Apollo Theater, "If you Black, you get more respect coming out of jail than school," they erupted in laughter, just as I did. Those who had the privilege of knowing Langston Hughes often talk about how much he laughed. "He laughed a lot. He liked to laugh and he liked to make people laugh," remembers Gertrude Jeannette, a friend of his and founder of the H.A.D.L.E.Y. Players theater group in Harlem. Hughes revealed in his 1940 autobiography *The Big Sea* that he was often "Laughing to keep from cryin'." When we consider the brutal reality that hides itself behind Rock's raucous routine—that a generation of young, gifted Black men and women have been wiped out as a result of mass incarceration—we find ourselves, just as Hughes did, "laughing to keep from crying."

Being Black in America means that you probably know, all too well, what it's like to have a friend, family member, or loved one *come home* after "serving" a bid in what writer and death-row inmate Mumia Abu-Jamal calls "hi-tech hell." Sad as it is, *comin' home*—because of the attack on poor urban Blacks by an unjust "justice" system—has indeed become a tradition, one that gnaws at the flimsy fabric of our already deeply fractured families. It has become, especially for young Black males, a kind of rite of passage into what poet Sonia Sanchez dubs a "makeshift manhood." Despite all of this, however, nothing beats having a formerly incarcerated loved one come home. Last June, my lil' cousin's homecoming was no exception.

The sun blushed across the sky as I waited for the mouth of the prison, made-up of stiff gates, to open wide enough to allow my cocoa-colored cousin to walk out. As I waited, I tried not to think about the fact that he'd be walking out of one prison and into another kind of prison. The correctional officers (COs) that patrolled his cell block were now police officers patrolling his block. The bars, like teeth that kept him confined to his cell, now covered most of the windows on most of the skinny houses in our neighborhood. The jobs available to him were, in scale, as low paying as the twelve cents an hour he earned in jail. The anger and frustration that boiled the blood of optionless inmates now paints the streets of Philadelphia red. One finds the same general sense of entrapment and nihilism inside and out—a double sentence. The late French philosopher Michel Foucault, in his observation of Attica prison in New York, observed that:

> *Society eliminates by sending to prison people whom prison breaks up, crushes, physically eliminates; the prison eliminates them by "freeing" them and sending them back to society. . . . The state in which they*

come out ensures that society will eliminate them once again, sending
them to prison.

The late Tupac Shakur, who grew up in the ghettos of East Harlem
and Baltimore and served stints in prison, may have articulated this
connection best in "Trapped":

> *Too many brothers daily heading for tha big pen*
> *Niggas comin' out worse off than when they went in.*

Contemporary scholars have come to similar conclusions, in many
cases viewing the ghetto and prison as two points on the same continuum of oppression. Sociologist Loïc Wacquant, professor at the University of California, Berkeley, sees the prison as a surrogate ghetto.
In "The New 'Peculiar Institution': On the Prison as Surrogate Ghetto,"
he writes that the ghetto and the prison are mutually reinforcing
"institutions of forced confinement":

> *This carceral mesh has been solidified by changes that have reshaped the*
> *urban "Black Belt" of mid-century so as to* make the ghetto more like
> a prison *and undermined the "inmate society" residing in U.S. pen-*
> *itentiaries in ways that* make the prison more like a ghetto. . . . *In*
> *the post-Civil Rights era, the remnants of the dark ghetto and an ex-*
> *panding carceral system have become linked in a single system that en-*
> *traps large numbers of younger black men, who simply move back and*
> *forth between the two institutions. This carceral mesh has emerged*
> *from two sets of convergent changes: sweeping economic and political*
> *forces have reshaped the mid-century "Black Belt" to make the ghetto*
> *more like a prison; and the "inmate society" has broken down in ways*
> *that make the prison more like a ghetto. The resulting symbiosis be-*
> *tween ghetto and prison enforces the socioeconomic marginality and*

symbolic taint of an urban black sub-proletariat. Moreover, by pro-
ducing a racialized public culture that vilifies criminals, it plays a
pivotal role in remaking "race" and redefining the citizenry.

Observing this, one can see why the line between prison culture and street culture, among Black youth, is, at best, thin. This is why, for example, one can look at the prisons and determine what the styles and trends are on the streets. The Wayans brothers mock this interconnectedness in their film *Don't Be a Menace to South Central While Drinking Your Juice in the Hood* (a spoof on the films *Juice, South Central, Higher Learning, Menace II Society, Poetic Justice, New Jack City, Dead Presidents,* and *Boyz n the Hood*) where Toothpick, a secondary character who has just been released from prison, still behaves as if he's locked up, using language exclusive to prisons like "phone check, nigga" and "I got top bunk."

An alarm sounded as a group of Black men, each clutching a clear plastic bag filled with their belongings, trekked up a semi-steep hill. When my cousin reached the top, I met him with an embrace—a deep, soulful embrace full of fraternity and love.

"I'm out!" he yelled as we drove down the avenue. The avenue in Philly is just like any other avenue in any Black urban city: a consumer mecca lined with pawnshops, check-cashing spots, and sneaker, jewelry, and hair accessory stores; none of which, with very few exceptions, is owned, operated, or managed by Black folks. I tried not to dwell on those dismal facts and focused on the beautiful reality that my cousin was finally HOME!

The ride home was full of updates about friends and family as well as frequent outpourings of *I missed you, I'm out, you're out,* and so on and so forth. I caught glimpses of him on the outskirts of my eye as we passed store after store after store. He turned to me.

"I ain't got no gear," he said, "but what's on my back—and this is what I was wearing when I got locked up three years ago," he added.

I understood both what he was saying and what he was asking. One of the visible differences between the inside/out is that you don't have to wear those dreaded orange or blue jumpsuits that are the standard in most prisons. Throughout history, fashion has been used as a nonverbal communicator of social class, gender, occupation, age group, history, ambition, and reality. As Alison Lurie writes in the *Language of Clothes,* "To choose clothes, either in a store or at home, is to define and describe ourselves." We see the implications of what we wear in Amiri Baraka's 1964 one-act play *Dutchman,* a poetic indictment of American racism and capitalism, which centers around an interracial clash on the subway between Lula, a white femme fatale, and Clay, a young Black man. At one point on their train ride, Lula snaps:

> *Everything you say is wrong. That's what makes you so attractive. Ha. In that funny book jacket with all the buttons. What've you got that jacket and tie on in all this heat for? And why're you wearing a jacket and tie like that? Did your people ever burn witches or start revolutions over the price of tea? Boy, those narrow-shoulder clothes come from a tradition you ought to feel oppressed by. A three-button suit. What right do you have to be wearing a three-button suit and a striped tie? Your grandfather was a slave, he didn't go to Harvard.*

I understood my cousin's need to *change clothes.* Plus, after all he'd been through—in the hellholes of the American injustice system—it was the least I could do.

"Let's get you some gear, then," I suggested.

"Really? You got me?" he checked respectfully.

"Of course man. I got you," I assured him, as I eased into a parking spot in front of a wide storefront boasting URBAN FLAVA—LATEST IN URBAN WEAR.

Regardless of their name or location—Dr. Jays in New York, Up Against the Wall in L.A. and D.C., City Blue and Net in Philadelphia— all of these "urban wear" shops are the same: they're all located in Black shopping districts, they cater to a young Black consumer demographic, and they are never Black-owned. Jerseys. Crisp white XXXL T-shirts. Firm, fitted hats. Colorful Nikes. A warehouse of overpriced items that both 50 Cent and my father agree to call "instant gratification."

My cousin hit the racks hard, flipping through hangers of starched cotton like an avid reader might fly through the pages of a good novel. He scanned: *EvisuTimberlandPolo 5iveJungleAdidasAkademiksAvirexCOOGI DickiesDKNYJeansEckoEnyceFreshJiveG-UnitGirbaudLacosteNikePhatFarmReebokRocawearSean JohnTheNorthFace,* until—

"Yeah," he said as he admired a blue shirt that reminded me of the type of shirt he just took off—prison blue.

"What you think?" he asked, as he held the shirt up against his sturdy frame.

"That's nice," a voice, laced with an accent I couldn't place, chimed in before I could. I turned around to find a shopgirl pulling a pair of pants off the rack.

"We've also got the pants to go with it," she added, as she offered the pants to my cousin. As she did, I noticed the tag on the pants.

STATE PROPERTY

18153

3X

"State Property?" I blurted out.

"Yeah, it's good," the shopgirl said.

"No, the fuck it ain't," my cousin said, his face wrinkled with scorn.

"Well, it's very, real popular. State Prop," she said.

"Where you from?" I asked, annoyed.

"Lebanon," she stated seriously.

"Do you know what this means, 'State Prop'?"

She pursed her lips and shrugged her shoulders, indicating she wasn't sure.

"It means us, Blacks, in prison. In jail. Modern-day slavery," I said, animating my words with my hands to which she simply smirked. As my cousin and I walked out of the store, I noticed that State Property, which I knew to be a term employed by the state to exercise governmental authority to possess property (us), had an entire section in the store. Thoughts of crushing glass, shaking gasoline out of a crimson canister, dousing the store, and striking a match crisscrossed my mind. But it wasn't the store's fault. They didn't manufacture the line.

The tragic irony is that Beanie Sigel, the front man for the clothing line, has fought valiantly to stay out of prison and even raps about the conditions that more than two million Black men find themselves in. In "What Ya Life Like," which is perhaps the best song, in any genre, ever written about the prison experience, Sigel addresses the painful reality of incarceration:

> *I know what it's like in hell, I did a stretch in a triflin' cell*
> *They got you stuck in the can, white man got you fuckin' your hand.*

"You know how you put your gun in your waistline and you gotta worry about it slipping? With these [State Property] clothes, you don't got to worry about that," Beans once explained. "You don't worry about having to run from the police neither, because State Property can withstand the search."

Or can they?

Just a few months after these comments, Beans ran from the cops, tossing aside a handgun during the chase through South Philly. He was later charged with attempted murder, and months later, despite testimony from Jay-Z, was sent to prison: becoming true *state property*!

"Why would he do that?" my cousin asked of Beans on our way home.

"The Panopticon," I replied.

"The what?" my cousin asked.

I told my cousin about the Panopticon, a type of prison building designed by English philosopher Jeremy Bentham in the late eighteenth century. The architecture of the Panopticon places a tower— *the tower of power*—central to a circular building that is divided into cells encircling the Panopticon's perimeter. The prisoners are isolated from each other by thick walls and their cells are backlit, making them open for inspection by anyone in the central tower who remains unseen. The basic idea of the design is to allow the prison guards to observe the prisoners without the prisoners being able to tell whether or not they are being observed, thus conveying a "sentiment of an invisible omniscience." Bentham saw his prison as "a new mode of obtaining power of mind over mind" where prisoners would behave like prisoners even in the absence of authority. The Panopticon was intended to be cheaper than the prisons of Bentham's time, as it required fewer staff. "Allow me to construct a prison on this model," Bentham told a Committee for the Reform of Criminal Law, "I will be the gaoler [jailer]. You will see . . . that the gaoler will have no salary—will cost nothing to the nation." As the watchmen cannot be seen, they need not be on duty at all times, effectively leaving the watching to the watched. According to Bentham's design, the prisoners would also be used as menial labor, walking on wheels to spin looms or run a water wheel. This would decrease the cost of the prison and give a possible source of income.

"So basically, brothas rockin' State Prop—that's the Panopticon. Right?" my cousin asked.

"Yeah, exactly, man," I responded.

"That's like when I was in the Box, and they watched me all the time. At least that's what they said," he explained.

The Box, or Special Housing Unit (SHU), is an especially cruel solitary confinement cell that is designed to keep inmates locked down for twenty-three hours a day for extended periods of time that range from a few months to a few years. More than 10 percent of New York's inmate population is confined to SHUs, which are electronically monitored, sixty-square-foot cells of concrete and steel that house two inmates each. SHUs prohibit educational and rehabilitation programs and allow just one hour of exercise time per day. Although human rights groups including Amnesty International have condemned SHUs as a measure of torture under international law, the number of newly erected SHUs continues to rise, normalizing this "torture."

SHUs are first cousins to Panopticons, which dictate behavior even after one is free from its restraints. It is this panoptical effect that, in part, has us—the descendants of enslaved Africans—not just paying for logos of oppression and then wearing them on our sleeves, chests, hats, and asses, but manufacturing them, as well. This is unacceptable. We have options. If our ancestors who were enslaved had options, then we have options. Frederick Douglass, who escaped the shackles of slavery in 1838, defined state property as a power by which the state "exercises and enforces a right of property in the body and soul of another." Douglass continues:

> *He is a piece of property—a marketable commodity, in the language of the law, to be bought or sold at the will and caprice of the master*

who claims him to be his property; he is spoken of, thought of, and
treated as property. His own good, his conscience, his intellect, his af-
fections, are all set aside by the master. The will and the wishes of the
master are the law of the slave. He is as much a piece of property as a
horse. If he is fed, he is fed because he is property. If he is clothed, it is
with a view to the increase of his value as property. Whatever of com-
fort is necessary to him for his body or soul that is inconsistent with
his being property is carefully wrested from him, not only by public
opinion, but by the law of the country. He is carefully deprived of
everything that tends in the slightest degree to detract from his value
as property.

What is imperative is that we make the connection between the
state property (via slavery) Douglass experienced and the clothes symbolic of where my cousin had just come from. The incarceration of
more than 1.5 million African-American men, most of whom are
poor and poorly educated, is a reinstitution of the institution of enslavement. We must ask the questions: Can ex-prisoners vote? Can
they get jobs? As with the case of slavery, today's institution of state
property strips men and women of their rights to citizenry even after
they've served their time. The State Property clothing line, then, for
me, represents a kind of death. An acceptance of one's condition to
the point of promotion. Rockin' our own despair. State Property is
the official clothier of modern-day slavery. Hitler's Sturmabteilung's
(or Storm Troopers') ultimate triumph required that the tortured Jewish victim be driven to a point where he could be led to the gallows
without protest, neglecting himself to the point where he ceases to
affirm his own identity, his own agency as a human being.

This is what Henry Highland Garnet, another Black body born
into slavery, alluded to when he said, "They endeavor to make you as
much like brutes as possible. When they have blinded the eyes of

your mind—when they have embittered the sweet waters of life—
when they have shut out the light which shines from the word of
God, then and not till then, has American slavery done its perfect
work."

*Let your motto be resistance, resistance, resistance. No oppressed people
have ever secured their liberty without resistance. What kind of resistance you had better make, you must decide by the circumstances that
surround you, and according to the suggestion of expediency.*

There is a difference, brothers and sisters, between being stuck in a
cell and being imprisoned. "Stone walls do not a prison make, Nor
iron bars a cage," wrote the English poet Richard Lovelace in *To
Althea, From Prison*. We can and, in fact, must realize that our conditions are prisonlike, but we mustn't think of ourselves as perpetual
prisoners. We mustn't think about our position as a fait accompli, as
written in stone.

'Cause I'm doin better now don't mean I never lost shit
I was married to a state of mind and I divorced it.
—THE ROOTS, "CLOCK WITH NO HANDS," GAME THEORY

We must divorce the prison mentality if we wish to be free. Assata
Shakur, the former Black Panther who escaped to Cuba from a super-
maximum-security prison in New Jersey, reminds us that "love is the
acid that eats away bars."

For no matter how they confine our bodies—in chains, shackles,
SHUs, Panopticons, ghettos—they can never imprison our souls!

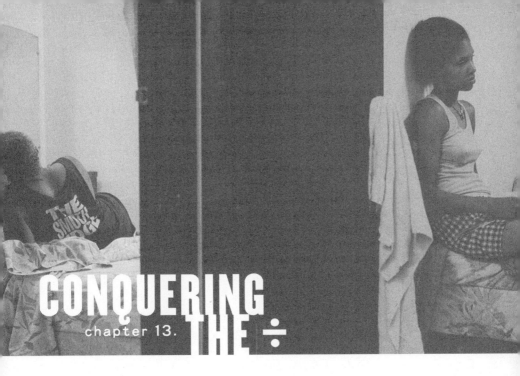

CONQUERING THE ÷

chapter 13.

Back in the days our parents used to take care of us,
Look at 'em now, they even fuckin scared of us.
—NOTORIOUS B.I.G.

I really hate the way my generation is always bitching
and moaning about the hip—hop generation.
—NIKKI GIOVANNI

Cayuga Park—hidden beneath burnt-brown train tracks at the foot of a dead-end street in San Francisco—is an eleven-acre walk-through tribute to mother nature; thick with memorials to its Native American namesake, meticulous gardens of sage and plum, and wood carvings with timely messages engraved upon them. One of the carvings, sculpted by groundskeeper Demetrio Bracero, has a message scrawled in freehand that freezes my stride:

The flowers of tomorrow are in the seeds of today

If the oak slab had a bit more space, the next line might read:

And the flowers of today were in the seeds of yesterday

In a world that seems obsessed with the right now, sometimes we lose sight of the reality that today is only what today is because of what yesterday was.

> If you ain't sayin nothin'
> Then you the system's accomplice.
> —THE ROOTS, "DON'T FEEL RIGHT," GAME THEORY

Years ago, a hungry reporter—when the teeth of my poems were first growing in—asked me, "Do you ever write poems that are NOT political?"

"Not political?" I posed back at her while, in my mind, I put my response together: "Everything's political. Everything. And things that seem apolitical are actually very political because they reinforce and maintain the status quo."

"So see," I told to the reporter, "I can't write about, say, flowers." Today, however, I take pride in writing about and, in fact, believing in flowers. For to believe in flowers is to believe in tomorrow.

The late Tupac Shakur wrote about flowers, too.

"Long live the rose that grew from concrete," he celebrates in an early poem. Even in his definition of THUG LIFE, Tupac infused the floral/natural element, explaining, "What you feed us as seeds, grows, and blows up in your face—that's THUG LIFE."

Tupac went on to create an ancronym from the words that best described his lifestyle; the same words tatted in dark blue-black ink across his chiseled cocoa-colored stomach: THE HATE YOU GAVE LIL INFANTS FUCKS EVERYBODY. Tupac's definition and acronym for "THUG LIFE" verbalize a potent anger that he—a burgeoning flower of the hip-hop generation—felt toward some in his parents' generation: the planters. Writer, scholar, and death-row inmate Mumia Abu-Jamal, whom Tupac considered one of his "real teachers," may have articulated this anger best in "Homeland and Hip-Hop."

For the music arises from a generation that feels with some justice that they have been betrayed by those who came before them. That they are at best tolerated in schools, feared on the streets, and almost inevitably destined for the hell holes of prison. They grew up hungry, hated and unloved. And this is the psychic fuel that seems to generate the anger that seems endemic in much of the music and poetry. One senses very little hope above the personal goals of wealth and the climb above the pit of poverty.

Twentieth-century Black thinkers like James Weldon Johnson observed, "The world does not know that a people is great until that people produces great literature and art.... And nothing will do more to change the mental attitude and raise his status than a demonstration of intellectual parity by the Negro through the production of literature and art." It is because of this that there has always been great attention and criticism given to Black art by Blacks. Both the blues and jazz music were perceived by an older, more church-rooted crowd to be raunchy, hedonistic, and not representative of "decent Black folk." Zora Neale Hurston once noted that the older generation believed that the "good-for-nothing, trashy Negro is the one the white people judge us all by. They think we're all just alike. My people! My people!" Throughout our history, this disconnect between generations is heard loudest in the firestorm about the younger generation's music.

During hip hop's early years, the strongest opposition to rap came from older Blacks. Aside from those in the Afrocentric and Black Nationalist movements, who initially embraced it as a vital tool for Black liberation, the consensus among older Blacks was that the music was ignorant and violent and promoted criminality.

I remember wandering into my dad's office at Temple University where he was chair of the African-American studies program, and being greeted not by him, but by Chuck D, Flavor Flav, Professor Griff, and DJ Lord of Public Enemy. As an Afrocentrist, my father recognized the importance of Public Enemy and their message; however, many of his colleagues didn't understand the value and saw the group as nothing more than rowdy hooligans rather than revolutionary spark plugs.

Despite hesitance from some elders, many in the hip-hop generation attempted to bridge the gap. One such try was in 1984, during Jesse Jackson's presidential campaign, when Grandmaster Flash, Melle Mel, and others teamed up to make "Jesse," a track promoting the civil rights leader's presidential run. The song's hook was a poignant analysis of the current state as well as a fraternal embrace of Jackson:

> Brothers stand together and let the whole world see
> Our brother Jesse Jackson go down in history.

Melle Mel had established himself as an emcee dedicated to addressing serious issues. In "White Lines, Don't Do It," Mel addressed the crack problem in the Black community long before it was at the forefront of most of our agendas. In "World War III," Mel rapped against the prospects of nuclear war. And in "Not Going to Play," Mel, along with Sun City and Run-D.M.C., addressed apartheid in South Africa. Despite the pentameters of praise delivered in "Jesse," Jackson opted not to use this song during his campaign. Many in the hip-hop community took that decision as not only a rejection of their music, but, ultimately, of them as well. Moreover, it would be a symbol of things to come. As legendary raptivist KRS-One remembers about the older generation's position on the emerging culture, "Our own people prevented our voices from being heard. And that's the real politics that need to be addressed."

Although there was an effort by some older Blacks to silence the voice of the rebellious eighties youth, hip hop's increasing power in the global marketplace—due to the discovery of a huge white base that brought about larger distribution deals—made it practically impossible to quiet the voices of rappers. So instead, the older generation used their voices to condemn the music that, because of its new foray into white America, was becoming increasingly problematic for many Blacks, old and young. The image of civil rights pioneers steamrolling and smashing hundreds of rap CDs was forever imprinted in our collective memories. The late C. Delores Tucker, a lifelong civil rights leader and activist, became known for the rallies and protests she led against what was dubbed "gangster rap." Tucker was a staunch believer that this subgenre of rap was a form of genocide and was destroying the minds of Black children, exploiting women, and glorifying gang and criminal culture. "It is a crime that we are promoting these kind of messages. The whole gangster rap industry is drug-driven, race-driven, and greed-driven, and it is not healthy for our children," declared Tucker. Tupac, who was a frequent target of Tucker's, retaliated through his music. On the album *All Eyez on Me*, Shakur rhymes: "Delores Tucker you's a motherfucka / Instead of tryna help a nigga you destroy your brotha." During one interview, Tucker clarified her position, demonstrating an understanding and appreciation for hip hop and explaining that she wasn't against hip hop.

I'm not complaining about hip hop. I'm talking about gangster-porno rap which is rap that glorifies murder, rape, drugs, guns, and is very misogynistic toward women by calling women demeaning names.

That is the kind of rap—gangsta porno rap—that we're against, not
hip hop, not rap in its purest form.

Tucker later went on to unsuccessfully sue Tupac for "damaging
her sex life" with her husband. Misunderstandings such as this contributed to the hip-hop generation's don't-give-a-fuck mind-set and
furthered a deep divide comparable to the one that separated the rebellious white hippy/activist/flower children of the sixties from their
white happy/consumer/cookie-cutter parents. Later, Tucker remarked
that "we're going to keep fighting it until it dies or we die." It's ironic
that a woman who fought on the front lines during the Civil Rights
and Black Power movements outlived Tupac. They both died, however, having never sat down with each other.

One hopes that misunderstandings such as these would allow the
hip-hop generation and civil rights generation to come together; however, a few years after Tupac's death, the public face to this gap would
be reopened with this hook:

Ah ha, hush that fuss
Everybody move to the back of the bus
Do you want to bump and slump with us
We the type of people make the club get crunk.

That was the chorus for "Rosa Parks," a hit single from the rap duo
OutKast. No matter where you were in the summer of '98, hood-to-
hood, "Rosa Parks" was on heavy rotation.

Although the song, which sports an upbeat tempo and party tone,
doesn't actually address who Rosa Parks was, most in the hip-hop
generation simply saw it as a harmless dance track named after a civil
rights pioneer. In fact, the song may have been a helpful reminder for
a generation who many believed "don't know their history." Many

people in the civil rights generation, however, took the song as a dis. The song's rotation was scratched when Rosa Parks, the matriarch of the Civil Rights Movement, took Big Boi (Antwan Patton) and André 3000 (André Benjamin) to court.

Parks is famous for her refusal on December 1, 1955, to obey bus driver James Blake's demand that she relinquish her seat to a white man. Her subsequent arrest and trial for this act of civil disobedience triggered the Montgomery Bus Boycott, one of the largest and most successful mass movements against racial segregation in history. The boycott also launched a young Martin Luther King Jr., one of the organizers of the boycott, to the forefront of the Civil Rights Movement. Her role in American history earned her an iconic status in American culture and her actions have left an enduring legacy for civil rights movements around the world.

In March 1999, Gregory Reed, attorney for Mrs. Parks, filed a lawsuit claiming that OutKast's song defamed his client, unjustly appropriated her name for commercial purposes, and, because of consumer confusion, hindered the sales of the Parks-authorized gospel album *A Tribute to Rosa Parks.* Reed, at this point in time, asked for an injunction and upward of $5 million. OutKast responded, just as numerous rappers and artists had previously responded in similar situations, by pointing to the First Amendment. So there it was: icons of the hip-hop generation versus an icon from the previous one. The case, in one sense, was seen as widening the gap between the generations. In another sense, however, the case revealed some of the keys to closing it.

Mrs. Parks said she was disturbed by the sexual references and vulgarity in the song. Lines like: "Bull doggin' hoes like them Georgetown Hoyas" and "Doing doughnuts 'round you suckas like them circles around titties" offended Parks and prompted the suit. In addition, the song throws around a civil rights–generation vocab no-no: "nigga." Regardless of the hip-hop generation's ranging views on "nigga," "nigguh," "niggah," or "ngh," the civil rights generation is almost unanimously against its use.

From the beginning, this dispute revealed one of the major challenges that has hindered intergenerational progress: communication.

"There's nothing wrong with the youth, unless you look at NBC and CBS and ABC," says comedian, writer, civil rights and antiwar activist Dick Gregory. "All we got to do is go and give the youth the truth, and they will respond." Gregory's analysis is an important one because one of the major factors that has contributed to the intergenerational disconnect is the way in which the older generation is exposed to the youth. Because of the decline of Black institutions where young and old can interact together, the older generation is mainly learning about young people not through illuminating conversations or engaging dialogues, but through mainstream media outlets, TV being the largest medium among them. BET, MTV, and the nightly news are the primary informants that shape their perceptions and vice versa. We know from the most recent research studies on the ethnographic effects of television, including those conducted by the Center for Media Literacy and Alliance for a Media Literate America, that TV not only plays a major role in teaching white America about us, but also, and perhaps most detrimentally, teaches us about us—the older generation of Black folks about their successors. Just as media is not a good third party to communicate, it's not a good learning tool, either, especially as far as images of young Blacks are concerned. Generations need to take time to get to know each other on a personal, familial, and communal level.

Tupac's genius lay in his ability to make keen observations on human relationships. He recognized this lack of communication and quality time. Consider what he said when asked about people who misperceive him: "Once people take the time to find out who I really am—they're surprised."

Any real attempt at conflict resolution, without direct communication and dialogue, only complicates the message and distances the generations still further, as we will see as this unfortunate case proceeds.

Although Parks's case was initially dismissed by U.S. District Court Judge Barbara Hackett in November 1999, Parks, in the summer of 2000, hired the late Johnnie Cochran to help her appeal the court's decision. Cochran, who ironically represented rappers Tupac Shakur, Sean Combs, and Snoop Dogg, took the case to the Sixth U.S. Circuit Court of Appeals, resulting in the case being remanded. Cochran explained, "Rosa Parks is an icon in this country. She's the mother of the civil rights movement," he said. "Because she stood up, we can all stand up." Cochran's message echoed that of Georgia congressman John Lewis, a mahogany man who marched beside Rosa Parks in the sixties. When asked about the case, he said, "Rosa Parks is a mother of the civil rights movement. It would be very unfortunate if people forgot her raw courage and remembered her as an elderly African-American lady who sued a rock band."

Both Cochran's and Lewis's statements reflected the idea that the younger generation had forgotten its history. Forgotten the marches. Protests. Fights. Pain. Despair. Spit. Sacrifice. Dogs. Cheeks. Crosses. Whips. Hate. Hoses. Hydrants. Sirens. Sweat. Fire. Panthers. Us. Shoes (worn). Epithets. Strange fruit. Pride. Solidarity. As John Leland writes of the hip-hop generation in *Hip: The History,* no group "has been less interested in the past, except as something to be scratched."

A pathetic example of this forgetfulness is when Joseph Skipper, a hip-hop generationer, broke into the then eighty-one-year-old Rosa Parks's home. Once he entered the house, he asked: "Hey, aren't you Rosa Parks?"

"Yes," Mrs. Parks said as she handed him three scrunched-up dollar bills.

"Give me more!" Skipper demanded.

When Parks couldn't come up with any more loot, Skipper punched Parks in the face. Soon after, he was caught and sentenced to fifteen years in prison. If we are to be successful, by the true measure of success rather than simply money, we must employ the principle of Sankofa—going back to the past to move forward in the future.

On April 15, 2005, just a week after Johnnie Cochran's funeral, the lawsuit was settled. OutKast and company agreed to pay an undisclosed monetary amount and to work with the Rosa and Raymond Parks Institute for Self Development in creating educational programs "to enlighten today's youth about the significant role Rosa Parks played in making America a better place for all races," said the court in a statement. OutKast also agreed to perform on a tribute CD and appear on an educational TV show about Parks's legacy. And finally, under the agreement, OutKast admitted no wrongdoing. This was a disaster. A disaster because once in the courtroom, all real communication between Parks and OutKast, representatives of two powerful generations, was severed. The potential for collective good was amputated. OutKast, along with their label, never admitted to any wrongdoing. It is imperative that all generations recognize that we need each other's support rather than contempt.

On October 24, 2005, Rosa Louise McCauley Parks, dubbed the mother of the modern-day Civil Rights Movement, passed away. This death, like those of Tucker, Cochran, and Tupac, raises the stakes and reminds us that time is running out. The post-hip-hop generation, whose promise is to heal relations between all generations and classes of Black people, must learn from the mistakes that were made in this case, as they are symbolic of larger intergenerational issues. In learning from these mistakes, solutions reveal themselves that will enable us to conquer the divide.

Even with the deaths of Tupac, Tucker, and Cochran, the fire that separates the hip-hop generation from their parents rages on. Bill Cosby is not the lone voice of his generation when he describes the hip-hop generation as "people putting their clothes on backwards . . . people with their hat on backwards, pants down around the crack . . . standing on the corner . . . these knuckleheads . . . with names like Shaniqua, Shaligua, Mohammed and all the crap and all of them are in jail." He goes on:

> This is a sickness, ladies and gentlemen, and we are not paying attention to these children. These are children. They don't know anything. They don't have anything. They're homeless people. All they know how to do is beg. And you give it to them, trying to win their friendship. And what are they good for? And then they stand there in an orange suit and you drop to your knees: "He didn't do anything. He didn't do anything." Yes, he did do it. And you need to have an orange suit on, too.

Cosby's comments, which he emphasizes were "out of love," expressed what most of us have heard in churches, schools, barber shops, beauty salons, and other community spots where young people interact with elders. It's more than a complaint, it is, rather, an indictment. An indictment that accuses the younger generation of dropping the ball, torch, and mantle. It more than suggests that the hip-hop generation has blown the opportunities the Civil Rights Movement created. Cosby says it explicitly:

I mean, this is the future, and all of these people who lined up and done—they've got to be wondering what the hell happened. Brown v. Board of Education—these people who marched and were hit in the face with rocks and punched in the face to get an education and we got these knuckleheads walking around who don't want to learn English . . . Brown v. Board of Education, where are we today? It's there. They paved the way. What did we do with it? The White Man, he's laughing—got to be laughing. Fifty percent drop out—rest of them in prison. . . . And these people don't know history, they don't know about who faced down bigots to help them.

A cinematic expression of this indictment can be seen in the Hughes Brothers' hood classic *Menace II Society*. When Caine, a teenager symbolic of the hip-hop generation and the protagonist of the film, gets arrested, he is interrogated by an intimidating middle-aged ultra-Black detective, who utters the infamous lines, "You know you done fucked up, don't you? You know it, don't you? You know you done fucked up."

What's interesting and often overlooked is how similar Tupac and Cosby are. Cosby opens the preceding speech with this statement:

I heard a prize fight manager say to his fellow who was losing badly, "David, listen to me. It's not what's he's doing to you. It's what you're not doing."

Similarly, Tupac ends his song "White Manz World" with this plea:

*Use your brain, use your brain
It ain't THEM that's killin' us it's US that's killin us*

It ain't THEM that's knockin' us off, it's US that's knockin' us off
I'm tellin' you better watch it, or be a victim.

Tupac's and Cosby's ideas of personal responsibility are stunningly similar. Cosby even indicts the parents of today and himself, as Tupac did:

We are not parenting.
You got to tell me that if there was parenting—help me—if there was parenting, he wouldn't have picked up the Coca-Cola bottle and walked out with it to get shot in the back of the head. He wouldn't have. Not if he loved his parents. And not if they were parenting! Not if the father would come home.
Let's start parenting.

Despite these similarities, many in the hip-hop generation embrace Pac's sentiments while denouncing Cosby.

Above the sunken black heads on the bus, a sign spoke of King. Not the Jordan King who I had just met behind bars, but Dr. Martin Luther King, whose photo was used to promote an annual celebration of the national holiday in his name. The tone of the incarcerated J. King's message, in many ways, echoed the tone of Dr. King who once said that "There is nothing more tragic than to sleep through a revolution." In that speech, delivered at Oberlin College and aptly titled "Remaining Awake Through a Great Revolution," Dr. King discussed the strides that had been made since "the Negro was first brought to this nation as a slave in 1619." Dr. King illustrated the then-recent developments that had been made—"the Supreme Court's decision outlawing segregation in the public schools, a

comprehensive Civil Rights Bill in 1964 . . . a new voting bill to guarantee the right to vote." Although pleased with some of the progress
being made, Dr. King was under no illusion:

> *All of these are significant developments, but I would be dishonest
> with you this morning if I gave you the impression that we have come
> to the point where the problem is almost solved. . . . We must face the
> honest fact that we still have a long, long way to go before the problem
> of racial injustice is solved. For while we are quite successful in break-
> ing down the legal barriers to segregation, the Negro is now con-
> fronting social and economic barriers which are very real. The Negro
> is still at the bottom of the economic ladder. He finds himself perish-
> ing on a lonely island of poverty in the midst of a vast ocean of mate-
> rial prosperity. Millions of Negroes are still housed in unendurable
> slums; millions of Negroes are still forced to attend totally inadequate
> and substandard schools.*

Simply replace "Negroes" with "Blacks" or "African-Americans" and
Dr. King's speech could be delivered today.

Dr. King gave that speech at the height of the Civil Rights Movement, an era remembered as a time of great struggle and sacrifice for
African-Americans. A time when many of our parents and grandparents marched like soldiers against the wretched army of racial oppression. A time when we sat-in in order to stand up to institutions of
hate and fear. A time when kings marched behind queens. A time
when "by any means necessary," "Black Power," "freedom now," "freedom ride," "freedom driver," and "we shall overcome" were not just
catchphrases on pinback buttons, but ways to live.

Many people often point to the rise of the Black middle class as
one of the triumphs of the Civil Rights Movement. Sociologist and
educator E. Franklin Frazier, in his seminal work *The Black Bour-*

geoisie, observed that the African-American middle class, during his lifetime (1894–1962), never constituted more than 5 percent of the African-American populace. Within a few years of Frazier's death, the Civil Rights Act of 1964 and the National Voting Rights Act of 1965 were passed, allowing for increased handfuls of Black folks to get a slice, however thin, of the American pie. Today the Black middle class makes up somewhere between 20 percent to 25 percent of the Black population.

Despite these gains, however, many of the ills that Dr. King and others organized against still plague us. Among African-American children under six years old, 50 percent live in poverty. Among African-American males between eighteen and thirty-four in Washington, D.C., 50 percent are in the criminal justice system. The Urban Institute estimates that 60 percent of America's poor youth are Black.

Integration wasn't the be-all and end-all as many thought it would be. Malcolm X once remarked that "An integrated cup of coffee isn't sufficient pay for four hundred years of slave labor." In 1962, in "Separation or Integration: A Debate" published in *Dialogue,* he wrote:

> *We are living in an era of great change; when dark mankind wants freedom, justice and equality. It is not a case of wanting integration or segregation, it is a case of wanting freedom, justice, and equality and human dignity . . . if integration is not going to return human dignity to dark mankind, then integration is not the solution to the problem.*

It is clear from the current state of Black America that integration has not returned "human dignity to dark mankind," even if a small number of Blacks have risen in class status.

The whole scene is strangely reminiscent of Amiri Baraka's short story "Neo-American," in which Tim Goodson, a Black mayor, runs the city with a clique of WaBenzis. WaBenzis are what many East Africans call the new ruling class; the word in Swahili literally means "men of the Mercedes-Benz." Despite the Black faces that now seem to call the shots in the story, the conditions of the masses of Black people haven't changed. One perceptive character asks, "And what we got here in this town?" He continues, "Niggers in high places, black faces in high places, but the same rats and roaches, the same slums and garbage, the same police whippin' your heads, the same unemployment and junkies in the hallways muggin' your old lady." Similarly, although there have been a great number of individual strides, the masses of Black people in America still live a life confined to the pits of poverty.

The Black middle class, however, has been trapped inside an illusion of symbols and tokens. In this illusion, they believe we can deconstruct institutional racism not by constructing Black institutions, but by the drip-drop approach in which Black America slowly assimilates into high-level positions. Sadly, it is this narrow thinking that causes liberal African-Americans to promote the advancement of Republican conservatives like Clarence Thomas or Condoleezza Rice despite the reality that their advancement works against their own purported ideological and social interests. Any strategy that sees race, Black or white, as more important than ideology is a failing one. In the wake of the civil rights and Black Power eras, a Black leadership has emerged that doesn't even live in the Black community. We must come to grips with the fact that symbols of progress are not substitutes for progress.

It is tragically true, as Lerone Bennett, Jr., writes in *The Shaping of Black America,* that "the great movement of the sixties destroyed the brutal and visible manifestations of racism, but it did not and could not at that time destroy invisible institutional manifestations of racism." He goes on to add that there are "still invisible Jim Crow signs on the walls of every American institution." And those signs still scream:

"Niggers" on the walls of inner—city schools;

"Niggers" in our crumbling neighborhoods;

"Niggers" in the wails of police sirens;

"Niggers" in the hospital where we are turned away;

"Niggers" in the laws;

"Niggers" at our job interviews.

It seems as though many of us have fallen asleep on the "comfortable mattress" that Jordan King warned of—we have become too comfortable and have stopped fighting for what most African-Americans still don't have. Consider the analogy of a sports team who has been held down illegally by unfair rules. As the team, after uphill battle upon uphill battle, starts to close the gap, they suddenly pull back, having mistaken their temporary momentum for victory. We must never forget that momentum; at its best, it is a symbol of the potential for a shift but it is not the shift. How can we, today, be content with momentum when we are still losing?

When I see the apathy of today, I'm reminded—no, *haunted*—by Malcolm X's words: "You don't stick a knife in a man's back nine inches and then pull it out six inches and say you're making progress." He adds: "No matter how much respect, no matter how much recognition, whites show towards me, as far as I'm concerned, as long as it is not shown to every one of our people in this country, it doesn't exist for me." Regardless of individual examples of success, myself included, we must not forget that those examples are merely tokens who do not accurately reflect the potential of the masses so long as savage inequalities exist throughout the institutions of America. As opera singer Leontyne Price once remarked, "All token blacks have the same experience. I have been pointed at as a solution to things that have not begun to be solved, because pointing at us token blacks eases the conscience of millions, and I think it is dreadfully wrong." Make no mistake, the struggle for justice, freedom, and equality is not over.

Amid so much apathy, I found myself on the bus ride from the prison, asking what happened? Where did the momentum go? Wasn't/isn't it so painfully clear that the conditions for most Blacks hadn't/haven't changed?

In 1959, at the height of the Cold War, Soviet leader Nikita Khrushchev came to America to meet with President Dwight Eisenhower, known to some as the "oatmeal president" for his dull demeanor. Despite this tag, however, he had been the first U.S. president to fly in a helicopter. So on this day, after a relatively unsuccessful dialogue session at Camp David, Eisenhower and Khrushchev boarded the *Seahorse,* Eisenhower's presidential helicopter, for a tour of suburban Pennsylvania. They hovered over the private opulence that American capitalism made possible: the humungous houses, shiny automobiles, and neat lawns. Eisenhower geared Khrushchev's gaze toward the ultramarine-blue swimming pools that bowled the area, then remarked, "That's why my people will never revolt." Eisenhower's logic was simple: material possessions, be they pools or twenty-two-inch rims, nullify and trap the middle class, thus preoccupying and preventing them from challenging the status quo.

While Khrushchev and Eisenhower were helicoptering over the burbs, warrior penman James Baldwin was in Atlanta covering a story about the small percentage of middle-class Blacks that lived there at the time. In a piece entitled "Nobody Knows My Name: A Letter from the South," published in *Partisan Review,* he described middle-

class African-Americans as being in "a really quite sinister position."
He elaborated:

> *They are in the extraordinary position of being compelled to work for*
> *the destruction of all they have bought so dearly—their homes, their*
> *comfort, the safety of their children. But the safety of their children is*
> *merely comparative; it is all that their comparative strength as a class*
> *has bought them so far; and they are not safe, really, as long as the*
> *bulk of Atlanta's Negroes live in such darkness. On any night, in that*
> *other part of town, a policeman may beat up one Negro too many, or*
> *some Negro or some white man may simply go berserk. And the island*
> *on which these Negroes have built their handsome houses will simply*
> *disappear.*

Since Baldwin's article, the Black middle class has grown. In 1960,
there were 385,586 middle-class African-Americans; in 1980 that
number jumped to 1,317,080; and in 1995, it mushroomed to nearly
seven million. What's more, the upper income bracket of African-
Americans increased fourfold between 1967 and 2003.

However, with this growth it seems as though something has been
lost. As NFL Hall of Famer and social activist Jim Brown told me on
his West Hollywood porch, "We have an African-American community that's headed nowhere because all of these individual millionaires are just individual millionaires with no effect upon nothing."

This "headed nowhere-ness" is fueled by a brand of vulgar individ-
ualism that promotes disassociation from poor Blacks and, in fact,
any of the social ills that confront us as a people, nation, and world.
We see this in the high-pitched rhetoric of comedian Chris Rock who
asks, "Who's more racist? Black people or white people?" His answer:
"Black people. Because we hate Black people, too. Everything white
people don't like about Black people, Black people *really* don't like

about Black people." He says there's a "civil war" being waged: "There's Black people, and there's niggas. And niggas have *got to go*." He goes on to say, "I love Black people, but I hate niggas."

This tone is echoed in a more serious (and scary) way in articles such as "The Manifesto of Ascendancy for the Modern American Nigger" by John Ridley, a Black man, published for the largely white readership of *Esquire*.

It's time for ascended blacks to wish niggers good luck. Just as whites may be concerned with the good of all citizens but don't travel their days worrying specifically about the well-being of hillbillies from Appalachia, we need to send niggers on their way.

This vile strain of thought is not only counterproductive, but to put it bluntly: counter-humanity. How can one be so stooped into his or her own self that they forget about their sister or brother? Can you imagine if Harriet Tubman took this attitude? John Brown? Nelson Mandela? Ella Baker? Rosa Parks? Gandhi? The unavoidable reality is that we are at our best as human beings when we realize that we're all tied together in a labyrinth of interrelation that culminates in our collective destiny. What may harm some of us directly harms all of us indirectly. Put another way, I can't be all that I can be until you are all you can be. I can never reach my full potential until others have reached theirs.

Many in the Black middle and upper classes have abandoned this idea of interrelatedness, claiming that "Blacks use charges of discrimination to avoid dealing with their cultural failings." Black conservatives like the Manhattan Institute's John H. McWhorter claim that Black people "spit in the eye of [their] grandparents" when they speak up and state that their lives are limited by racism. However, "contrary to McWhorter's assertion," as Algernon Austin argues, ignoring racism and discrimination is "spitting in the eye of everyone, Black and White, who struggled for civil rights in the 1950s and 1960s." What is most disturbing about any argument, on either side, is the oversight of not taking into serious consideration the role history plays in the present. When one combines a vulgarly individualistic society with lack of historical understanding (that is: how history affects the present), the result is a flimsy attack on poor people that overemphasizes "personal responsibility." These narrow, harsh, and inflammatory arguments overlook all of the structural and institutional factors (low wages, chronic underemployment, job/capital flight, downsizing and outsourcing, poorly funded schools) that create and perpetuate Black poverty. They fail to realize that self-help does not eradicate poverty and create jobs in our communities. This is not to say that personal responsibility isn't important, but we must recognize that without proper social justice, personal responsibility is impossible to exercise. The point, here, is not to blame today's plight on the Black middle class, but rather to show, as John Donne once wrote, that "No man is an island, entire of itself; every man is a piece of the continent, a part of the main . . . any man's death diminishes me, because I am involved in mankind; and therefore never send to know for whom the bell tolls; it tolls for thee." A failure to act would result in the continued and sustained attack on Black lives and perpetuate the suffering that the majority of Africans in this country face.

Over thirty-five years ago, Dr. Martin Luther King Jr. warned, "injustice anywhere is a threat to justice everywhere" and that "oppressed people cannot remain oppressed forever" because "the urge for freedom will eventually come." Without a doubt, African-Americans have made significant economic and political strides since the sixties, but not overwhelming ones—at least not overwhelming enough to discuss the civil rights era in the past tense.

The challenges we, all of us, face today are immense and demand a coordinated, grassroots approach—city by city and block by block—to address all the social, economic, and mental health issues that many Black women and men are experiencing in the nation's urban centers. All of these things make one thing painfully clear: We ain't free, yet. The civil rights struggle was one of guaranteeing the basic civil rights of Black Americans (and other non-whites).

We live in an era today when, as Cornel West describes, "All people with black skin and African phenotype are subject to potential white supremacist abuse. Hence, all Black Americans have some interest in resisting racism."

Let us embrace the traditional African idea of ubuntu, which means "humanity toward others"; I am because we are; I am what I am because of what we all are. A person becomes human through other persons; a person is a person because of other persons. Ubuntu insists that we all be open and available to others; that we affirm and encourage others to reach their potential. In its splendid, substantial simplicity, ubuntu reassures us that we, as humans, are all a part of a greater whole and, because of that, we feel the oppression of others because we ourselves are others. This does not mean that we should deny personal enrichment; however, we must at the same time advance and promote community enrichment.

The post-hip-hop generation will stand up to the structures that maintain poverty in our society. It is an absolute tragedy that hundreds of thousands of children, 562,000, go to bed hungry in the richest nation in the world. King said that:

> One day we must ask the question, "Why are there forty million poor people in America?" And when you begin to ask that question, you are raising questions about the economic system, about a broader distribution of wealth. When you ask that question, you begin to question the

capitalistic economy. And I'm simply saying that more and more,
we've got to begin to ask questions about the whole society . . .

That day has come. It is up to the post-hip-hop generation to create a new world. Historical circumstances have birthed us into an unjust world, but isn't it our personal responsibility to make sure we don't grow old in it? We must not become accustomed to the cruel and harmful; inhumane and unjust; criminal and vile.

This means beginning to carve, out of the hard stones of our history, a place for ourselves—one that, as poet/activist Amina Baraka says, is not "about the business of destroying ourselves, but uplifting ourselves." We need not be intimidated by our parents' stories of struggle, but instead take their stories out of the closets of invisibility, and wear them as inspiration. When we realize that all things grow with love and that the seed is hope and the flower is joy. When we realize as Rosa Parks said in an interview shortly before her death that "We still have a long way to go." It is time to move together as one.

That includes civil rights leaders working with us, rather than publicly criticizing us, to develop and hone leaders. Revolutionary leader Che Guevara told his comrades, "One of your duties is to create the people to replace us." The civil rights generation must adhere to this and know that the strides they made become diminished if we cannot build upon them. Great leadership is not about great individual talent or great oratory, but about intergenerational mantle-passing. Great leadership must be nurtured, matured, and spring from a community that values collectivity, love, and compassion. When this doesn't happen, the individual talent and great speeches that are present in every generation will become tools employed exclusively for self-advancement—even at the expense of a community. In this leadership-less abyss, a rapper, for example, who rhymes about destroying his community via drugs, murder, and sexism is celebrated by that same community for the personal accomplishment of becoming a professional recording artist. This is why leadership must be fostered in strong communities by incorruptible leaders with a strong sense of sociopolitical struggle. With once vibrant communities decimated, no unified political agenda, and a safe, corporate "leadership" base, one quickly realizes why the fog is so thick.

We are the light that promises to burn the fog away. Garvey asked, "Can we do it?" Of course we can. Although things have been rough, we are still the seeds of our planters. And it was Henry David Thoreau who said, "Though I do not believe that a plant will spring up where no seed has been, I have great faith in a seed. Convince me that you have a seed there, and I am prepared to expect wonders."

Back in Cayuga Park, among the trees and gardens, there lies a path that weaves through the organized chaos. It's called the Path of Hope. The path of hope for us is real when we recognize that we all need each other equally. When we come to see as the African proverb tells us: It is new broom that sweeps clean, but it is the old broom that knows the corners.

The path of hope leads us to recognize the tremendous efforts of people, young and old, committed to bridging the gap. Young people like Pierce Freelon, the twenty-two-year-old founder of Blackademics, a Web site that has blossomed into the premiere online roundtable for young Black thinkers. The site has effectively created a national and international dialogue between the generations. Through thought-provoking blog posts and insightful interviews with older luminaries like bell hooks, Jesse Jackson, John Hope Franklin, Maya Angelou, and Angela Davis, the site has created a dialogue that is helping conquer the divide. All bridges between young and old must begin at the scratch line of communication. Perhaps the best example of this is Nikki Giovanni, a poet who is truly watering the thorn for the sake of the rose. Born in 1943, Giovanni got "Thug Life" tatted on her arm to show her "solidarity with the younger generation" after Tupac's death. Giovanni explains that it was "a way of saying to the younger generation that the older generation mourns with you." As all of us, younger and older, march into the unknowns of our collective future, let us remember the compassion, sensitivity, tenderness, and love that Freelon and Giovanni share with each other. Let us embrace the earth, seeds, and planters all at once, understanding that we must work in tandem with each other—echoing the life cycle of nature—if we wish to survive.

chapter 14.

A LESSON BEFORE DYING:
A PHONE INTERVIEW WITH HIP HOP

> How much is it going to cost to buy you out of
> buying into a reality that originally bought you?
> —SAUL WILLIAMS

[ringing]

Yo.

Hip hop?

What's up.

Thanks for your time.

No doubt.

Can you hear me okay?

Yeah, but I'm on a cordless phone so if I stray too far from the base I might lose you.

Huh, I figured you would have a strong signal.

I do, just so long as I stay close to the base.

All right, so, stay close.

I will.

Ready?

Shoot.

So, can you tell me where you're from?

Originally, of course, I'm from Africa. The Motherland. I mean, it ain't hard to tell—just peep my first name.

Hip? I didn't know that was African.

Well, now ya know.

The word "hip" comes out of the Wolof language, spoken by the Wolof people in Senegal, Gambia, and Mauritania. In Wolof, there's a verb, *"hipi,"* which means "to open one's eyes and see." So, *hipi* is a term of enlightenment. My first name means "to see or to be enlightened," ya dig.

Definitely, definitely, I can dig it.

That's Wolof, too.

What—*dig*?

Un-hunh, it comes from the Wolof word *"dega,"* which means "to understand." So, you know, there's nothin' new under the sun. It all goes back. Whether we know it or not, it's all rooted in Africa.

I guess it's like that proverb that says: "Even in a foreign habitat, a snail never loses its shell."

That's exactly what it's like.

Or as Malcolm X said: "If a cat has kittens in an oven, that doesn't make them biscuits." [laughter]

That's why my godfather named himself Afrika Bambaataa and called his crew the Zulu Nation. That's *hipi, dega?*

Yes, yes I do. Any more Wolof?

Actually, yeah—honky.

Honky? As in—

Yeah, as in honky. It comes from the Wolof word *"honq,"* which means "pink man."

Damn. That's interesting. All right, well, since you brought it up, what's your take on the large group of whites that enjoy you and your music?

To be honest, that word you just used—"enjoy"—I take issue with that word, man. White people have always "enjoyed" Black performers— that ain't nothin' new. During the most violent, virulent, and vehemently racist times in America, whites shelled out mad loot to watch Black performers do their thing—smile, shuck, dance—as if everything was cool when in reality Blacks were "swinging from southern trees like strange fruit." The only way entertainers could make it back then, from a financial standpoint, was to show them pearly whites and avoid addressing the brutality that was really going down. When white folks went out or listened to music, they didn't wanna be reminded of the conditions that they created. They just wanted to . . . "enjoy" themselves.

A'ight, so now fast-forward.

My music is ghetto music—period.

It arises from a people, a beautiful people, who have been oppressed to the full extent of that word; a people who are forced to live
under conditions that are inhumane and unjust. Yet, the part of me
that the *honqs dega* is the shit that, just like back in the day, never calls
their oppression out.

Peep game: They'll not only listen, but they'll spend money to hear
Black men lie about killin' other Black men; lie about sellin' crack to
Black people; lie about pimpin' Black women. On the other hand,
though, not only will they NOT spend money, but they won't even listen to rappers who tell the truth about the oppressive conditions that the
community really faces; who tell the truth about the prison industrial
complex; who tell the truth about the school system; who tell the truth
about police brutality; who tell the truth about the U.S. government.

And do you know why?

Why?
Do you know who David Banner is—the rapper?

Of course. He made "Like a Pimp."
David Banner tells us the answer.

He breaks the whole thing down when he says: "They want black
artists to shuck and jive, but they don't want us to tell the real story
because they're connected to it!"

So because they're connected to it, they fetishize Black disenfranchisement and transform the ghetto into a glossy magazine spread,
uprooting it from the chain of injustices that created it, thus discon-
necting themselves from it—like voyeurs.

Okay, but do you think that perhaps for whites listening to your music, it
may bring them closer to the ghetto and compel them to help out there?
Help out?

Listen, the people in the ghetto have never been the problem. The people in the ghetto don't make decisions to bulldoze their homes and build freeways through their neighborhoods. The people in the ghetto don't redline their own neighborhoods. The people in the ghetto don't deny themselves loans and mortgages. The people in the ghetto don't cut funding for their children's schools. The people in the ghetto don't put more cops in their streets. The people in the ghetto don't install cameras to monitor themselves 24–7.

The people in the ghetto don't have any political power, so if white folks who like my music want to help, they need to go back to their communities and help out. The reality is that their communities need the most help because racism is so rampant there. So they need to study history, not just my history, but American history so they can properly understand who I am. Then they need to educate their communities. But that hasn't been happening. So, as a result, the dismal conditions that I was born into in the late seventies in the Bronx—despite all the whites that listen to my music today—haven't changed.

So, I don't know what it really means to have all these frat boys banging my music as they study to maintain a racist status quo—to keep the progenitors and custodians of me oppressed.

You really think they're studying to keep Blacks oppressed?

Well, yes.

The education that they're getting is teaching them to maintain the status quo. Teaching them to keep the world, give or take a few inches, as is. So whenever you don't oppose a system, then by default, by your inaction, you support it. So whether conscious of it or not, they will, even if it's by doing nothing, fall in line with the continued oppression.

Do you think that whites—

Yo, no disrespect, man, but I'd like to move on from the whole white thing. You got other questions?

Yeah, no doubt. All right, so, Black people, then?

For them, I am the latest weapon in a long line of weapons that have been created, out of necessity, to uplift and aid them in their struggle for liberation.

But you said yourself, there's a lot of negativity out there that promotes stereotypes.

Exactly. Weapons are like time.

Time?

Yeah, time.

Time can either be used constructively or destructively. You can either waste it or you maximize it. But time itself stays neutral. The same is true for a weapon, any weapon: it can either be used by the oppressed to liberate themselves or used against the oppressed.

So, you said you're a new weapon?

Yeah, but keep in mind that everything that is new is, by that very fact, very traditional. So I'm right in the tradition.

So being a part of that tradition, do you really think your music can liberate Black people?

Well, not by myself, of course. But in the context of a movement, my music can be the soundtrack.

Look at the freedom songs during the Civil Rights Movement. Those songs were the soul of that movement; the fire and fiber they needed to keep on keepin' on. Those songs were designed for one purpose: to invigorate and call to action. To prepare people for struggle, to elevate their consciousness.

You've got these big powerful voices singing, "Woke Up This Morning with My Mind Stayed on Freedom," I mean, that's revolutionary. Or, even "We Shall Overcome"—that's a declaration of victory. Those songs inspired people to challenge oppression, ignited their feet, and united them for a common cause. The music was the fuel. The music was the weapon.

Even Dr. King himself admitted that "through this music, the Negro is able to dip down into wells of a deeply pessimistic situation and danger-fraught circumstances and to bring forth a marvelous, sparkling, fluid optimism. He knows it is still dark in his world, but somehow, he finds a ray of light."

That's my tradition.

Is your music, today, providing that "ray of light" for your generation?
The ray is definitely there, but the movement is missing. So, you have emcees who are using me to uplift, educate, and inspire, but no foot soldiers on the ground to make the rhymes reality.

So, when it's all said and done, more has been said than done . . .

And that's not what I'm about.

I've got a first and a last name and they're connected. I already told you that hip was to enlighten. Well, "hop" is an Old English word that means "to spring into action." So what I'm about is enlightenment, then action. Without the enlightenment, you're not going to know what to do, but without the hop or the action, well, then it's just rhymes. Those freedom songs in the sixties, without the movement, what would they be?

So is that what KRS—One means when—

Yes! That's what he means when he rhymes in "Hip-Hop Lives": "*Hip n hop is more than music / Hip is the knowledge / Hop is the movement / Hip n hop is the intelligent movement.*"

Would you say your musi—

C'mon . . . [sigh] My bad for interrupting you, man, but you keep asking about my music. *Is my music this . . . Is my music that . . .*

I'm more than just music, but that's all you focusin' on.

Fair enough. What other components would you like to address?

The spiritual dimension.

Don't wrench me out of my context.

The masses bore me out of resistance and rebellion.

The most powerful part about me is my spirit—the spirit of resistance. Of rebellion against oppression. An outlaw.

Now, don't get it twisted, I'm not talking about a poor Black person that runs around terrorizing their own hood, terrorizing other poor, disenfranchised people. That's not an outlaw.

You remember what Ras Baraka said on The Fugees jawn "Manifesto/Outro"?

Um, refresh my memory.

On the outro, Ras says:

It's easy to kill niggas cuz they look like you, they smell like you, shit, they even live on your same mothafuckin' block. The only problem we have is killin' the people who don't look like us, who oppress us.

So I was born from those kicks of oppression . . . and we're still getting kicked.

And this is born out of the ghetto experience?

Yeah, but when I say "ghetto," I'm really talkin' about a whole notha', deeper level. Like, I might be young, I'm only in my thirties, but I'm coming out of a spiritual tradition of rebellion. It goes way back.

How far back?

I mean, it goes back to 1526 when the first Africans arrived here in shackles and just a few months later, killed their massas.

Where was your spirit when slavery was widespread?

In the fields.

X, who is sometimes called the "fire prophet," told you that during slavery, there were "two kinds of Negroes: house Negroes and field Negroes."

The field Negroes were the masses of people. There were always more field Negroes than house Negroes.

The house Negro, who, though still enslaved, "lived in the house with master, dressed pretty good, ate pretty good because they ate his food—what he left," would "give their life to save the master's house." Although he was only getting leftovers and was still a slave, he lived better than the field Negro. If massa said, "we got a good house here," the house Negro would respond by saying, "yeah, we got a good house here."

Now, what about the field Negro.

The field Negro "caught hell," ate left-leftovers, and dressed like a field mule because that's what he was. Underfed and overworked.

When the slave master's house—the "big house"—caught on fire, the house Negro, hand-me-down firefighter, would try harder than the master to put the flame out. While the field Negro would "pray for a strong wind to come along."

So when I was born, what did I say?

"We don't need no water, let the motherfucka burn?"

Exactly. "Burn, motherfucka, burn!"

And do you know what Dr. King told Harry Belafonte right before he died?

What?

He said: "I sit here deeply concerned that we're leading our nation on an integration trip that has us integrating into a burning house."

That's heavy. Do you think people know the house is burning?

They know, in their gut, that it ain't right.

But most oppressed people are too preoccupied with the day-to-day struggle to think about the bigger picture. Do you know what Harriet Tubman said?

She said a lot of things.

Well, one thing she said was that she freed a thousand slaves but she coulda freed a thousand more, if only they knew they were slaves.

So people don't even question their condition anymore. They believe as they are taught; and they are taught that they are inferior and that their inferiority is the reason for their condition. Charles Hamilton Houston said it best when he said: "As long as ignorance prevails, blacks will be the tools of the exploiting class."

That's why *hipi* is so important. To combat the ignorance so people will know the real from the fake. Rap from traps.

The radio—is that (t)rap? Or is there some positive there?

I'm not even gonna get into that.

Why not?

Man, discussin' corporate radio—*Hot this, Jammin' that, Q this, Blazin' that*—is like debating the pros and cons of rape.

But I will say this: Once you educate people about their history, about me, about themselves, they won't even want to listen to what those stations are playing now. And that's how those stations will die.

What about people who say you're dead?

Again, education. I'm not talkin' about school, but real education. Saying I'm dead is a shock thing, it makes people pay attention. Like, look, if you don't watch out, Imma die.

I'm not dead, but that doesn't mean that I can't die. It doesn't mean that I'm healthy either. I need to be conserved.

And in the end, people only conserve what they love, and they only love what they understand, and they will only understand what they are taught.

So you have to teach them.

That's why you see the misogyny, the self-hatred—Black people are not being taught to love themselves. So Black people don't conserve themselves or each other.

It's time to change that.

Word. Word. Well thank you.

[silence]

Hello . . . ? Hello . . . ? Hip hop? You still there?

Yes, still here. I ain't going nowhere. I think I've got to put this phone back on the base and charge it, though.

All right, well thanks so much for your time.

Peace and remember to tell the people: I am their weapon! Peace.

> Give light and the people
> will find their own way.
> —ELLA BAKER

BIBLIOGRAPHY

Abu-Jamal, Mumia. *All Things Censored.* New York: Seven Stories Press, 2001.

———. *Death Blossoms: Reflections from a Prisoner of Conscience.* Farmington, PA: Plough Publishing House, 1997.

———. *Live from Death Row.* New York: Harper Perennial, 1996.

———. *We Want Freedom: A Life in the Black Panther Party.* Boston: South End Press, 2004.

Asante, M. K., Jr. *Beautiful. And Ugly Too.* Trenton, NJ: Africa World Press, 2005.

———. *Like Water Running off My Back: Poems.* Trenton, NJ: Africa World Press, 2002.

Asante, Molefi K. *The Afrocentric Idea.* Philadelphia, PA: Temple University Press, 1998.

———. *Afrocentricity: The Theory of Social Change.* Chicago: African-American Images, 2003.

———. *Erasing Racism: The Survival of the American Nation.* New York: Prometheus Books, 2003.

———. *The History of Africa.* New York: Routledge, 2007.

Asim, Jabari. *The N Word: Who Can Say It, Who Shouldn't, and Why.* New York: Houghton Mifflin, 2007.

Baraka, Amiri. *Blues People: Negro Music in White America*. New York: Harper Perennial, 1999.

The Black Dot. *Hip Hop Decoded: From Its Ancient Origin to Its Modern Day Matrix*. New York: Mome Publishing, 2005.

Bogdanov, Vladamir. *All Music Guide to Hip-Hop: The Definitive Guide to Rap & Hip-Hop*. San Francisco: Backbeat Books, 2003.

Boyd, Herb, ed. *Race and Resistance: African Americans in the 21st Century*. Cambridge, MA: South End Press, 2002.

Boyd, Todd. *The New H.N.I.C.: The Death of Civil Rights and the Reign of Hip Hop*. New York: New York University Press, 2003.

Bracey, John H., Jr. and Manisha Sinha, eds. *African American Mosaic: A Documentary History from the Slave Trade to the Twenty-first Century, Volume Two: From 1865 to the Present*. Upper Saddle River, NJ: Pearson/Prentice Hall Textbooks, 2004.

Bynoe, Yvonne. *Stand & Deliver: Political Activism, Leadership, and Hip Hop Culture*. New York: Soft Skull Press, 2004.

Capital D. *Fresh Air: Hip Hop Lit and Lyrics*. Chicago: Writer's Bloc., 1998.

Chang, Jeff. *Can't Stop Won't Stop: A History of the Hip-Hop Generation*. New York: St. Martin's Press, 2005.

Chuck D. *Fight the Power: Rap, Race, and Reality*. New York, Delacorte Press, 1997.

Cobb, William Jelani. *The Devil & Dave Chappelle: And Other Essays*. New York: Thunder's Mouth Press, 2007.

———. *To the Break of Dawn: A Freestyle on the Hip-Hop Aesthetic*. New York: New York University Press, 2007.

Conyers, James L., Jr. *African American Jazz and Rap: Social and Philosophical Examinations of Black Expressive Behavior*. Jefferson, NC: McFarland, 2001.

Davis, Ossie. *Life Lit by Some Large Vision: Selected Speeches and Writings*. New York: Atria Books, 2006.

Devaney, Micaela. *The Poetry of the Streets*. Norton, MA: Wheaton College, 2002.

Douglas, Emory. *Black Panther: The Revolutionary Art of Emory Douglas*. New York: Rizzoli, 2007.

Dyson, Michael Eric. *Between God and Gangsta Rap: Bearing Witness to Black Culture*. New York: Oxford University Press, 1996.

———. *Holler If You Hear Me: Searching for Tupac Shakur*. New York: Basic Civitas Books, 2001.

Eure, Joseph D. *Nation Conscious Rap: The Hip Hop Vision*. New York: PC International Press, 1991.

Fanon, Frantz. *The Wretched of the Earth.* New York: Grove Press; reprint edition, 2005.

Fernando, S. H. *The New Beats: Exploring the Music, Culture, and Attitudes of Hip-Hop.* New York: Anchor Books Doubleday, 1994.

Flanders, Julian. *From Rock and Pop to Hip Hop.* London: Brown Partworks, 2001.

Flores, Juan. *From Bomba to Hip-Hop: Puerto Rican Culture and Latino Identity.* New York: Columbia University Press, 2000.

Forman, Murray. *The Hood Comes First: Race, Space, and Place in Rap and Hip Hop.* Middletown, CT: Wesleyan University Press, 2002.

Forman, Murray and Mark Anthony Neal, eds. *That's The Joint! The Hip-Hop Studies Reader.* New York: Routledge, 2004.

Freire, Paulo. *Pedagogy of the Oppressed.* New York: Continuum, 2006.

Fricke, Jim. *Yes Yes Y'all: The Experience Music Project Oral History of Hip-Hop's First Decade.* Cambridge, MA: Da Capo Press, 2002.

George, Nelson. *Hip Hop America.* New York: Viking, 1998.

Hager, Steven. *Hip Hop: The Illustrated History of Break Dancing, Rap Music, and Graffiti.* New York: St. Martin's Press, 1984.

Haskins, Jim. *The Story of Hip-Hop: From Africa to America, Sugar Hill to Eminem.* London: Penguin, 2000.

Hilfiker, David. *Urban Injustice: How Ghettos Happen.* New York: Seven Stories Press, 2002.

Hinds, Selwyn Seyfu. *Gunshots in My Cook-Up: Bits and Bites from a Hip-Hop Caribbean Life.* New York: Atria Books, 2002.

hooks, bell. *Black Looks: Race and Representation.* Boston: South End Press, 1992.

———. *We Real Cool: Black Men and Masculinity.* New York: Routledge, 2003.

Jackson, George. *Blood in My Eye.* Baltimore, MD: Black Classics Press, 1990.

———. *Soledad Brother: The Prison Letters of George Jackson.* Chicago: Lawrence Hill Books, 1994.

Jackson, Robert. *The Last Black Mecca: A Black Cultural Awareness Phenomena and Its Impact on the African American Community.* Chicago: Research Associates, 1994.

Kelley, Norman. *R & B, Rhythm and Business: The Political Economy of Black Music.* New York: Akashic, 2002.

Kitwana, Bakari. *The Hip Hop Generation: Young Blacks and the Crisis in African-American Culture.* New York: Basic Civitas Books, 2002.

———. *The Rap on Gangsta Rap: Who Run It?: Gangsta Rap and Visions of Black Violence.* Chicago: Third World Press, 1994.

Kondo, Baba Zak A. *The Black Student's Guide to Positive Education.* Baltimore, MD: Nubia Press, 1996.

KRS-One. *Ruminations.* New York: Welcome Rain Publishers, 2003.

Kunjufu, Jawanza. *Hip-Hop vs. MAAT: A Psycho/Social Analysis of Values.* Chicago: African American Images, 1993.

Leland, John. *Hip: The History.* New York: Harper Perennial, 2004.

Lhamon, W. T. *Raising Cain: Blackface Performance from Jim Crow to Hip Hop.* Cambridge, MA: Harvard University Press, 1998.

Loewen, James W. *Lies My Teacher Told Me: Everything Your American History Textbook Got Wrong.* New York: Touchstone, 1996.

Lornell, Kip. *The Beat: Go-Go's Fusion of Funk and Hip Hop.* New York: Billboard, 2001.

Lusane, Clarence. *Pipe Dream Blues: Racism & the War on Drugs.* Boston: South End Press, 1991.

Maxwell, Ian. *Phat Beats, Dope Rhymes: Hip Hop Down Under Comin' Upper.* Middletown, CT: Wesleyan University Press, 2003.

Mazur, Eric Michael and Kate McCarthy. *God in the Details: American Religion in Popular Culture.* New York: Routledge, 2001.

McCarthy, Cameron. *Sound Identities: Popular Music and the Cultural Politics of Education.* New York: Peter Lang, 1999.

Melling, Phillip H. *Americanization and the Transformation of World Cultures: Melting Pot or Cultural Chernobyl?* Lewiston, NY: Edwin Mellen Press, 1996.

Mitchell, Tony. *Global Noise: Rap and Hip-Hop Outside the USA.* Middletown, CT: Wesleyan University Press, 2001.

Morgan, Joan. *When Chickenheads Come Home to Roost: My Life as a Hip-Hop Feminist.* New York: Simon & Schuster, 2000.

Paniccioli, Ernie. *Who Shot Ya?: Three Decades of Hiphop Photography.* New York: Amistad, 2002.

Perkins, William Eric. *Droppin' Science: Critical Essays on Rap Music and Hip Hop Culture.* Philadelphia: Temple University Press, 1996.

Pinn, Anthony B. *Noise and Spirit: The Religious and Spiritual Sensibilities of Rap Music.* New York: New York University Press, 2003.

Potter, Russell A. *Spectacular Vernaculars: Hip-Hop and the Politics of Postmodernism.* Albany, NY: State University of New York Press, 1995.

Rivera, Raquel Z. *New York Ricans from the Hip Hop Zone.* New York: Palgrave Macmillan, 2003.

Ro, Ronin. *Gangsta: Merchandizing the Rhymes of Violence.* New York: St Martin's Press, 1996.

Rose, Tricia. *Black Noise: Rap Music and Black Culture in Contemporary America.* Middletown, CT: Wesleyan University Press, 1994.

Ross, Lawrence C., Jr. *The Ways of Black Folks: A Year in the Life of a People.* New York: Dafina Books, 2003.

Runell, Marcella, Tatiana Forero Puerta, and Martha Diaz. *The Hip-Hop Education Guidebook, Volume 1.* New York: The Hip-Hop Association, 2007.

Sexton, Adam. *Rap on Rap: Straight-Up Talk on Hip-Hop Culture.* New York: Delta, 1995.

Shabazz, David L. *Public Enemy #1.* Clinton, SC: Awesome Records, 1999.

Shabazz, Julian L. *The United States of America vs. Hip-Hop: The Historical & Political Significance of Rap Music.* Hampton, VA: United Brothers, 1992.

Shomari, Hashim A. *From the Underground: Hip Hop Culture As an Agent of Social Change.* Fanwood, NJ: X-Factor Publications, 1995.

Spady, James G. *Street Conscious Rap.* Philadelphia: Black History Museum Umum/Loh Pub, 1999.

Spencer, Jon Michael. *The Emergency of Black and the Emergence of Rap.* Durham, NC: Duke University Press, 1991.

Toop, David. *Rap Attack 3: African Rap to Global Hip Hop.* London: Serpent's Tail, 2000.

Touré. *Never Drank the Kool-Aid: Essays.* New York: Picador, 2006.

Ture, Kwame. *Stokley Speaks: From Black Power to Pan-Africanism.* Chicago: Lawrence Hills Books, 2007.

Watkins, S. Craig. *Representing: Hip Hop Culture and the Production of Black Cinema.* Chicago: University of Chicago Press, 1998.

West, Cornel. *Race Matters.* Boston: Beacon, 1993.

Williams, Saul. *The Dead Emcee Scrolls: The Lost Teachings of Hip-Hop.* New York: Pocket Books, 2006.

Wimsatt, William Upski. *Bomb the Suburbs.* New York: Soft Skull Press, 1999.

———. *No More Prisons.* New York: Soft Skull Press, 2002.

FILMOGRAPHY

500 Years Later. Dir. Owen Alik Shahadah. Prod. M. K. Asante, Jr. Halaqah Media and Asante Filmworx, 2005.

The Agronomist. Dir. Jonathan Demme. Prod. Jonathan Demme. Clinica Estetico and HBO, 2003.

Amandla! Revolution in Four Part Harmony. Dir. Lee Hirsch. Prod. Johnathan Dorfman. ATO Pictures and Kwela Productions, 2002.

Bastards of the Party. Dir. Cle Shaheed Sloan. Prod. Antoine Fuqua. Fuqua Films, 2005.

Battle of Algiers. Dir. Gillo Pontecorvo. Prod. Antonio Musu. Casbah Film and Igor Film, 1966.

Black to Our Roots. Dirs. Tresubira Whitlow and Jacqueline Olive. Habesha Films, 2006.

Brother Minister: The Assassination of Malcolm X. Dirs. Jack Baxter and Jefri Aalmuhammed. Prod. Lewis Kesten. X-ceptional Productions, 1994.

Classified X. Dir. Mark Daniels. Prod. Yves Jeanneau. Centre National de la Cinématographie, 1998.

Color Adjustment. Dir. Marlon Riggs. Prod. Vivian Kleiman. Signigyin' Works, 1992.

The Corporation. Dir. Mark Achbar. Prod. Mark Achbar. Big Picture Media Corporation, 2003.

The Coup: The Best Coup DVD Ever. Dir. Chris Wroubel. Prod. Chris Wroubel. MVD, 2005.

Daughters of the Dust. Dir. Julie Dash. Prod. Julie Dash. American Playhouse, 1991.

Ethnic Notions. Dir. Marlon Riggs. Prod. Marlon Riggs. KQED TV, 1986.

The Eyes of the Rainbow. Dir. Gloria Rolando. Prod. Gloria Rolando, 1997.

Fahrenheit 9/11. Dir. Michael Moore. Prod. Jim Czarnecki. Lions Gate Films, 2004.

Favela Rising. Dirs. Jeff Zimbalist and Matt Mochary. Prod. RaviAnne. THINKFilm & HBO/Cinemax Documentary Films, 2005.

Fela Kuti—Music Is the Weapon. Dir. Jean-Jacques Flori. UMVD, 1982.

The First Amendment Project: Poetic License. Dir. Mario Van Peebles. Sundance Channel Home Entertainment, 2004.

The Fog of War: Eleven Lessons from the Life of Robert S. McNamara. Dir. Errol Morris. Prod. Julie Ahlberg. Sony Pictures Classics, 2003.

The Fourth World War. Dir. Rick Rowley. Prod. Rick Rowley. Big Noise Films, 2003.

The Freshest Kids: A History of the B-Boy. Dir. Israel. Prod. Quincy Jones III. QD3 Entertainment, 2002.

Hip-Hop: Beyond Beats & Rhymes. Dir. Byron Hurt. Prod. Stanley Nelson. God Bless the Child Productions, 2006.

An Inconvenient Truth. Dir. Davis Guggenheim. Prod. Lawrence Bender. Lawrence Bender Productions and Participant Productions, 2006.

James Baldwin: The Price of the Ticket. Dir. Karen Thorsen. Prod. Karen Thorsen. American Masters, 1989.

Letter to the President. Dir. Thomas Gibson. Prod. Quincy Jones III. QD3 Entertainment, 2005.

Life and Debt. Dir. Stephanie Black. Prod. Stephanie Black. Tuff Gong Pictures, 2001.

Manufacturing Consent. Dirs. Mark Achbar and Peter Wintonick. Prod. Dennis R. Murphy. Necessary Illusions/National Film Board of Canada, 1992.

Mumia: A Case for Reasonable Doubt? Dir. John Edginton. Prod. Sarah Teale. Otmoor Productions, 1996.

The Murder of Emmett Till. Dir. Stanley Nelson. Prod. Stanley Nelson. Firelight Media, 2003.

The Murder of Fred Hampton. Dir. Howard Alk. Prod. Mike Gray. The Film Group, Chicago, 2007.

Negroes with Guns: Rob Williams and Black Power. Dir. Sandra Dickson. Prod. Charles Hobson. The Documentary Institute, 2004.

"Paul Robeson: Here I Stand," *American Masters.* Dir. St. Claire Bourne. Prod. Chiz Schultz. WNET/Thirteen and Menair Media International Inc., 1999.

Rize. Dir. David LaChapelle. Prod. Marc Hawker. David LaChapelle Studios, 2005.

Sankofa. Dir. Haile Gerima. Prod. Haile Gerima. Channel Four Films, 1993.

Slam. Dir. Marc Levin. Prod. Henri M. Kessler. Off Line Entertainment Group, 1998.

The Spook Who Sat by the Door. Dir. Ivan Dixon. Prod. Ivan Dixon. Bokan, 1973.

What We Want, What We Believe: The Black Panther Party Library. 2006.

When the Levees Broke: A Requiem in Four Acts. Dir. Spike Lee. Prod. Spike Lee. 40 Acres & A Mule Filmworks and HBO, 2006.

When We Were Kings. Dir. Leon Gast. Prod. Leon Gast. Das Films, 1996.

Zapatista. Dir. Benjamin Eichert. Big Noise Films, 1999.

INDEX